The Caribbean Basin
to the Year 2000

Westview Replica Editions

The concept of Westview Replica Editions is a response to the continuing crisis in academic and informational publishing. Library budgets for books have been severely curtailed. Ever larger portions of general library budgets are being diverted from the purchase of books and used for data banks, computers, micromedia, and other methods of information retrieval. Interlibrary loan structures further reduce the edition sizes required to satisfy the needs of the scholarly community. Economic pressures on the university presses and the few private scholarly publishing companies have severely limited the capacity of the industry to properly serve the academic and research communities. As a result, many manuscripts dealing with important subjects, often representing the highest level of scholarship, are no longer economically viable publishing projects--or, if accepted for publication, are typically subject to lead times ranging from one to three years.

Westview Replica Editions are our practical solution to the problem. We accept a manuscript in camera-ready form, typed according to our specifications, and move it immediately into the production process. As always, the selection criteria include the importance of the subject, the work's contribution to scholarship, and its insight, originality of thought, and excellence of exposition. The responsibility for editing and proofreading lies with the author or sponsoring institution. We prepare chapter headings and display pages, file for copyright, and obtain Library of Congress Cataloging in Publication Data. A detailed manual contains simple instructions for preparing the final typescript, and our editorial staff is always available to answer questions.

The end result is a book printed on acid-free paper and bound in sturdy library-quality soft covers. We manufacture these books ourselves using equipment that does not require a lengthy make-ready process and that allows us to publish first editions of 300 to 600 copies and to reprint even smaller quantities as needed. Thus, we can produce Replica Editions quickly and can keep even very specialized books in print as long as there is a demand for them.

About the Book and Authors

The Caribbean Basin to the Year 2000:
Demographic, Economic, and Resource-Use Trends in Seventeen Countries
A COMPENDIUM OF STATISTICS AND PROJECTIONS
Norman A. Graham and Keith L. Edwards

Bringing together a wealth of data not easily obtainable elsewhere, this book comparatively analyzes long-term demographic, economic, and resource-use trends in seventeen Caribbean basin countries. More than one hundred tables and figures provide information on a wide range of topics, including fertility rates, income distribution, energy consumption, arable land per capita, receipts from tourism, foreign trade, oil and mineral resources, and U.S. military assistance. The authors point to the potentially destabilizing role of rapid population growth, limited natural resources, weak national economic performance, and income disparities, incorporating a variety of forecasting techniques to examine the impact of these factors for each country to the year 2000. The study concludes with an assessment of the implications of the findings for U.S. security and economic interests.

Norman A. Graham, manager of international studies at The Futures Group, is co-author of The U.S. Export-Import Bank: Policy Dilemmas and Choices (Westview, 1984) and The United States and Multilateral Diplomacy. Prior to joining The Futures Group, he served as a research associate with the United Nations Institute for Training and Research. Keith Edwards is an economist at The Futures Group with responsibility in the areas of innovation studies, technology assessment, and economic forecasting.

The Caribbean Basin to the Year 2000

Demographic, Economic, and Resource-Use Trends in Seventeen Countries

A COMPENDIUM OF STATISTICS
AND PROJECTIONS

by Norman A. Graham
and Keith L. Edwards

in association with:
James J. Emery
Michael F. Oppenheimer
John G. Stover
Joseph H. Wex

WESTVIEW PRESS / BOULDER AND LONDON

Copyright © 1984 by The Futures Group

Published in 1984 in the United States of America by
Westview Press, Inc.
5500 Central Avenue
Boulder, Colorado 80301
Frederick A. Praeger, Publisher

Library of Congress Cataloging in Publication Data
Graham, Norman A.
  The Caribbean Basin to the Year 2000.
  (A Westview replica edition)
  1. Caribbean Area--Economic conditions--1945-   . 2. Economic forecasting
--Caribbean Area. 3. Caribbean Area--Population. 4. Population forecasting--
Caribbean Area. 5. Natural resources--Caribbean Area. 6. Natural resources--
Caribbean Area--Forecasting. I. Edwards, Keith L. II. Title.
HC151.G72 1984   330.9182'1   84-2242
ISBN 0-86531-830-1

Printed and bound in the United States of America

10 9 8 7 6 5 4 3

Contents

Tables and Figures

ix

xii

Acknowledgments

The authors would like to acknowledge the individual contributions made by several members of the staff of The Futures Group. In particular, we would like to note the general advisory role played by Michael F. Oppenheimer, Vice President for International Programs, and substantive contributions of James Emery and Joseph Wex as panelists for the trend impact analyses of mineral resources for several countries. James Emery also provided the treatment of trends in tourism contained in Chapter 4, and Joseph Wex contributed much of the section on political instability in the same chapter. John Stover, Manager of Analytic Services, provided helpful advice on data sources and many technical suggestions for the use of GLOBESCAN in forecasting social and economic trends in the region.

We also would like to acknowledge the valuable assistance provided by our consultants to the study. Frank P. Le Veness of St. John's University, David J. Louscher of the University of Akron, and Abraham Lowenthal, Secretary of the Latin American Program of the Smithsonian Institution, reviewed an initial draft of the study and made many useful suggestions.

Finally, the authors would like to acknowledge the superb editorial assistance provided by Cathy Johnson and Beverly Pitts, and the efforts of Marion Healy, Gail Layden and June Osborne in preparing the final manuscript for publication.

The research for this study was originally supported by the Department of State under contract No. 17722-220002. The Department, however, bears no responsibility for the findings, analyses and conclusions contained in this volume.

Norman A. Graham
Keith L. Edwards

1
Introduction and Overview

INTRODUCTION

Considerable analysis and policy prescription have been directed toward developments and emerging problems in the Caribbean basin countries of late. Certainly, there is no shortage of views on the ways in which these developments and problems pose policy and security challenges for U.S. policymakers; and President Reagan's Caribbean Basin Initiative (CBI) and Central American policy have generated considerable analysis and debate.[1] Most of this writing and research, however, has generally taken a near-term view, focusing on proximate threats and policy guidance and ignoring or insufficiently treating the major long-term demographic, economic and resource use trends in the region. This study is an initial attempt to explore these trends and their implications for U.S. interests and security in the long term.

The study is essentially a comparative analysis of demographic, economic and resource use trends in seventeen Caribbean basin countries. A variety of techniques was used to forecast these trends to the year 2000 for each country. These techniques and the assumptions and data used in their application are discussed in considerable detail in Chapter 2.

OVERVIEW

In general, the results of the projections and analysis make it clear that many of the Caribbean basin countries face a long-term struggle against severe demographic and economic pressures. This, of course, assumes no dramatic improvements in their trade and aid environments and no drastic policies to curb population growth in the near future. It also assumes, however, some fertility decline, varying from country to country according to recent trends, and moderate economic growth, both of which may not in fact occur in all cases. These trends, of course, can only worsen for several countries if the present conflict and instability in Central America continues or widens.

Table 1.1 summarizes the projections for the future growth of total population in the region, given current and expected age distributions, fertility rates, life expectancy and migration patterns in each of the countries. The total population in the Caribbean basin will likely increase by nearly 50 percent to more than 77 million by the year 2000. Population

1

TABLE 1.1
Total population of the principal countries in the Caribbean
basin for 1982 and 2000

Country	Total Population in 1982	Total Population in 2000
Cuba	9,853,100	11,600,800
Guatemala	7,694,000	12,636,100
Dominican Republic	6,249,500	9,276,900
Haiti	6,110,800	9,628,200
El Salvador	5,094,600	8,718,100
Honduras	3,947,500	6,923,800
Nicaragua	2,922,100	5,172,500
Costa Rica	2,315,300	3,345,400
Jamaica	2,261,900	2,821,600
Panama	1,987,200	2,858,600
Trinidad and Tobago	1,203,400	1,479,000
Guyana	921,800	1,236,200
Suriname	413,400	693,400
Barbados	268,000	310,700
Bahamas	250,500	342,900
Belize	169,200	257,600
Grenada	116,600	171,400
Total	51,778,900	77,473,200

growth in the countries of the region will by no means be uniform,
however; demographic pressures are clearly more severe in some countries
than in others. Even with some decline in total fertility rates (the average
number of children born per woman), the populations of El Salvador,
Guatemala, Haiti, Honduras, and Nicaragua will all increase dramatically
by the year 2000. Each of these countries will likely experience an annual
population growth rate of 2.5 percent or greater.

Continued high levels of rural to urban migration together with high
fertility in cities mean that the urban populations of Caribbean basin
countries will grow at an even faster pace. Table 1.2 shows that, in all
cases, the urban population will likely grow substantially as a percentage of
the total population. In Belize, Cuba and Grenada the urban populations
will exceed 70 percent of the total by the year 2000, while in every other
country except Guyana, Haiti and Trinidad and Tobago the percentage
urban will exceed 50 percent.

As a country's total population grows substantially, so too does the
size of its labor force. In the absence of rapid economic growth, this
obviously leads to increased unemployment pressure, as the number of new
jobs required to meet increased numbers of new entrants into the labor
force grows dramatically each year. Table 1.3 depicts the growth in the

TABLE 1.2
Growth in the size of the urban population in Caribbean
basin countries

Country	1982 Urban Population as a Percentage of Total Population	2000 Urban Population as a Percentage of Total Population
Bahamas	59.6%	67.0%
Barbados	40.1	51.3
Belize	62.1	72.2
Costa Rica	44.4	55.9
Cuba	66.4	75.2
Dominican Republic	52.9	66.6
El Salvador	41.9	52.6
Grenada	51.4	91.2
Guatemala	39.9	51.6
Guyana	22.1	30.0
Haiti	26.1	39.3
Honduras	37.0	51.0
Jamaica	51.4	64.2
Nicaragua	54.6	65.9
Panama	55.6	67.0
Suriname	45.2	54.1
Trinidad and Tobago	21.9	31.1

size of the labor force expected for each of the seventeen Caribbean basin countries between 1982 and 2000. Not surprisingly, the largest increases will be registered by El Salvador, Guatemala, Haiti, Honduras and Nicaragua--each nearly doubling the size of its labor force by the year 2000, but Belize, the Dominican Republic, Grenada and Suriname will also experience rapid growth in the labor force. As the table also indicates, all Caribbean countries should experience some improvement in the labor force dependency ratio, that is, in the number of dependents per 100 workers. El Salvador, Haiti, Honduras, Nicaragua and Suriname, however, will still have a very unfavorable ratio--more than 80 dependents for every 100 workers. This ratio is in great contrast to a typical industrial country in which each dependent is generally supported by 2-3 workers.

Demographic pressures will obviously be most destabilizing for countries with limited natural resources or those generally faced with weak economic performance. Table 1.4 provides an indication of those countries most likely to face increased economic deprivation by ranking the principal countries in the Caribbean basin by gross national product and income per capita. Using the fairly optimistic World Bank assumptions for growth in gross national product, five countries--Nicaragua, El Salvador, Guyana, Honduras and Haiti--will still be limited to an annual income per capita level of less than $1,000 in the year 2000.[2] This is in contrast to Trinidad

TABLE 1.3
Labor force size and dependency ratios in Caribbean
basin countries

Country	Labor Force Size		Dependency Ratio (Number of Dependents Per 100 Workers)	
	1982	2000	1982	2000
Bahamas	89,700	147,800	83.8	52.8
Barbados	100,200	124,100	56.6	46.6
Belize	37,478	70,442	116.0	68.2
Costa Rica	713,000	1,097,200	68.3	58.1
Cuba	3,118,400	3,933,700	58.9	48.5
Dominican Republic	1,713,300	2,920,600	84.9	63.6
El Salvador	1,783,900	3,247,600	92.7	81.1
Grenada	29,833	54,480	98.6	60.0
Guatemala	2,462,500	4,299,500	87.0	75.9
Guyana	238,000	375,400	74.6	50.9
Haiti	2,427,000	3,925,400	87.5	83.1
Honduras	849,800	1,634,000	101.1	83.5
Jamaica	788,400	1,202,800	79.3	52.3
Nicaragua	938,100	1,791,200	100.2	87.1
Panama	1,159,600	1,842,900	75.9	59.2
Suriname	106,300	201,100	110.7	82.7
Trinidad and Tobago	475,000	626,300	56.8	47.5

and Tobago, the Bahamas, and Barbados--countries that are projected to
attain annual income per capita levels in excess of $5,000 by the year 2000.

While projected growth in GNP and income per capita provides some
rough indication of the economic pressures and deprivation likely to face
Caribbean basin countries in the future, it does not address the problem of
internal disparities in wealth and deprivation. An examination of change in
income distribution is obviously preferable, but reliable national data on
this question are extremely difficult to obtain. Rough estimates of change
in income distribution have been calculated, however, using the limited
data available. Table 1.5 presents the results of these calculations and
projections. The projections suggest some improvement in the distribution
of income in each case, in line with the growth in income per capita.
Nevertheless, by the year 2000 less than 30 percent of the populations of El
Salvador, Haiti, Honduras and Nicaragua will enjoy an annual income in
excess of $1,000, and the same will be true for less than 50 percent of the
populations of Belize, Grenada, Guatemala and Guyana. At present, there
is no reason to expect dramatic improvement in the income disparities and
relative deprivation that characterize the populations of many of these
countries.

TABLE 1.4
Total gross national product and income per capita for the principal countries in the Caribbean basin, 1982 and 2000 (1980 U.S. dollars)

Country	Gross National Product (Millions of U.S. Dollars) 1982	2000
Cuba	$9,274.2	$17,477.1
Guatemala	8,654.8	22,249.5
Dominican Republic	6,986.0	18,390.8
Trinidad and Tobago	5,676.8	16,855.8
Costa Rica	4,243.7	10,936.4
Panama	3,435.3	8,529.5
El Salvador	2,957.3	7,502.5
Jamaica	2,471.2	6,260.3
Honduras	2,245.4	5,583.1
Nicaragua	2,075.5	5,094.0
Haiti	1,460.5	3,657.8
Suriname	1,098.3	2,782.4
Bahamas	878.6	2,225.9
Barbados	796.9	1,883.3
Guyana	561.1	837.1
Belize	167.8	396.5
Grenada	83.9	198.2

Country	Income Per Capita 1982	2000
Trinidad and Tobago	$4,434.3	$10,618.2
Bahamas	3,296.6	6,101.5
Barbados	2,795.0	5,697.6
Suriname	2,192.0	3,310.5
Costa Rica	1,684.4	3,004.4
Panama	1,478.0	2,551.1
Guatemala	1,056.3	1,655.1
Dominican Republic	1,016.1	1,774.4
Jamaica	985.5	1,933.3
Belize	931.9	1,446.9
Cuba	884.8	1,416.1
Grenada	676.1	1,087.4
Nicaragua	653.4	898.9
Guyana	555.1	617.6
El Salvador	547.4	811.5
Honduras	531.8	754.0
Haiti	233.0	369.5

TABLE 1.5
Income distribution in Caribbean basin countries

Country	1982 Percentage of Population with Incomes Above:			2000 Percentage of Population with Incomes Above:		
	Poverty Line	$1000	$5000	Poverty Line	$1000	$5000
Bahamas	98.6%	88.8%	17.2%	99.2%	94.2%	64.6%
Barbados	98.3	86.1	12.7	99.2	93.6	46.6
Belize	94.2	24.0	5.0	96.7	37.3	9.1
Costa Rica	98.0	54.6	8.4	98.9	84.1	14.6
Cuba	98.1	33.4	0.0	98.9	83.3	0.0
Dominican Republic	95.2	29.9	4.8	97.8	58.6	9.7
El Salvador	85.8	14.6	2.5	91.0	26.7	3.7
Grenada	91.5	16.9	3.7	95.6	36.8	4.6
Guatemala	95.5	30.0	4.9	97.1	48.0	9.3
Guyana	83.8	14.5	4.4	97.2	32.9	5.0
Haiti	48.9	5.2	1.8	73.4	10.8	3.4
Honduras	73.8	14.8	4.2	82.7	22.9	4.6
Jamaica	87.2	29.2	4.9	97.1	55.3	11.9
Nicaragua	89.7	15.6	4.2	95.0	25.9	4.6
Panama	95.8	58.5	4.9	97.6	84.2	11.7
Suriname	93.0	77.4	6.4	99.4	95.9	16.7
Trinidad and Tobago	98.9	85.6	26.0	99.8	97.0	72.2

Table 1.6 presents a rough inventory of mineral resources in the Caribbean basin. Five countries might be described as resource rich at present: Trinidad and Tobago has substantial proven oil reserves; Jamaica, Suriname and Guyana have substantial bauxite reserves; and Cuba is well endowed in several metals, particularly nickel. Panama also appears to have considerable potential for mineral exploitation, particularly in copper reserves.

Future production levels and the extent to which these countries can obtain a significant economic return on their mineral resources through expanded trade will be constrained and influenced, however, by a large number of domestic and international factors. Forecasts incorporating many of these factors into trend impact analyses suggest that Trinidad and Tobago, Cuba and, to a lesser extent, Jamaica (due primarily to recent U.S. policy decisions) are likely to enjoy the fruits of expanded trade in their key mineral resources, while bauxite production and trade in Suriname and Guyana are likely to stagnate and offer no great stimulus to the economies.

Table 1.7 summarizes U.S. trade with the principal countries in the Caribbean basin for 1981 and 1982. Overall, the United States experienced a negative balance of trade with the region of more than

TABLE 1.6
Mineral resources of Caribbean basin countries

Country	Energy Resources	Other Mineral Resources
Bahamas		Aragonite, salt
Barbados	Petroleum (1 million barrels of proven reserves)	
Belize		
Costa Rica	Hydroelectric	Gold, manganese, bauxite (150 million metric tons), copper
Cuba		Nickel, chromium, cobalt, copper, manganese ore, petroleum, iron ore
Dominican Republic		Gold, silver, bauxite, copper, lime, mercury, nickel
El Salvador	Hydroelectric	
Grenada		
Guatemala	Petroleum (16 million barrels of proven reserves)	Nickel, lead, copper, antimony, tungsten, feldspar, limestone, marble
Guyana	Hydroelectric	Bauxite, gold, diamonds
Haiti		Bauxite (mines closed), copper, gold, marble (limited)
Honduras	Hydroelectric	Silver, gold, lead, mercury, tin, copper, iron ore
Jamaica		Bauxite (substantial), petroleum, lime, salt
Nicaragua	Natural gas, hydroelectric	Gold, silver, lead, zinc
Panama	Hydroelectric	Copper, manganese, iron ore, asbestos
Suriname	Hydroelectric	Bauxite (substantial), copper, gold, iron ore, lead
Trinidad and Tobago	Petroleum (700 million barrels of proven reserves), natural gas	

TABLE 1.7
U.S.-Caribbean basin trade in 1981 and 1982
(in million U.S. dollars)

Country	1981 U.S. Exports	1981 U.S. Imports	1981 U.S. Balance
Panama	832.5	296.6	535.9
Dominican Republic	762.3	922.4	-160.1
Trinidad and Tobago	681.4	2,214.9	-1,533.5
Guatemala	550.2	347.1	203.1
Jamaica	468.1	357.0	111.1
Bahamas	434.5	1,243.2	-808.7
Costa Rica	370.4	365.4	5.0
Honduras	337.8	431.2	-93.4
El Salvador	302.3	258.5	43.8
Haiti	296.1	276.4	19.7
Nicaragua	182.3	140.3	42.0
Barbados	145.9	80.7	65.2
Suriname	136.8	179.4	-42.6
Guyana	105.2	104.1	1.1
Belize	65.0	42.2	22.8
Total	5,670.8	7,259.4	-1,588.6

Country	1982 U.S. Exports	1982 U.S. Imports	1982 U.S. Balance
Trinidad and Tobago	880.1	1,628.4	-748.3
Panama	825.2	250.8	574.4
Dominican Republic	649.2	622.5	26.7
Bahamas	584.6	1,045.2	-460.6
Jamaica	460.0	278.1	181.9
Guatemala	385.4	330.1	55.3
Costa Rica	327.0	358.1	-31.1
Haiti	292.6	309.9	-17.3
El Salvador	264.4	310.0	-45.6
Honduras	261.5	359.6	-98.1
Barbados	152.3	106.6	45.7
Suriname	126.7	60.1	66.6
Nicaragua	117.6	86.9	30.7
Belize	59.9	38.5	21.4
Guyana	55.3	70.7	-15.4
Total	5,441.8	5,855.5	-413.7

Source: U.S. Department of Commerce.

$1.5 billion in 1981 and more than $400 million in 1982. Panama, the Dominican Republic, Trinidad and Tobago, Guatemala, Jamaica and the Bahamas accounted for the largest amounts of exports from the United States, but Trinidad and Tobago (due to substantial petroleum exports) and the Bahamas still enjoyed balance-of-trade surpluses with the United States of $1.5 billion and $800 million, respectively, in 1981, and nearly $750 million and $460 million, respectively, in 1982.

IMPLICATIONS FOR U.S. INTERESTS AND POLICY

Some of these trends are quite alarming. Even if one uses the fairly optimistic economic growth assumptions suggested by the World Bank, five countries--Nicaragua, El Salvador, Guyana, Honduras and Haiti--will still be limited to an annual income per capita level of less than $1,000 in the year 2000, according to projections.

Other countries, most notably Costa Rica, the Dominican Republic, Jamaica and Suriname, find themselves in a fragile economic state because of a combination of high-priced imports of oil and manufactured goods from the West and low world market prices for their own raw material and agricultural exports. Costa Rica's external debt situation has become alarming, as a consequence, and the populations of the other three face the prospect of increased economic deprivation, unless the trade picture improves considerably.

The rich bauxite deposits of Guyana, Jamaica and Suriname will mean little if the world bauxite market does not improve substantially. Of the three, Jamaica's position appears the most promising because of recent U.S. policy statements, but the rising levels of external debt and unemployment are worrisome.

Belize, Panama and Grenada have also suffered troublesome balance-of-trade deficits in recent years, and the immediate prospects for improvement are not good. Sugar prices have hurt Belize, and foreign investors are wary because of the threat of incursions by Guatemala. The beneficial economic impact of British troops stationed in the country to guard against this threat, however, has helped to offset the imbalances. Similarly, Panama's trade deficits, largely stemming from expensive petroleum import requirements, have been offset somewhat by the income generated from the canal and its related support services. External debt is growing, and unemployment is severe; but there is some long-term prospect for improvement, as Panama's mineral resources are exploited to a greater degree.

Grenada's economy is also fragile, and the long-term prospects are not good. But the fact that the economy is not overly dependent on export income from any one commodity has helped to keep Grenada out of economic crisis.

Cuba is well endowed in several metals, and our forecasts suggest that its trade in nickel is likely to grow substantially, thanks to new production capacity and expected increases in exports of the cobalt by-product to the Soviet Union. But, from all available indications, Cuba's recent economic performance has been stagnant at best, and recent declines in sugar income have forced officials to attempt to reschedule external debt payments to several Western nations.

The economy of Barbados has also been hurt by sugar prices, as well as from a decline in its income from tourism, but it appears rather less fragile than most of the neighboring economies. The economic strong points in the Caribbean basin, however, are Trinidad and Tobago, and to a lesser extent, the Bahamas.

Severe population pressures together with economic weakness tend to set the stage for political instability in many of the Caribbean basin countries. In this sense, the countries that appear most vulnerable are El Salvador, Guatemala, Guyana, Haiti, Honduras, Nicaragua, and perhaps to a lesser extent, Belize, Costa Rica, and the Dominican Republic.

Although rapid population growth does not lead inevitably to political instability or regional conflict, it can in many cases be a key factor in the process that produces instability. Moreover, there is an abundance of potential "triggering mechanisms" at work in the region, in the form of long-standing territorial disputes and national rivalries, opposition and guerrilla movements, insurgent activities by foreign governments, and flagrant human rights violation by authoritarian regimes and political movements.

There are clear threats to U.S. interests in this potential increased political instability. Regime changes in themselves can obviously harm political and economic relations between the United States and Caribbean basin countries, as we have seen in Cuba, Nicaragua and Grenada. To the extent that certain types of new regimes are deemed undesirable by U.S. officials or potentially threatening to stability, prosperity and democracy in the region, the demographic and economic sources of discontent threatening several friendly governments must be viewed with alarm. Much of Central America is in turmoil, and present active conflicts threaten to spread. While there may be few core or primary U.S. interests directly threatened by this potential for increased conflict and instability, there are obvious interests at stake.

Concern about threats to U.S. interests in the Caribbean basin has risen recently, and the region appears to be passing out of a long period of U.S. neglect. Key threatened countries have been singled out recently for expanded security assistance in a near-term effort to protect perceived U.S. interests. But there are also significant opportunities for a constructive U.S. role in the long-term rehabilitation and development of the region through increased U.S. economic and technical assistance, trade and investment. The initial excitement created by the announcement of the Caribbean Basin Initiative indicated that a major program of economic and technical assistance and trade reform would be warmly welcomed by hard-pressed regional leaders. As yet, however, the initiative has failed to live up to the expectations that were raised in the region.

NOTES

1. See, for example, the articles in the Summer 1982 issue of Foreign Policy by Abraham F. Lowenthal, Peter Johnson, Rafael Hernandez-Colon, Baltasar Corrada, Sidney Weintraub, Richard E. Feinberg and Richard S. Newformer; see also: Robert Pastor, "Sinking in the Caribbean Basin," Foreign Affairs, Vol. 60, No. 5 (Summer 1982), pp. 1038-1058; and Abraham F. Lowenthal, "The Caribbean," The Wilson Quarterly (Spring 1982), pp. 113-141. On Central America alone, see: Richard E. Feinberg, "Central America: No Easy Answers," Foreign Affairs, Vol. 59,

No. 5 (Spring 1981), pp. 1121-1146; The Report of the President's National Bipartisan Commission on Central America (New York: Macmillan Co., 1984); Martin Diskin, ed., Trouble in Our Backyard: Central America and the United States in the Eighties (New York: Pantheon Books, 1984); and Robert S. Leiken, ed., Central America: Anatomy of Conflict (New York: Carnegie Endowment for International Peace, 1984).

    2. These assumptions are taken from the World Bank's World Development Report for 1981 and 1982.

2
Method and Data Sources

PLAN OF PRESENTATION

Aside from the overview in Chapter 1 and this method discussion, the present volume consists of three main parts. By profiling economic, social and natural resource trends and attributes for each of the seventeen countries examined in the study, Chapter 3 provides a useful starting point and a firm basis for the analysis and assessments contained in the subsequent chapters. Data for the individual country profiles were collected from a wide variety of national and international sources. Forecasts of selected demographic and economic trends were then made using an updated version of the GLOBESCAN data base and socioeconomic forecasting system developed by The Futures Group. These forecasts are reported on a country-by-country basis, and a variety of economic, social and natural resource attribute data are summarized.

During the course of this data collection and analysis it was determined that at least five countries in the Caribbean basin had significant mineral resources that have important implications both for their future economic well-being and for U.S. economic interests in the region. As a consequence, these five countries (Cuba, Guyana, Jamaica, Suriname and Trinidad and Tobago) were singled out for an intensive mineral resource forecast using trend impact analysis (TIA), an approach to interrupted time series analysis and forecasting developed by The Futures Group. The results of these five analyses are also summarized in Chapter 3, as part of the individual country profiles and forecasts.

Subsequent chapters in this study build directly upon the work performed for Chapter 3. Chapter 4 consists of a series of analyses that focus on the impact of interactions among the demographic, economic and environmental trends in each country. Specifically, it examines the impact of rapid population growth and natural resource use in several of the countries on:

- arable land per capita
- the balance between agricultural production and consumption
- income per capita growth
- energy consumption
- forestry usage
- water availability
- pollution control and land restoration

- tourism
- political instability

Chapter 5 then contains a preliminary assessment of the implications of the preceding findings for U.S. interests and policy. It addresses the following general questions:

- What threats to the United States or U.S. interests will stem from demographic, natural resource use and economic trends in the Caribbean basin?
- Given the potential for political instability in certain countries, what are the implications for U.S. security, trade and investment relations and political relations?
- In what ways can U.S. foreign assistance and expertise help to alleviate population pressures and environmental deterioration?
- To what extent can foreign assistance requirements be met by private-sector investment?
- What is the potential for increased trade and investment in the Caribbean basin?

Several of these questions are examined in part by considering the possible effects of a reduced fertility scenario for the rapid population growth countries, as well as the potential effects of major changes in trade restrictions and energy costs for those countries most affected by the global recession.

METHODOLOGY

Demographic Projections

The demographic projections in this report have been made using the cohort projection technique. With this approach, each age group (cohort) in the population is followed as it ages through the age groups 0-4 to 75 and over. As each cohort ages, it is diminished in size by deaths and may be increased or decreased by migration. The size of the 0-4 cohort is determined by the number of births.

The mortality rate for each age group is determined by the life expectancy and a model life table. Life expectancy indicates the average number of years of life expected for a newborn baby at the prevailing mortality rates. The model life table indicates the mortality rate for each age group that results in the given life expectancy. This mortality pattern varies from country to country. The projections in this report are based on a set of model life tables that contain four different mortality patterns for both males and females. For each country, the pattern that most closely fits the country's own mortality pattern is used. The model life tables are those of Coale and Demeny.[1]

The number of births was calculated by using the total fertility rate, the age distribution of fertility and the number of women in the reproductive ages. The total fertility rate for any period is the number of children that would be born to a woman during her lifetime if she followed the average childbearing rates for that period. The age distribution is simply the percentage of those births that occurs during different ages. Total births were calculated by multiplying the total fertility rate by the percentage of births that occurs at each age, multiplying this result by the number of women of that age and summing the results for all ages from 15 to 49.

The values of life expectancy and fertility used to produce these projections are taken from the United Nations estimates. Specifically, they are the assumptions used in the 1980 UN assessment of world population growth and are shown in Table 2.1. (The gross reproduction rate is the average number of female births that would occur to a woman following the prevailing childbearing rates. The total fertility rate is equal to the gross reproduction rate divided by one plus the sex ratio at birth.)

For the countries shown in Table 2.2, international migration is an important component of population growth and has, accordingly, been taken into account. The number and size of households are also projected for each country. The changing household size was calculated from the changing age structure of the population and does not include any consideration of changing lifestyles that could also affect household size. The urban and rural population were based on assumed urbanization rates, taken from the 1978 UN assessment. The definition of urban population is the one prevailing in each country.

Economic Projections

The projections of gross national product were based on growth rate assumptions used by the World Bank; projected growth rates were adjusted downward, however, in a few cases (e.g., Guyana) where they appeared overoptimistic in light of the real economic prospects of the country in question. Actual growth rates for the period 1980-1985 are the average of the World Bank assumptions and the historical growth rates for the period 1970-1979. Income per capita was calculated by multiplying GNP by the ratio of income to GNP and dividing by the population. The size of the labor force was calculated assuming a constant participation rate for the population between the ages of 15 and 64. The dependency ratio is the population under age 15 and over age 64 divided by the population aged 15 to 64 multiplied by 100.

Income Distribution Projections

Data on income distribution are not easily obtained and are in fact available for only sixty-six countries in the world. These data were used in cross-country regression analyses to develop two sets of equations. The first set provides an estimate of income distribution in a country for which no specific data are available. The second set contains projection equations used to project future income distribution based on the current distribution and changes in the level of economic and social development. These equations are shown in Tables 2.3 and 2.4. The projection equations are based on the results for the set of countries for which data are available. For use with any individual country these equations were normalized to the distribution for that country in the base year.[2] The projections of income distribution for each country and region were combined with the projections of income per capita to estimate the number of people in each income category.

TABLE 2.1
Fertility and life-expectancy assumptions in the Caribbean basin

Country	Gross Reproduction Rates		Life Expectancy			
			1980-1985		1995-2000	
	1980-1985	1995-2000	Males	Females	Males	Females
Bahamas	1.67	1.20	68.6	71.9	71.3	74.0
Barbados	1.00	1.02	68.8	73.5	70.8	75.0
Belize	2.41	1.71	64.1	67.9	68.1	71.9
Costa Rica	1.55	1.40	68.7	73.3	70.4	75.4
Cuba	0.96	1.02	71.8	75.2	72.2	76.7
Dominican Republic	2.07	1.56	60.7	64.6	66.1	70.2
El Salvador	2.71	2.17	52.6	67.1	69.4	73.3
Grenada	2.12	1.26	66.5	72.8	70.0	75.2
Guatemala	2.52	2.10	59.7	61.8	66.8	69.3
Guyana	1.59	1.07	67.7	73.3	69.9	75.2
Haiti	2.80	2.51	51.2	54.4	56.7	60.2
Honduras	3.14	2.44	58.2	61.7	66.0	69.7
Jamaica	1.60	1.02	69.0	73.5	70.8	75.0
Nicaragua	3.03	2.46	55.8	59.5	62.8	66.8
Panama	1.74	1.39	68.5	73.0	70.4	75.4
Suriname	2.77	1.80	66.3	71.5	69.8	75.0
Trinidad and Tobago	1.10	0.95	67.1	73.0	71.3	74.0

Source: World Population Prospects as Assessed in 1980 (Department of International Economic and Social Affairs, Population Division, United Nations, 1981).

TABLE 2.2
Caribbean countries where international migration
is an important component of population growth

Cuba	Haiti
Dominican Republic	Jamaica
El Salvador	Nicaragua
Grenada	Suriname
Guyana	Trinidad and Tobago

The estimate of the population with incomes below the poverty line
was based on income per capita, the distribution of income and the poverty
line. The selection of one poverty line to use for seventeen different
countries is difficult because of different conditions in each country and
different conceptions of poverty. While various demarcations of a poverty
line have been used in the past, the cutoff used here is based on studies in
India that have estimated the per capita income required to allow people
to obtain a nutritionally adequate diet at about $136 (in 1980 U.S. dollars).
Although this income level could be higher or lower for other countries, it
is used here as the best single measure available of a poverty line.

Trend Impact Analysis

The minerals forecasts in this report make use of trend impact
analysis (TIA). TIA is an analytic procedure developed by The Futures
Group that divides the task of extrapolation in such a way that humans and
computers are assigned precisely the task that each does best. First, the
computer extrapolates from the history of a trend. Second, the analyst
specifies a set of unique future events and how the extrapolation would be
changed by the occurrence of each of these events. The computer then
uses these judgments to modify the trend extrapolation. Finally, the
analyst evaluates the resultant adjusted extrapolation and modifies the
input data to the computer in those cases where the output appears
unreasonable.

The output of a TIA is comprised of a median (center) forecast with a
lower and upper forecast, a table of events with event impact and
probability judgments, and a graph of the forecast showing a range of
uncertainty. Also, event probabilities in the text of the report are given in
the following manner: (.30 by 1985, .50 by 1990). These concepts are
graphically illustrated in Figures 2.1 through 2.3, which show a TIA
forecast of Cuba's nickel production to the year 1990.

DATA SOURCES

Data used in this report are drawn from files of the United Nations,
the World Bank, the International Monetary Fund, the U.S. Department of
Commerce and other international organizations and governmental
agencies. This is supplemented by data drawn from The Futures Group's
own files, a data source developed during studies in some forty countries.

TABLE 2.3
Estimation equations for income distribution

Percent of Income Accruing to Following Population Groups (Starting with the Poorest)	Constant	Ln (GNP/Cap)	Percent GDP in Agriculture	Secondary School Enrollment	Socialism*	R^2
0–10	1.43				2.40 (5.7)	.35
10–20	1.21		0.02 (2.4)	0.02 (3.9)	2.47 (5.2)	.50
20–30	1.93		0.03 (2.8)	0.04 (5.4)	2.23 (4.7)	.53
30–40	2.65		0.03 (2.9)	0.04 (6.2)	2.05 (4.3)	.56
40–50	3.63		0.03 (3.0)	0.05 (7.0)	1.85 (4.0)	.58
50–60	5.03		0.01 (2.8)	0.05 (7.6)	1.53 (3.6)	.60
60–70	6.95		0.02 (2.4)	0.04 (7.7)	1.01 (2.5)	.59
70–80	10.35			0.03 (7.1)		.44
80–90	12.78	0.48 (2.4)			-1.52 (-2.1)	.12
90–100	52.50		-0.19 (-2.5)	-0.29 (-6.8)	-11.71 (-3.8)	.57

Numbers in parentheses represent T. scores.
*Variable equals 1 if the country is socialist, otherwise it equals 0.

TABLE 2.4
Projection equations for income distribution

Percent of Income Accruing to Following Population Groups (Starting with the Poorest)	Constant	Ln (GNP/Cap)	(Ln (GNP/Cap))²	Percent Urban	Population Growth Rate	Socialism*	R^2
0-10	1.43					2.41 (5.7)	.35
10-20	11.14	-2.95 (2.1)	0.25 (2.3)			3.08 (6.3)	.44
20-30	17.32	-4.16 (-2.8)	0.31 (2.7)	.02 (1.6)	-0.36 (-1.8)	2.63 (4.5)	.48
30-40	15.74	-3.48 (-2.3)	0.29 (2.4)		-0.39 (-1.9)	2.37 (3.9)	.47
40-50	16.16	-3.36 (-2.3)	0.29 (2.4)		-0.38 (-1.8)	2.21 (3.7)	.48
50-60	16.57	-3.13 (-1.8)	0.28 (2.0)		-0.42 (-1.8)	1.87 (2.7)	.42
60-70	15.11	-2.60 (-2.0)	0.25 (2.5)			1.75 (3.7)	.43
70-80	9.53		0.05 (5.5)				.32
80-90	12.45	0.53 (2.7)				-1.57 (-2.1)	.14
90-100	-9.60	19.61 (2.0)	-1.32 (-2.4)			-18.22 (-5.4)	.43

Numbers in parentheses represent T. scores.
*Variable equals 1 if the country is socialist, otherwise it equals 0.

20

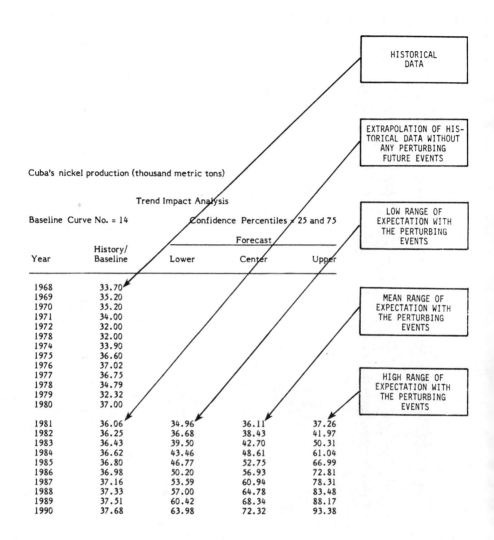

Figure 2.1 Typical TIA forecast

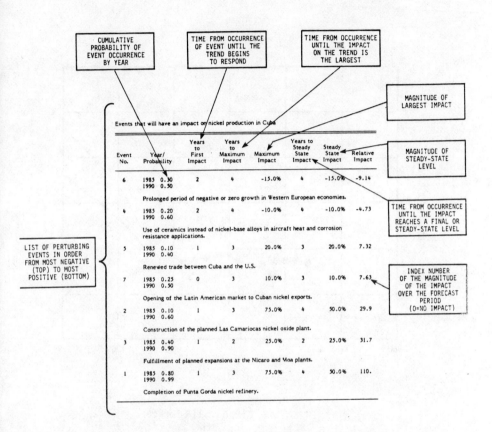

Figure 2.2 Table of events

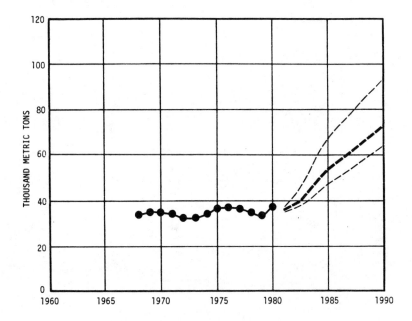

Figure 2.3 Graph of TIA forecast

These data are based on information drawn from censuses, statistical yearbooks, and development plans of the individual countries. General published sources used in the study include:

Demography

Population by Age and Sex. The total population of the country by five-year age cohorts and by male and female sex for 1980. Sources: Selected World Demographic Indicators by Countries, 1950-2000, prepared by the United Nations Population Division and World Population Prospects as Assessed in 1980 (Department of International Economic and Social Affairs, Population Division, United Nations, 1981).

Total Population. Total population in 1980. Source: World Population Prospects as Assessed in 1980 (Department of International Economic and Social Affairs, Population Division, United Nations, 1981).

Population in Urban Areas. The percentage of the population living in urban areas, where the definition of urban areas is the one adopted by each country. Source: Selected World Demographic Indicators by Countries, 1950-2000.

Average Household Size. The average number of people per household. Source: Estimates and Projections of the Number of Households by Country, 1975-2000 (Population Division, International Economic and Social Affairs, United Nations, 1981).

Economics

GNP Gross national product expressed in millions of 1980 U.S. dollars. Sources: World Bank Atlas (Washington, D.C.: World Bank, 1982) and International Financial Statistics (Washington, D.C.: International Monetary Fund, various issues).

GNP Per Capita. Gross national product per capita expressed in 1980 U.S. dollars. Source: calculated by dividing GNP by population.

GNP Per Capita Growth Rate. The average annual real growth rate of GNP per capita. Source: World Bank Atlas.

Labor Force Size. The size of the economically active population. These figures are based on country censuses and surveys and, therefore, depend on each country's definition of labor force. Sources: 1950-2000 Labour Force (Geneva: International Labour Office, 1977); 1981 Yearbook of Labour Statistics (Geneva: International Labour Office, 1981); individual country development plans and other reports.

Income Distribution. The percentage of national income accruing to each decile of some population group. The table on the left of each data sheet shows the distribution for households, if available. The first line shows the percentage of total income accruing to the poorest 10 percent of households. The second line shows income accruing to the next poorest 10 percent, and so on, up to the richest 10 percent of households. The table on the right shows the distribution of income by another

24

population group, if available. These groups include population, income recipients and economically active population. Source: Jain, Shail, Size Distribution of Income (Washington, D.C.: World Bank).

External Debt. Debt in U.S. dollars owed to nonresidents and repayable in foreign currency, goods or services that have an original or extended maturity of over one year. Including public debt, publicly guaranteed debt, and external private nonguaranteed debt. Sources: World Debt Tables, 1981 (Washington, D.C.: External Debt Division, Economic Analysis and Projections Department, World Bank, 1981); and International Financial Statistics.

Natural Resources

Arable Land. Land under temporary crops, permanent crops and land temporarily fallow or idle. Source: FAO Production Yearbook (Rome: Food and Agriculture Organization, 1979).

Forested Area. Land under natural or planted stands of trees, whether productive or not, and includes land from which forests have been cleared but that will be reforested in the foreseeable future. Source: FAO Production Yearbook.

Proven Oil and Gas Reserves. Source: Energy in the Developing Countries, 1980 (Washington, D.C.: World Bank).

Hydroelectric Potential. Estimated gross theoretical capacity including all installed and installable capacity, assuming average flows. Source: Energy in the Developing Countries, 1980.

Proven Coal Reserves. Source: Energy in the Developing Countries, 1980.

Principal Mineral Resources. Sources: The Europa Yearbook 1981: A World Survey (London: Europa Publications Limited, 1981); Encyclopedia of the Third World (by G. T. Kurian; Facts on File, 1979); and OECD Interfutures Project (calculations based on data from U.S. Bureau of Mines and other national data sources from member states).

NOTES

1. Ansley J. Coale and Paul Demeny, Regional Model Life Tables and Stable Populations (Princeton, N.J.: Princeton University Press, 1966).
2. The data from the sixty-six countries for which income distributions have been surveyed are known to be highly prone to error. The regression equations are based on these data. Therefore, the user of these estimates and projections of income distribution should be aware of the fact that this information has built-in inaccuracies. This information should be used primarily to indicate orders of magnitude of how income may be distributed in a country.

3
Country Profiles

This chapter summarizes economic, social and natural resource trends and attributes for each of the seventeen Caribbean basin countries examined in this study. Forecasts of selected demographic and economic trends are provided in each case, and mineral resource forecasts using trend impact analysis are provided for the five countries that have proven economically significant mineral reserves: Cuba, Guyana, Jamaica, Suriname and Trinidad and Tobago.

THE BAHAMAS

The Bahamas are a group of 700 islands stretching in a southeasterly direction from off West Palm Beach, Florida, to north of Haiti. Twenty-nine of the islands are inhabited but over three-quarters of the population live on New Providence and Grand Bahama islands.

A former British colony, the Bahamas gained self-governing status in 1964 and complete independence in 1973. Eighty-five percent of the population are descendants of African slaves with the remainder being of North American or British origin. The nominal head of state is the queen, and she is represented in the Bahamas by a governor-general. The parliament is divided into a House of Assembly and Senate whose members are elected to six-year terms and appointed by the governor-general, respectively. The prime minister is Lynden O. Pinding, who has held the post since independence was granted in 1967.

Demography

The Bahamian population in 1980 totaled 241,000, of which 119,800 were males and 121,200 were females. Approximately 52 percent of the population were fourteen years of age or younger while 3.4 percent were sixty-five or older. Thus, over 53 percent of the population theoretically fall into the employable category. The average Bahamian household size in 1980 was 4.3 persons, and 58.9 percent of the population resided in urban areas.

Economy

The largest component of the Bahamian economy is tourism, which contributes approximately 75 percent to the total GNP. Nearly two million

25

people visit the main tourist areas--Nassau/Paradise Island, Freeport/ Lucaya, and the Family Islands--each year, and tourist expenditures topped $500 million in 1978. Most of the investment in the tourist industry comes from extraterritorial entities, but the government-owned Hotel Corporation also has a substantial stake in the industry, including ownership of several major hotels.

Tough secrecy laws, combined with the absence of corporate, capital gains, profits, and income tax, make the Bahamas a veritable haven for financial institutions. This opportunity has not been neglected as over 300 bank and trust companies have set up shop on the island as a result. The Bahamas rank second only to London in volume of Eurocurrency transactions. The refining and transshipment of petroleum is of great importance to the Bahamian economy. In addition, agriculture and fishing contribute 2-3 percent of the GNP.

Bahamian exports rose 237.3 percent from 1970 to 1975 and 118 percent from 1975 to 1980, while imports rose 646 percent and 120 percent, respectively, over the same periods. The large jump in imports and exports during the 1970-1975 period reflected the then-realized value of the Bahamas as a petroleum transshipment center. Fully 96 percent of Bahamian exports are petroleum and petroleum products, while 94 percent of the imports are petroleum. Eighty-eight percent of Bahamian exports enter the United States and 3 percent go to the United Kingdom. The principal import partners are Saudi Arabia (35 percent), Nigeria (13 percent), Angola (11 percent), Iran (10 percent), Libya (10 percent), and the United States (6 percent).

Investment in the Bahamas by U.S. companies amounted to $763 million in 1975 and $2.7 billion in 1980. Return on these investments was $358 million in 1975 and $915 million in 1980. Three hundred million dollars of the 1975 investment total were associated with the finance and insurance industries. By 1980 this figure had increased to $1.96 billion.

Mineral Commodities

Aragonite, a type of limestone, and salt are the only minerals found in the Bahamas, and neither plays a very significant role in the economy or foreign trade of the Bahamas.

Forecasts

Our GLOBESCAN forecasts suggest that the population of the Bahamas will rise to 290,500 in 1990 and 342,900 in 2000 (Table 3.1). This represents increases of 20.5 percent in the 1980-1990 period and 18 percent in the 1990-2000 period. Average household size will decline from 4.3 in 1980 to 4.0 in 1990 and 3.4 in the year 2000. The urban segment of the total population will increase to 62.4 percent in 1990 and 67 percent in the year 2000.

The male/female population ratio will shift from an almost 50/50 split in 1980 to a 49/51 split in the year 2000. The population below fourteen years of age will be 30 percent of the total population, while those over sixty-four years will comprise 5.7 percent. Over 56 percent of the population will thus be in the "work-force" category, putting some pressure on the economy to provide jobs for this growing segment.

TABLE 3.1
GLOBESCAN medium growth demographic projections
for the Bahamas

Year	Population (Thousands)	Household Size	Households (Thousands)	Urban Population (Thousands)	Rural Population (Thousands)
1980	241.0	4.3	55.7	141.9	99.1
1981	245.7	4.3	57.0	145.6	100.2
1982	250.5	4.3	58.4	149.3	101.3
1983	255.5	4.3	59.9	153.1	102.4
1984	260.5	4.2	61.3	156.9	103.5
1985	265.6	4.2	62.9	160.9	104.6
1986	270.4	4.2	64.9	164.8	105.6
1987	275.3	4.1	66.9	168.8	106.5
1988	280.3	4.1	69.1	172.9	107.4
1989	285.4	4.0	71.3	177.0	108.3
1990	290.5	4.0	73.5	181.3	109.2
1991	295.5	3.9	76.1	185.7	109.8
1992	300.6	3.8	78.8	190.2	110.4
1993	305.8	3.7	81.6	194.8	111.0
1994	311.1	3.7	84.5	199.6	111.5
1995	316.4	3.6	87.4	204.4	112.0
1996	321.5	3.6	90.0	209.2	112.3
1997	326.8	3.5	92.7	214.2	112.6
1998	332.1	3.5	95.5	219.3	112.8
1999	337.5	3.4	98.3	224.4	113.0
2000	342.9	3.4	101.2	229.8	113.2

Population by age and sex

1985 (Thousands)				2000 (Thousands)		
Males	Females	Total	Age	Males	Females	Total
15.0	15.3	30.3	0-04	17.3	17.8	35.1
19.1	18.6	37.8	5-09	16.3	16.7	33.0
18.9	18.2	37.1	10-14	15.2	15.7	30.9
14.4	14.6	29.0	15-19	14.6	15.1	29.7
10.1	10.6	20.7	20-24	18.7	18.4	37.1
8.8	9.1	17.9	25-29	18.4	18.0	36.3
9.7	9.7	19.4	30-34	13.9	14.4	28.3
8.3	7.9	16.2	35-39	9.4	10.4	20.1
6.6	6.5	13.1	40-44	8.4	8.9	17.3
5.3	5.4	10.7	45-49	9.2	9.4	18.6
4.2	4.5	8.7	50-54	7.7	7.6	15.3
3.9	4.2	8.1	55-59	6.0	6.1	12.1
3.1	3.0	6.1	60-64	4.6	4.9	9.5
1.9	2.6	4.5	65-69	3.3	3.8	7.2
1.3	1.8	3.2	70-74	2.8	3.2	6.0
1.1	1.8	2.9	75+	2.8	3.6	6.4
131.5	134.1	265.6	TOTAL	168.9	174.0	342.9

Our GLOBESCAN forecasts suggest that Bahamian GNP will rise from its 1980 level of $800 million to $1.3 billion in 1990 and $2.2 billion in the year 2000 (Table 3.2). This represents increases of 64.4 percent between 1980 and 1990 and 69 percent between 1990 and 2000, and assumes annual growth rates of 4.8 percent from 1980 to 1985 and 5.4 percent from 1985 to 2000. Growth rates of this order will thus require continued growth in the banking and tourist industries coupled with larger petroleum refining revenues. Substantial investments by foreigners in the manufacturing sector would also be a factor in the attainment of the forecasted growth rates. Per capita income will double over the forecast period--from $3,120 in 1980 to $6,101 in the year 2000--and the labor force will experience average annual increases of 3.8 percent.

BARBADOS

Barbados has a land area of only 431 square kilometers, which makes it one of the most densely populated countries in the world. The capital, Bridgetown, is located along the southwest coast of the country. The population is mostly comprised of individuals of African origin (80 percent); 16 percent of the population are of mixed descent and 4 percent are of European extraction.

As an independent member of the British Commonwealth of Nations, Barbados has the queen of England as its nominal head. She is represented on the island by a governor-general who exercises protocol functions. A former member of the now-defunct West Indian Federation, Barbados gained full independence from England in 1966. The country is ruled under a democratic system modeled on the British system, with the government controlled by a cabinet, which is in turn responsible to the parliament. The cabinet is headed by a prime minister, currently J. M. G. "Tom" Adams.

Demography

The Barbadian population numbered 263,000 in 1980, with females comprising 54 percent of that total. Thirty-five percent of the population were in the nonproductive categories of fourteen years of age or younger and sixty-five years of age or older; 39 percent lived in urban areas. The average household size in 1980 was 3.6 persons.

Economy

The Barbadian GNP totaled $760 million in 1980, and the 5 percent real increase in GDP over 1979 represented the fifth consecutive year that the Barbadian GDP had experienced real growth. The Barbadian labor force numbered 97,000 with 12.6 percent unemployed in 1980--a reduction from 12.8 percent in 1979. The 1980 inflation rate was 14.4 percent

Prior to 1969, the largest foreign exchange earner and, thus, the most important sector of the Barbadian economy, was agriculture. The backbone of agriculture has long been sugar production. Because Barbados is a member of the ACP countries, its product is somewhat insulated from the vagaries of the spot market. The major problems facing the sugar industry are a lack of workers (as young persons refuse to take jobs as canecutters, etc.) and wage militance of the present sugar workers. Other agricultural crops include sea island cotton and vegetables.

TABLE 3.2
GLOBESCAN economic projections for the Bahamas

Year	GNP in 1980 US$ (Millions)	Per Capita Income	Labor Force (Thousands)	Dependency Ratio (Per 100)
1980	800.0	3120.3	84.2	88.4
1981	838.4	3207.2	86.9	86.1
1982	878.6	3296.6	89.7	83.8
1983	920.8	3388.4	92.6	81.5
1984	965.0	3482.8	95.6	79.3
1985	1011.3	3579.8	98.7	77.2
1986	1066.0	3705.8	102.2	74.1
1987	1123.5	3836.4	105.8	71.1
1988	1184.2	3971.5	109.5	68.3
1989	1248.1	4111.4	113.4	65.6
1990	1315.5	4256.2	117.4	63.0
1991	1386.6	4410.1	120.8	61.1
1992	1461.4	4569.6	124.3	59.2
1993	1540.4	4734.9	127.8	57.4
1994	1623.5	4906.2	131.5	55.7
1995	1711.2	5083.6	135.3	54.0
1996	1803.6	5272.6	137.7	53.8
1997	1901.0	5468.6	140.2	53.5
1998	2003.7.	5671.9	142.6	53.3
1999	2111.9	5882.8	145.2	53.1
2000	2225.9	6101.5	147.8	52.8

Income distribution--population with incomes above:

Year	Poverty Line (Thousands)	$1000 (Thousands)	$2000 (Thousands)	$5000 (Thousands)	$10000 (Thousands)
1980	237.3	212.5	166.5	36.8	10.5
1981	242.0	217.4	173.9	39.8	10.8
1982	246.9	222.5	181.6	43.1	11.0
1983	251.8	227.6	189.7	46.6	11.3
1984	256.8	232.9	198.2	50.4	11.6
1985	261.9	238.3	207.0	54.6	11.9
1986	266.8	243.6	213.3	60.1	12.3
1987	271.7	249.0	219.8	66.2	12.7
1988	276.8	254.5	226.4	73.0	13.1
1989	281.9	260.2	233.3	80.4	13.6
1990	287.2	266.0	240.3	88.6	14.0
1991	292.2	271.5	246.6	97.3	15.6
1992	297.4	277.0	253.1	106.9	17.2
1993	302.6	282.7	259.7	117.4	19.1
1994	307.9	288.5	266.5	129.0	21.2
1995	313.4	294.4	273.4	141.7	23.5
1996	318.5	299.9	279.5	154.9	27.1
1997	323.8	305.5	285.7	169.4	31.3
1998	329.2	311.2	292.0	185.3	36.1
1999	334.6	317.1	298.5	202.6	41.6
2000	340.2	323.0	305.2	221.5	48.0

Although the number of tourists visiting Barbados in 1980 represented the first decline in over five years, the receipts garnered by the tourist industry were up 24.5 percent over the previous year because of higher prices charged by establishments. Recession in the Western countries, coupled with the perception of Barbados as a relatively expensive resort, has combined to depress 1981 figures: the number of tourists visiting Barbados was down 5-8 percent from the comparable 1980 period.

The government is mounting a strong campaign to diversify the Barbadian economy away from the traditional agricultural and tourist sectors and, to that end, it has attempted to make the country attractive as a manufacturing and offshore banking center. There has been some success in the manufacturing sector which now employs 16,000 workers and contributes 14 percent to the GDP, but only minimal progress has been made in attracting financial institutions.

Despite high sugar prices, Barbados experienced a trade deficit of $315.4 million in 1980. The balance of payments, however, recorded a $12.5 million surplus. Exports increased 56.9 percent over 1979 totals, while imports showed a 26.3 percent increase from the previous year's total--this despite the harm to Barbados' exports to Jamaica and Guyana from the imposition of import restrictions by these fellow CARICOM members. The major Barbadian exports are sugar and sugarcane byproducts, clothing, and electrical components. Its major export markets are the United States (34 percent), CARICOM (27 percent), and the United Kingdom (10 percent). The main imports are food, machinery, manufactured goods and chemicals, with 25 percent of the imports originating from the United States, 19 percent from the United Kingdom, 16 percent from other CARICOM members, and 7 percent from Canada.

Mineral Commodities

Barbados has proven petroleum and natural gas reserves; petroleum is presently being exploited at the rate of 1,200 barrels/day. No other significant mineral deposits are presently under development.

Forecasts

Our GLOBESCAN population forecasts show the Barbadian population increasing at a relatively slow rate over the forecast period (see Table 3.3). The population will grow from 263,000 in 1980 to 288,600 in 1990 and 310,700 in the year 2000, increases of 9.7 percent over the 1980-1990 period and 7.6 percent over the 1990-2000 period. This reflects a continuing adjustment to the limited size and overcrowded nature of the island. Barbados was one of the pioneers of family planning, and the island's Family Planning Association receives substantial financial support from the government. Household size will decline from 3.6 persons in 1980 to 3.1 persons in 1990 and 3.0 persons in 2000, while the urban population will grow to 44.1 percent and 51 percent of the total population. This suggests significant movement from rural to urban areas and the need for expansion of economic and social networks to deal with the influx. Females will comprise approximately 53 percent of the population in the year 2000, up from 50 percent in 1980. The population outside of the productive category (fourteen years of age and younger and sixty-five years of age and older) will drop from 35 percent in 1980 to 31.8 percent in the year 2000.

TABLE 3.3
GLOBESCAN medium growth demographic projections
for Barbados

Year	Population (Thousands)	Household Size	Households (Thousands)	Urban Population (Thousands)	Rural Population (Thousands)
1980	263.0	3.6	73.7	103.1	159.9
1981	265.5	3.5	75.6	105.2	160.3
1982	268.0	3.5	77.5	107.4	160.6
1983	270.6	3.4	79.5	109.6	161.0
1984	273.1	3.3	81.5	111.8	161.3
1985	275.7	3.3	83.6	114.1	161.6
1986	278.3	3.3	85.3	116.7	161.6
1987	280.8	3.2	86.9	119.2	161.6
1988	283.4	3.2	88.6	121.9	161.5
1989	286.0	3.2	90.3	124.5	161.5
1990	288.6	3.1	92.0	127.3	161.3
1991	290.8	3.1	93.2	130.2	160.6
1992	293.0	3.1	94.3	133.1	159.9
1993	295.2	3.1	95.4	136.1	159.1
1994	297.4	3.1	96.6	139.2	158.2
1995	299.6	3.1	97.7	142.3	157.3
1996	301.8	3.1	98.8	145.6	156.2
1997	304.0	3.0	99.9	148.9	155.1
1998	306.2	3.0	101.1	152.3	153.9
1999	308.5	3.0	102.2	155.8	152.6
2000	310.7	3.0	103.3	159.4	151.3

Population by age and sex

1985 (Thousands)				2000 (Thousands)		
Males	Females	Total	Age	Males	Females	Total
11.1	12.4	23.5	0-04	11.2	12.5	23.7
11.2	11.3	22.6	5-09	10.8	12.2	23.0
11.3	11.4	22.7	10-14	11.4	12.9	24.2
13.4	13.4	26.8	15-19	10.8	12.3	23.1
15.4	15.5	30.8	20-24	11.0	11.2	22.2
14.3	14.4	28.7	25-29	11.0	11.2	22.2
11.2	12.3	23.6	30-34	12.9	13.2	26.1
9.2	9.2	18.4	35-39	14.8	15.2	30.0
5.1	6.1	11.2	40-44	13.7	14.1	27.8
5.1	6.1	11.2	45-49	10.7	12.0	22.6
4.0	6.1	10.1	50-54	8.6	8.9	17.4
3.9	6.0	10.0	55-59	4.6	5.8	10.4
3.9	4.9	8.8	60-64	4.4	5.6	10.0
3.7	5.7	9.5	65-69	3.2	5.3	8.5
3.5	4.5	8.0	70-74	2.8	4.7	7.5
3.9	6.0	9.9	75+	4.5	7.4	11.9
130.1	145.6	275.7	TOTAL	146.3	164.4	310.7

Gross national product will increase by 46.5 percent between 1980 and 1990 and 69.2 percent between 1990 and 2000 to total $1.1 billion in 1990 and $1.9 billion in the year 2000 (see Table 3.4) and, coupled with low population growth, will result in significant gains in per capita income: from $2,716 in 1980 to $3,625 in 1990 and $5,697 in the year 2000. Growth rates of 4.8 percent annually from 1980 to 1985 and 5.4 percent were assumed for the GNP forecasts and this compares favorably with growth rates of 4.4 percent during the 1970s. The 27.9 percent labor force growth over the entire forecast period--from 97,000 in 1980 to 124,100 in the year 2000--suggests that unemployment will not much exceed present-day levels.

BELIZE

Belize is a former British colony bounded to the north and west by Mexico, to the south and west by Guatemala, and with the entire eastern portion fronting the Caribbean Sea. The Belizean population is comprised of Africans, Creoles, Amerindians and Mestizos. English is the official language. Belize is a sparsely populated country with a land area of 2,305 square kilometers (8,866 square miles) which, prior to 1973, was called British Honduras. Belize gained full internal self-governing status in 1964 and full independence from Britain in 1981.

One of the most pressing concerns for Belizeans has been an ongoing border dispute with Guatemala, a dispute that has necessitated the maintenance of a British garrison in Belize. At a meeting in London in early 1981 between Guatemalan, British, and Belizean ministers, the Guatemalans promised to drop their claim if certain conditions were met by Belize. (These conditions included: Guatemalan facilities at Belizean seaports; permission for Guatemala to construct two oil pipelines across Belize; and shared use of some uninhabited islets and reefs that lie east of Belize's southernmost coastline.) The conditions were agreed to by the Belizean premier, George Price. The queen of England is the nominal head of state, and she is represented in the country by a governor-general.

Demography

The population of Belize in 1980 was 162,000, of which 81,000 were males and 80,900 were females. Primarily due to high emigration levels, Belize has experienced only moderate population growth. According to U.S. government estimates, approximately 35,000 Belizeans are employed in the United States--almost as many people as are working in Belize. The consequence of these high levels of emigration has been to skew the population to the nonproductive categories: almost 54 percent of the population are fifteen years of age and younger or sixty-five years of age and older.

Fully 61 percent of the population lived in urban areas in 1980; 50 percent of the population lived in the six major urban cities, and 33 percent lived in Belize City alone.

Economy

The Belizean economy grew modestly in 1980 and 1981 after experiencing real average annual growth rates of 5.5 percent during most of the

TABLE 3.4
GLOBESCAN economic projections for Barbados

Year	GNP in 1980 US$ (Millions)	Per Capita Income	Labor Force (Thousands)	Dependency Ratio (Per 100)
1980	760.0	2716.3	97.0	58.8
1981	778.2	2755.4	98.6	57.7
1982	796.9	2795.0	100.2	56.6
1983	816.0	2835.1	101.8	55.6
1984	835.6	2875.9	103.5	54.5
1985	855.7	2917.2	105.2	53.5
1986	901.9	3046.8	106.4	53.1
1987	950.6	3182.1	107.7	52.6
1988	1001.9	3323.4	109.0	52.2
1989	1056.0	3471.0	110.3	51.7
1990	1113.1	3625.1	111.7	51.3
1991	1173.2	3792.5	112.9	50.9
1992	1236.5	3967.5	114.0	50.4
1993	1303.3	4150.6	115.2	50.0
1994	1373.7	4342.2	116.4	49.5
1995	1447.8	4542.6	117.6	49.1
1996	1526.0	4753.2	118.9	48.6
1997	1608.4	4973.5	120.2	48.1
1998	1695.3	5204.0	121.5	47.6
1999	1786.8	5445.2	122.8	47.1
2000	1883.3	5697.6	124.1	46.6

Income distribution--population with incomes above:

Year	Poverty Line (Thousands)	$1000 (Thousands)	$2000 (Thousands)	$5000 (Thousands)	$10000 (Thousands)
1980	258.4	225.5	157.0	32.2	10.9
1981	260.9	228.1	160.5	33.1	11.1
1982	263.5	230.8	164.1	34.0	11.3
1983	266.0	233.5	167.7	34.9	11.5
1984	268.6	236.3	171.5	35.9	11.8
1985	271.2	239.1	175.3	36.9	12.0
1986	273.9	242.7	182.4	41.1	12.4
1987	276.6	246.5	189.7	45.7	12.8
1988	279.3	250.2	197.4	50.9	13.3
1989	282.1	254.1	205.3	56.7	13.7
1990	284.8	258.0	213.6	63.1	14.2
1991	287.1	261.2	219.1	69.8	16.1
1992	289.4	264.5	224.8	77.3	18.3
1993	291.8	267.9	230.6	85.6	20.8
1994	294.1	271.3	236.6	94.7	23.7
1995	296.5	274.7	242.7	104.8	26.9
1996	298.8	277.8	247.5	111.8	29.2
1997	301.1	281.0	252.3	119.2	31.8
1998	303.4	284.3	257.3	127.2	34.5
1999	305.8	287.5	262.3	135.7	37.5
2000	308.1	290.8	267.5	144.7	40.8

1970s. Being an import-dependent country, Belize has been susceptible to imported inflation from the developed Western countries. The high inflation rates (estimates range from 12 to 18 percent) that prevail in the country have been one of the major culprits in the current economic slowdown.

The key element of the Belizean economy is agriculture, with sugar accounting for over 50 percent of export earnings and 23 percent of GDP. High sugar production in 1980, coupled with high sugar prices, caused export earnings from sugar to exceed 1979 levels by 50 percent, but the increased production was not enough to prevent Belizean output from falling below its International Sugar Agreement quota. Other problems facing the sugar industry include smut infestation, an inadequate supply of both skilled and unskilled labor, and low productivity in relation to other sugar-producing countries. The recent decline in sugar prices is a major threat to the economy.

The government's view is that agriculture is the best development vehicle for Belize and, to that end, the Economic Plan 1980-1983 emphasized expansion and development of the agricultural sector and improved productivity. The fact that 35 percent of the GDP, 85 percent of the exports, and 40 percent of the country's employment are provided by agriculture attests to its importance to the Belizean economy. Other important sectors include forestry, fishing, manufacturing (mostly for local consumption), and service industries (of which tourism is the most important).

The Guatemala-Belize border dispute was simultaneously injurious and beneficial to the Belizean economy. It was injurious in that many investors refused to risk their capital as the conflict persisted, and beneficial to the extent that the British garrison in the country--stationed to ensure that Guatemala did not invade--injected in excess of $10 million annually into the economy. Independence puts Belize in a position to receive aid from institutions such as the Inter-American Development Bank but will eventually result in the loss of the expenditures of the British soldiers.

The large outflow of Belizeans has a two-edged effect on the country's economy. Economic growth is slowed because of the exodus of skilled workers but, at the same time, the remittances of these emigres to relatives in Belize go a long way to reducing the current account deficit.

In the past, Belize has consistently experienced balance-of-trade deficits: $28 million in 1977; $26.2 million in 1978; $31.5 million in 1979; and $9.8 million in 1980. The precipitous decline in the deficit between 1979 and 1980 was primarily due to increased re-exports (Mexico being the prime target) and high sugar prices. Exports amounted to $130.9 million; re-exports, $45.9 million; and imports, $140.6 million in 1980. The major Belizean exports are bananas, sugar, clothing, citrus fruits, lobsters and fish; its major trading partners are the United States, the United Kingdom, Mexico, Canada, and other CARICOM members. Belize imports food, consumer goods, building materials, vehicles, and machinery from the United States, the United Kingdom, Jamaica, and Canada. Approximately 49 percent of Belizean exports reach the United States, while 46 percent of Belizean imports originate in the United States.

Minerals

Belize does not have any known deposits of important minerals.

Forecasts

The Belizean population will increase 25 percent by 1990, when it will number 203,100, and another 27 percent by 2000, when the total will be 257,600 (see Table 3.5). The number of productive persons will increase appreciably. In 1980, 54 percent of the population could be classified as nonproductive; by 2000 this figure will fall to 40 percent. Household size will show a significant decline over the forecast period: from 5.0 persons in 1980 to 4.2 persons in 1990 and 3.5 persons in 2000. The number of households will increase from 32,727 in 1980 to 48,840 in 1990 and 73,391 in the year 2000. Urban residents will comprise 67 percent of the population by 1990 and 72 percent by the year 2000.

Under the World Bank growth assumptions, Belizean GNP will more than double over the life of the forecast period. From $160 million in 1980, GNP may well rise to $234 million by 1990 and $396 million by the year 2000 (see Table 3.6). This represents annual growth rates of 4.8 percent between 1980 and 1985 and 5.4 percent between 1985 and 2000 (as compared to a growth rate of 3.3 percent in 1979). With GNP rising faster than population, significant gains will be made in per capita income--$928 in 1980; $1,084 in 1990; and $1,446 in the year 2000. The labor force will increase from 34,500 in 1980 to 52,544 in 1990 and 70,442 in the year 2000, while the dependency ratio will fall from 116/100 in 1980 to 78/100 in 1990 and 68.2/100 in the year 2000.

COSTA RICA

The Republic of Costa Rica, located along one of the narrowest portions of Central America, is bounded by Nicaragua to the north and Panama to the south. It has a land area of 51,022 square kilometers (19,700 square miles). The dominant grouping in the population is of European descent, many of whom are of pure Spanish stock. Descendants of Jamaicans comprise the only significant minority group as the indigenous Indian population continues to decline. The official language in Costa Rica is Spanish, but an English Creole is spoken by black Costa Ricans.

Costa Rica has strong democratic traditions and historically has been the most stable of the Central American countries. Except for two short periods, Costa Ricans have enjoyed uninterrupted democratic rule since 1889. The government is divided into three branches--executive, legislative, and judicial--with executive powers vested in the president. Legislative powers are embodied in a 57-member Legislative Assembly whose members are elected to four-year terms. The present Costa Rican president, elected by popular vote in February and inaugurated in May of 1982, is Luis Alberto Monge.

Demography

The Costa Rican population numbered 2,211,000 in 1980, with almost equal representation from males and females. Thirty-eight percent of the

TABLE 3.5
GLOBESCAN medium growth demographic projections
for Belize

Year	Population (Thousands)	Household Size	Households (Thousands)	Urban Population (Thousands)	Rural Population (Thousands)
1980	162.0	5.0	32727.3	98.5	63504.0
1981	165.6	4.9	33974.6	101.7	63866.5
1982	169.2	4.8	35269.5	105.0	64203.1
1983	173.0	4.7	36613.7	108.4	64512.3
1984	176.8	4.7	38009.2	112.0	64792.2
1985	180.7	4.6	39457.8	115.6	65041.0
1986	184.9	4.5	41177.8	119.5	65489.3
1987	189.3	4.4	42972.7	123.4	65912.2
1988	193.8	4.3	44845.9	127.5	66307.8
1989	198.4	4.2	46800.7	131.7	66674.4
1990	203.1	4.2	48840.7	136.1	67009.9
1991	208.0	4.1	51080.8	140.5	67542.8
1992	213.1	4.0	53423.6	145.1	68052.8
1993	218.3	3.9	55873.9	149.8	68537.9
1994	223.7	3.8	58436.5	154.7	68996.6
1995	229.1	3.7	61116.7	159.7	69426.8
1996	234.6	3.7	63395.3	164.6	69914.9
1997	240.1	3.7	65758.8	169.7	70378.8
1998	245.8	3.6	68210.5	175.0	70816.9
1999	251.6	3.6	70753.6	180.4	71227.3
2000	257.6	3.5	73391.4	186.0	71608.3

Population by age and sex

1985 (Thousands)				2000 (Thousands)		
Males	Females	Total	Age	Males	Females	Total
11.9	11.8	23.7	0-04	17.3	17.3	34.6
14.6	14.3	28.8	5-09	15.6	15.7	31.3
14.1	13.8	27.9	10-14	13.5	13.6	27.1
11.2	11.1	22.3	15-19	11.5	11.6	23.1
8.4	8.4	16.8	20-24	14.2	14.0	28.2
5.2	5.5	10.8	25-29	13.6	13.5	27.1
4.0	4.1	8.2	30-34	10.8	10.9	21.6
3.8	3.6	7.5	35-39	8.0	8.2	16.2
3.4	3.5	7.0	40-44	5.0	5.4	10.3
3.2	3.1	6.3	45-49	3.8	4.0	7.8
2.6	2.5	5.1	50-54	3.5	3.4	7.0
2.1	2.2	4.3	55-59	3.1	3.3	6.3
1.9	2.1	4.0	60-64	2.7	2.8	5.5
1.6	1.5	3.1	65-69	2.0	2.1	4.2
1.1	1.2	2.3	70-74	1.4	1.7	3.1
1.2	1.4	2.6	75+	1.9	2.3	4.1
90.3	90.4	180.7	TOTAL	128.0	129.6	257.6

TABLE 3.6
GLOBESCAN economic projections for Belize

Year	GNP in 1980 US$ (Millions)	Per Capita Income	Labor Force (Thousands)	Dependency Ratio (Per 100)
1980	160.0	928.4	34500.0	116.0
1981	163.8	930.2	35958.4	111.7
1982	167.8	931.9	37478.4	107.5
1983	171.8	933.7	39062.6	103.5
1984	175.9	935.5	40713.8	99.6
1985	180.1	937.3	42434.9	95.8
1986	189.9	965.1	44287.7	91.9
1987	200.1	993.7	46221.5	88.2
1988	210.9	1023.2	48239.7	84.6
1989	222.3	1053.5	50346.0	81.1
1990	234.3	1084.7	52544.3	77.8
1991	247.0	1116.0	54471.9	75.6
1992	260.3	1148.2	56470.1	73.5
1993	274.4	1181.3	58541.7	71.5
1994	289.2	1215.4	60689.3	69.5
1995	304.8	1250.5	62915.7	67.5
1996	321.3	1287.5	64353.7	67.7
1997	338.6	1325.6	65824.6	67.8
1998	356.9	1364.9	67329.1	67.9
1999	376.2	1405.3	68868.0	68.1
2000	396.5	1446.9	70442.1	68.2

Income distribution--population with incomes above:

Year	Poverty Line (Thousands)	$1000 (Thousands)	$2000 (Thousands)	$5000 (Thousands)	$10000 (Thousands)
1980	152.7	38.9	21.0	8.0	6.9
1981	156.0	39.8	21.5	8.2	7.1
1982	159.4	40.6	22.0	8.3	7.2
1983	162.9	41.5	22.4	8.5	7.4
1984	166.4	42.4	22.9	8.7	7.5
1985	170.1	43.3	23.4	8.9	7.6
1986	174.6	45.9	24.3	9.3	7.9
1987	179.3	48.8	25.2	9.7	8.2
1988	184.1	51.8	26.2	10.2	8.5
1989	189.0	54.9	27.2	10.7	8.7
1990	194.1	58.3	28.2	11.2	9.0
1991	199.0	61.4	29.2	12.1	9.3
1992	204.2	64.7	30.3	13.2	9.6
1993	209.4	68.2	31.4	14.4	9.9
1994	214.8	71.8	32.5	15.7	10.3
1995	220.3	75.7	33.6	17.0	10.6
1996	225.8	79.4	35.7	18.2	10.9
1997	231.4	83.3	37.9	19.4	11.2
1998	237.1	87.3	40.2	20.7	11.6
1999	243.0	91.6	42.6	22.0	11.9
2000	249.0	96.1	45.3	23.5	12.3

population were fourteen years of age or younger and 4 percent were sixty-five or older. The majority of the population, 56.6 percent, lived in rural areas in 1980, and the average household size was 5.2 persons.

Economy

Although better known for its agricultural products--coffee, bananas, sugar, and cocoa--Costa Rica has built up a significant industrial base over the years, to the extent that the industrial contribution to the GDP is 27 percent greater than the agricultural contribution. This industrial base has allowed Costa Rica to benefit immensely from the Central American Common Market (CACM) and has contributed to the fact that Costa Ricans have the highest per capita GDP of the Central American countries.

Costa Rica's 1980 GNP totaled $3,820 million and per capita GNP was $1,726. Gross domestic product grew at an average annual rate of 6.5 percent between 1960 and 1970, 6 percent between 1970 and 1979, and 1.2 percent in 1981. The increasing importance of industry in the Costa Rican economy is illustrated by the fact that GDP in industry grew by an average annual rate of 9.4 percent between 1960 and 1970 and by 8.5 percent between 1970 and 1979. Conversely, GDP in agriculture experienced average annual growth rates of 5.7 percent between 1960 and 1970 and 2.6 percent between 1970 and 1979. The labor force numbered 712,500 in 1980 and the inflation rate was 18.1 percent.

Coffee and bananas historically have been the bulwarks of the Costa Rican economy, but since 1960 the government has sought to diversify away from that base. The vehicles chosen were sugar and beef and, more recently, the development of an industrial sector. The formation of the CACM was instrumental in the development of the industrial sector in that it widened the effective market and made possible economies of scale in the production of certain light manufactures.

Costa Rica has always imported more than it has exported, but the drop of world coffee prices and the rise in oil prices have exacerbated its trade deficit. According to former Vice President Jose Miguel Alfaro, "In 1970, one bag of coffee bought 100 barrels of oil. Today one bag of coffee buys just three barrels of oil." The Costa Rican trade deficit has increased from $85 million in 1970, to $200.6 million in 1975 and $511.1 million in 1980. The major Costa Rican exports are coffee (34 percent), bananas (8 percent), and beef (9 percent); the major export partners are the United States (33 percent), the Federal Republic of Germany (14 percent), Guatemala (8 percent), and El Salvador (6 percent); the latter two are CACM members. The principal Costa Rican imports are machinery and transport equipment (31 percent), manufactures (31 percent), chemicals (17 percent), and fuel (10 percent); the principal import partners are the United States (34 percent), Japan (14 percent), Guatemala (7 percent), and El Salvador (6 percent).

The record trade deficits, coupled with high oil prices, low world coffee prices, and high interest rates, have driven Costa Rica to the brink of bankruptcy. The Costa Rican debt stands at $3.2 billion, of which 41 percent are held by commercial banks, 30 percent by international financial organizations, and 14 percent by foreign governments. The remaining debt is denominated in Eurobonds and foreign CDs. The weight of the debt has forced Costa Rica to seek a renegotiation of its loans and standby arrangements with the International Monetary Fund. An extended fund facility negotiated with the IMF fell through in the Summer of 1981 because Costa Rica failed to carry out the austerity measures called for under the agreement. Costa Rica, which has not made any interest or principal payments on its debt since June 1981, has agreed to make token payments to its debtors to demonstrate its determination to repay loans. The government also is working closely with an IMF team to negotiate another standby facility, without which the commercial institutions will not advance further credit to Costa Rica.

Minerals

The only minerals currently mined in Costa Rica are gold and manganese, but the country is estimated to have 150 million metric tons of bauxite reserves and considerable copper reserves awaiting exploitation.

Forecasts

The Costa Rican population is projected to reach 2,759,700 in 1990 and 3,345,400 in the year 2000 (see Table 3.7), with increases of 25 percent between 1980 and 1990 and 21 percent between 1990 and 2000. There will be a significant decline from the 1980 level in the percentage of the population falling into the nonproductive category. In 1980, 42 percent of the population were classified as such, but by the year 2000 this will decline to 36 percent. Household size will average 4.6 persons in 1990 and 4.4 persons in 2000, down from a 5.2 average in 1980, but the number of households will increase 41 percent between 1980 and 1990 and 77 percent over the entire forecast period. Households totaled 425,000 in 1980 but will reach 600,000 in 1990 and 754,000 in the year 2000. By 1990, 49 percent of the population will reside in urban areas, and this will increase to 60 percent by the year 2000.

Gross national product will almost triple between 1980 and 2000. From a total of $3.8 billion in 1980, Costa Rican GNP will exceed $6 billion by 1990 and will amount to $10.9 billion in the year 2000 (see Table 3.8). The growth rates assumed for the GNP forecast--4.9 percent from 1980 to 1985 and 5.4 percent from 1984 to 2000--are slightly lower than the 6 percent rate that was recorded in 1978. Per capita income will nearly double over the same period, starting from $1,586 in 1980 and growing to $2,152 in 1990 and $3,004 in the year 2000. An average of 22,600 people will enter the labor force annually between 1980 and 1990 and 22,700 people annually between 1990 and 2000. The total labor force in 1990 will be 939,200 and 1,166,800 in the year 2000.

CUBA

Cuba is located 90 miles south of Florida and 100 miles east of Mexico's Yucatan peninsula. The inhabitants, mainly mulattoes but with significant numbers of Caucasians and Negroes, are Spanish-speaking and were, prior to government restrictions on religious freedom, strong Roman Catholics.

In 1959, the government of Fulgencio Batista was overthrown by forces led by Fidel Castro Ruz who subsequently imposed a Marxist-Leninist system of government on the country. Castro currently is

TABLE 3.7
GLOBESCAN medium growth demographic projections
for Costa Rica

Year	Population (Thousands)	Household Size	Households (Thousands)	Urban Population (Thousands)	Rural Population (Thousands)
1980	2213.0	5.2	425.6	960.4	1252.6
1981	2263.6	5.1	441.9	993.5	1270.1
1982	2315.3	5.0	458.8	1027.6	1287.7
1983	2368.3	5.0	476.4	1063.0	1305.3
1984	2422.4	4.9	494.7	1099.5	1322.9
1985	2477.8	4.8	513.6	1137.3	1340.5
1986	2531.8	4.8	529.8	1176.9	1354.9
1987	2586.9	4.7	546.6	1217.9	1369.1
1988	2643.3	4.7	563.8	1260.2	1383.0
1989	2700.9	4.6	581.6	1304.1	1396.8
1990	2759.7	4.6	600.0	1349.5	1410.2
1991	2815.7	4.6	614.4	1395.5	1420.2
1992	2872.7	4.6	629.1	1443.1	1429.7
1993	2931.0	4.5	644.2	1492.2	1438.7
1994	2990.4	4.5	659.7	1543.1	1447.3
1995	3051.0	4.5	675.5	1595.7	1455.3
1996	3107.7	4.5	690.6	1647.1	1460.6
1997	3165.5	4.5	706.0	1700.3	1465.3
1998	3224.4	4.5	721.7	1755.1	1469.3
1999	3284.4	4.5	737.8	1811.7	1472.7
2000	3345.4	4.4	754.3	1870.1	1475.3

Population by age and sex

Males	Females	Total	Age	Males	Females	Total
	1985 (Thousands)				2000 (Thousands)	
160.2	154.5	314.8	0-04	188.7	182.3	371.0
146.9	142.6	289.5	5-09	179.3	174.8	354.1
135.7	131.8	267.5	10-14	169.4	165.6	335.0
141.4	138.1	279.5	15-19	156.3	153.2	309.5
136.8	133.9	270.7	20-24	143.7	141.4	285.1
118.5	115.7	234.2	25-29	131.9	130.3	262.2
93.8	92.8	186.6	30-34	136.5	136.2	272.7
72.1	70.9	143.0	35-39	131.5	131.6	263.2
55.3	54.9	110.2	40-44	113.4	113.3	226.7
45.1	45.8	90.9	45-49	88.9	90.2	179.1
38.7	39.5	78.1	50-54	67.2	68.0	135.2
32.1	33.1	65.2	55-59	50.0	51.7	101.7
24.6	26.7	51.3	60-64	39.0	41.8	80.9
18.8	20.1	38.8	65-69	31.0	34.2	65.2
13.1	15.1	28.2	70-74	22.7	26.0	48.7
12.9	16.4	29.3	75+	24.1	31.2	55.3
1245.9	1231.8	2477.8	TOTAL	1673.7	1671.7	3345.4

TABLE 3.8
GLOBESCAN economic projections for Costa Rica

Year	GNP in 1980 US$ (Millions)	Per Capita Income	Labor Force (Thousands)	Dependency Ratio (Per 100)
1980	3820.0	1586.3	670.0	71.3
1981	4026.3	1634.6	691.2	69.8
1982	4243.7	1684.4	713.0	68.3
1983	4472.9	1735.7	735.6	66.9
1984	4714.4	1788.5	758.8	65.5
1985	4969.0	1843.0	782.8	64.1
1986	5237.3	1901.1	801.9	63.7
1987	5520.1	1961.0	821.5	63.3
1988	5818.2	2022.8	841.6	62.9
1989	6132.4	2086.6	862.1	62.4
1990	6463.5	2152.4	883.2	62.0
1991	6812.6	2223.5	903.1	61.6
1992	7180.4	2297.0	923.6	61.3
1993	7568.2	2373.0	944.5	60.9
1994	7976.9	2451.4	965.9	60.5
1995	8407.6	2532.5	987.7	60.2
1996	8861.6	2620.5	1008.7	59.7
1997	9340.1	2711.6	1030.2	59.3
1998	9844.5	2805.8	1052.0	58.9
1999	10376.1	2903.4	1074.4	58.5
2000	10936.4	3004.3	1097.2	58.1

Income distribution--population with incomes above:

Year	Poverty Line (Thousands)	$1000 (Thousands)	$2000 (Thousands)	$5000 (Thousands)	$10000 (Thousands)
1980	2165.5	1133.9	491.7	170.3	94.7
1981	2216.4	1197.1	525.0	182.0	97.8
1982	2268.4	1263.9	560.7	194.4	100.9
1983	2321.7	1334.3	598.7	207.6	104.1
1984	2376.2	1408.7	639.3	221.8	107.4
1985	2432.0	1487.2	682.7	236.9	110.9
1986	2486.3	1561.7	728.7	250.4	114.2
1987	2541.8	1639.9	777.7	264.6	117.7
1988	2598.6	1722.1	830.0	279.6	121.2
1989	2656.6	1808.4	885.9	295.5	124.9
1990	2716.0	1898.9	945.5	312.3	128.7
1991	2772.4	1982.0	1008.7	327.5	132.3
1992	2829.9	2068.7	1076.2	343.5	136.0
1993	2888.7	2159.3	1148.2	360.2	139.9
1994	2948.6	2253.7	1225.0	377.8	143.8
1995	3009.8	2352.3	1306.9	396.2	147.8
1996	3067.1	2438.1	1387.8	413.2	153.9
1997	3125.5	2527.0	1473.7	431.0	160.1
1998	3185.0	2619.1	1564.9	449.5	166.6
1999	3245.6	2714.6	1661.8	468.8	173.4
2000	3307.3	2813.6	1764.7	488.9	180.5

President of Cuba, first secretary of the Cuban Communist Party and president of the Council of State and Council of Ministers. The Cuban government has committed itself to assisting revolutionary forces in overthrowing democratic governments and helping friendly governments to repulse external foes or suppress internal dissidents. To this end, Cuba has between 15,000 and 19,000 soldiers in Angola; between 11,000 and 15,000 soldiers in Ethiopia; and numerous military advisors, medical personnel, teachers, and intelligence personnel in Nicaragua.

Demography

There were 9,729,000 people living in Cuba in 1980; of this total, 4.9 million were male and 4.7 million were female. The average household size in 1975 (the latest data available) was 4.3 persons per household. In 1980, 54 percent of the population were of working age; 31.8 percent were children below the age of fifteen. Urban areas support 65.4 percent of the Cuban population.

Economy

As a consequence of its alignment with the Soviet Union and other Eastern bloc nations, Cuba has been denied access to U.S. markets and to certain sources of international finance. The inability to sell its major export products--sugar, nickel and tobacco--to the United States has placed Cuba in the position of being almost entirely dependent on Russia for its economic survival. (It is estimated that Russian aid and subsidies to Cuba exceed $3 billion dollars annually.) The weakness of the Cuban economy is emphasized by the fact that notwithstanding the billions of rubles poured into the economy by the Soviets, average annual real per capita growth over the 1960-1978 period was -1.2 percent. Economic performance may have improved in recent years, but government reports of a 1982 growth rate in excess of 10 percent seem highly exaggerated, particularly given recent declines in the price of sugar and Cuba's severe external debt problem.

The mainstay of the Cuban economy historically has been sugar, closely followed in importance by tobacco and nickel. Approximately half of Cuba's sugar exports go to Eastern bloc nations at heavily subsidized prices, with the remainder being sold on the open market. The recent sugar glut has wreaked havoc with Cuba's foreign currency earnings. Other agricultural goods produced in Cuba include rice, bananas, potatoes and citrus fruits. There has been a marked attempt to diversify the Cuban economy away from agriculture and mining and toward the industrial and manufacturing sectors, but success in this venture has been limited.

The major portion of Cuba's trade in the past twenty years has been conducted with Eastern bloc states; this was accentuated when Cuba joined CMEA (the Eastern bloc common market) in 1972. Eighty percent of Cuba's exports involve sugar, and 80 percent of all Cuban exports are destined for CMEA countries (65 percent to the Soviet Union; 15 percent to the remainder). Cuba's principal imports are machinery and transport equipment, industrial materials, food and live animals, and petroleum. Forty-nine percent of Cuban imports originate from the Soviet Union, 14 percent from other Communist countries, and 6 percent from Spain. Japan and Canada also play significant roles in Cuban imports. Since Cuba deals with CMEA countries mostly on a barter basis, it encounters difficulty finding the hard currency to import needed goods from Western countries.

Cuba's foreign debt is purported to be $10.5 billion, $7.3 billion of which is owed to the Soviet Union. Of the remaining Cuban debt, $1.8 billion is owed to Western governments and $1.2 billion to Western banks. Finding difficulty in meeting debt payments, Cuban officials began negotiations in late 1982 with several Western economics ministers in an effort to reschedule the debt.

Mineral Commodities

The mineral industry in Cuba is dominated by nickel production—nickel sulfide smelter concentrate and nickel oxides. Cuba is the world's fourth-largest producer of nickel, and nickel exports to non-CMEA countries account for between 10 percent and 12 percent of hard currency earnings. In addition to nickel, other minerals produced in Cuba are cement, chromium, cobalt, copper, manganese ore, crude petroleum, petroleum products, and crude steel.

Forecasts

Our forecasts suggest that Cuba's population will increase by 7.6 percent from 1980 levels to a total 10.5 million by 1990, and will increase further to 11.6 million by 2000—an increase of 10.7 percent (see Table 3.9). Household size will decrease from 4.3 in 1980 to 3.6 in 1990 and 3.5 in 2000. Decreasing household size coupled with an increasing population will cause an increase in the number of households: 2.3 million in 1980, 2.9 million in 1990, and 3.3 million in 2000.

By 1990, the percentage of the population living in urban areas will have increased by 5.1 percent to 7.3 million; there will be a further increase by the year 2000 when 75 percent (8.7 million) of the population will be residing in urban areas. The makeup of the population in 2000 will be very similar to the 1980 population in regard to male-female distribution. There will, however, be a shift in the age of the population. The largest segments of the 1980 population were the 5-9 (10.9 percent), 10-14 (11.9 percent), and 15-19 (11.6 percent) age groups. The largest segments in the 2000 population will be the 25-29 age group (8.7 percent), the 30-34 age group (9.4 percent), and the 35-39 age group (9.1 percent).

Our economic forecasts suggest that Cuban GNP may well increase to $12.2 billion in 1990 and $17.5 billion in 2000 (see Table 3.10). Moderate average annual GNP growth rates between 1985 and 2000, coupled with low population growth rates, will result in significant gains in per capita income that will increase from $844 in 1980 to $1,091 in 1990 and $1,416 in 2000. Growth rates of this order appear quite possible when viewed in the context of potential nickel production.

The prospects for Cuba's future nickel production were examined, using trend impact analysis (TIA). This analysis led us to forecast a substantial growth in production—by as much as 111 percent—from 1981 to 1990. This contrasts with a growth of only 8 percent over the 1968-1980 period. The forecast reflects the impact of several important events on future production of nickel in Cuba; they are listed from most negative to most positive in Table 3.11. The TIA forecast is illustrated graphically in

44

TABLE 3.9
GLOBESCAN medium growth demographic projections
for Cuba

Year	Population (Thousands)	Household Size	Households (Thousands)	Urban Population (Thousands)	Rural Population (Thousands)
1980	9732.0	4.3	2273.8	6364.7	3367.3
1981	9792.4	4.2	2330.4	6454.3	3338.0
1982	9853.1	4.1	2388.4	5645.2	3307.9
1983	9914.2	4.1	2447.9	6637.4	3276.9
1984	9975.7	4.0	2508.8	6730.8	3244.9
1985	10037.6	3.9	2571.2	6825.6	3212.0
1986	10123.8	3.8	2630.3	6934.1	3189.7
1987	10210.8	3.8	2690.8	7044.3	3166.4
1988	10298.5	3.7	2752.6	7156.3	3142.1
1989	10386.9	3.7	2815.9	7270.1	3116.8
1990	10476.1	3.6	2880.6	7385.7	3090.5
1991	10589.7	3.6	2932.4	7518.0	3071.8
1992	10704.6	3.6	2985.2	7652.6	3051.9
1993	10820.7	3.6	3038.8	7789.7	3030.9
1994	10938.0	3.5	3093.5	7929.3	3008.7
1995	11056.6	3.5	3149.1	8071.3	2985.3
1996	11163.4	3.5	3180.7	8197.8	2965.6
1997	11271.2	3.5	3212.7	8326.2	2944.9
1998	11380.0	3.5	3244.9	8456.7	2923.3
1999	11489.9	3.5	3277.5	8589.2	2900.6
2000	11600.8	3.5	3310.5	8723.8	2877.0

Population by age and sex

1985 (Thousands)				2000 (Thousands)		
Males	Females	Total	Age	Males	Females	Total
415.8	397.8	813.5	0-04	486.1	463.9	949.9
428.3	411.6	839.9	5-09	482.1	462.8	944.9
528.0	507.9	1035.9	10-14	456.9	440.4	897.4
577.2	555.1	1132.3	15-19	404.7	388.3	793.1
560.6	539.6	1100.1	20-24	416.4	400.5	816.9
383.3	373.2	756.4	25-29	510.9	493.9	1004.7
360.1	351.8	711.9	30-34	555.8	539.2	1095.0
336.0	330.7	666.7	35-39	539.0	524.9	1063.9
301.1	296.7	597.8	40-44	366.1	360.1	726.3
261.1	256.8	517.9	45-49	341.1	337.0	678.2
206.2	206.4	412.6	50-54	313.1	313.1	626.2
186.5	189.2	375.7	55-59	273.1	275.7	548.9
154.5	157.9	312.3	60-64	226.9	231.8	458.7
136.4	136.7	273.1	65-69	166.5	176.2	342.8
108.9	109.0	217.9	70-74	133.7	146.7	280.4
137.6	136.0	273.6	75+	173.8	199.9	373.7
5081.4	4956.2	10037.6	TOTAL	5846.3	5754.5	11600.8

TABLE 3.10
GLOBESCAN economic projections for Cuba

Year	GNP in 1980 US$ (Millions)	Per Capita Income	Labor Force (Thousands)	Dependency Ratio (Per 100)
1980	8741.8	844.4	2993.7	63.7
1981	9004.1	864.3	3055.4	61.3
1982	9274.2	884.8	3118.4	58.9
1983	9552.4	905.7	3182.7	56.7
1984	9839.0	927.1	3248.3	54.5
1985	10134.1	949.0	3315.3	52.5
1986	10509.1	975.8	3368.0	51.3
1987	10897.9	1003.3	3421.6	50.2
1988	11301.2	1031.5	3476.0	49.1
1989	11719.3	1060.6	3531.3	48.1
1990	12152.9	1090.5	3587.5	47.0
1991	12602.6	1118.7	3624.4	47.1
1992	13068.9	1147.6	3661.6	47.2
1993	13552.4	1177.3	3699.2	47.3
1994	14053.9	1207.8	3737.1	47.4
1995	14573.9	1239.0	3775.5	47.5
1996	15113.1	1272.6	3806.6	47.7
1997	15672.3	1307.0	3838.0	47.9
1998	16252.2	1342.4	3869.6	48.1
1999	16853.5	1378.8	3901.5	48.3
2000	17477.1	1416.1	3933.7	48.5

Income distribution--population with incomes above:

Year	Poverty Line (Thousands)	$1000 (Thousands)	$2000 (Thousands)	$5000 (Thousands)	$10000 (Thousands)
1980	9528.2	2663.5	363.6		
1981	9594.8	2960.1	381.6		
1982	9661.8	3289.8	400.5		
1983	9729.4	3656.2	420.4		
1984	9797.4	4063.4	441.3		
1985	9865.8	4516.0	463.2		
1986	9955.2	4906.5	514.9		
1987	10045.4	5330.8	572.5		
1988	10136.3	5791.8	636.5		
1989	10228.1	6292.7	707.6		
1990	10320.8	6836.8	786.7		
1991	10436.6	7114.5	901.0		
1992	10553.7	7403.5	1031.8		
1993	10672.1	7704.2	1181.6		
1994	10791.8	8017.1	1353.1		
1995	10912.9	8342.7	1549.6		
1996	11021.9	8592.1	1727.7		
1997	11132.0	8849.0	1926.2		
1998	11243.1	9113.6	2147.6		
1999	11355.4	9386.1	2394.4		
2000	11468.8	9666.8	2669.5		

TABLE 3.11
Events that will have an impact on nickel production in Cuba

Event No.	Year/ Probability	Years to First Impact	Years to Maximum Impact	Maximum Impact	Years to Steady State Impact	Steady State Impact	Relative Impact
6	1985 0.30 1990 0.50	2	4	-15.0%	4	-15.0%	-9.14
	Prolonged period of negative or zero growth in Western European economies.						
4	1985 0.20 1990 0.60	2	4	-10.0%	4	-10.0%	-4.73
	Use of ceramics instead of nickel-base alloys in aircraft heat and corrosion resistance applications.						
5	1985 0.10 1990 0.40	1	3	20.0%	3	20.0%	7.32
	Renewed trade between Cuba and the U.S.						
7	1985 0.25 1990 0.50	0	3	10.0%	3	10.0%	7.63
	Opening of the Latin American market to Cuban nickel exports.						
2	1985 0.10 1990 0.60	1	3	75.0%	4	50.0%	29.9
	Construction of the planned Las Camariocas nickel oxide plant.						
3	1985 0.40 1990 0.90	1	2	25.0%	2	25.0%	31.7
	Fulfillment of planned expansions at the Nicaro and Moa plants.						
1	1985 0.80 1990 0.99	1	3	75.0%	4	50.0%	110.
	Completion of Punta Gorda nickel refinery.						

Figure 3.1. In our view, completion of the Punta Gorda nickel refinery will have a positive impact on Cuba's nickel production in that its refining capacity will be doubled. Cuba's need for foreign currency--a need that is fulfilled to some extent by nickel sales--should assure the government's commitment to swift completion of the plant (.80 by 1985; .99 by 1990). Soviet interest in obtaining the cobalt which is extracted from Cuban nickel ore in part accounts for this investment in refining operations. There is thus likely to be strong, stable Soviet interest in expanded Cuban nickel production.

On the other hand, a prolonged period of negative or zero economic growth in Western Europe would have a negative effect on Cuba's nickel production. The major purchasers of Cuban nickel are West Germany, Italy and the Netherlands, and a slowdown in their economies will be reflected in reduced nickel usage due to a cutback in industrial activity. As orders for nickel are curtailed, Cuban officials will be forced to reduce production. According to the forecast, there is a moderate likelihood (.30 by 1985; .50 by 1990) of such an event occurring.

The Nicaro and Moa plants are nickel refineries that were owned by American companies prior to being expropriated by Cuba. Smelting capacity at these plants is presently at the same level as pre-Castro days, and nickel mining is forced to keep pace with smelting capacity. If the capacity at those two plants were expanded (.40 by 1985; .90 by 1990), nickel production would be positively affected.

Construction of the Las Camariocas nickel plant (.10 by 1985; 60 by 1990) would have much the same effect as the preceding positive impacts. By increasing smelting capacity, it provides a vehicle through which Cuban nickel production could be substantially increased.

DOMINICAN REPUBLIC

Hispaniola, an island situated between Cuba and Puerto Rico, is now shared by two countries: French-speaking Haiti occupies the western one-third and Spanish-speaking Dominican Republic the remainder. The Dominican Republic encompasses 48,464 square kilometers (18,712 square miles) of Hispaniola, and its border with Haiti extends for 310 kilometers (193 miles). There are some 1,600 kilometers (1,000 miles) of coastline in the Dominican Republic; the capital, Santo Domingo, is located on the southern coastline which fronts the Caribbean Sea.

The inhabitants of the Dominican Republic are primarily of mixed descent, but 16 percent are Caucasian and 11 percent are of Negro descent. The official language is Spanish, and the official religion is Roman Catholicism.

The Dominican Republic is a stable, multiparty democracy, with over twenty active political parties. Under the present constitution, power in the Dominican Republic is divided among independent executive, legislative and judicial branches. The head of the executive branch is the president, a position presently held by Salvador Jorge Blanco who was elected by popular vote in May 1982.

Demography

There were six million people living in the Dominican Republic in 1980. A significant percentage of the population (47 percent) fall into the

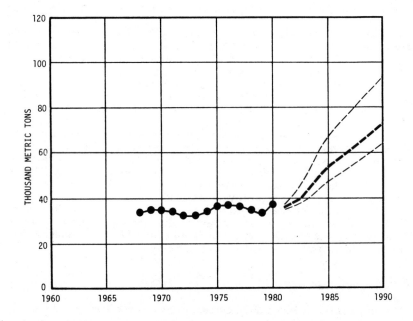

Figure 3.1 Forecast of Cuba's nickel production

		Forecast		
Year	History/ Baseline	Lower	Center	Upper

Trend Impact Analysis

Baseline Curve No. = 14   Confidence Percentiles = 25 and 75

Year	History/ Baseline	Lower	Center	Upper
1968	33.70			
1969	35.20			
1970	35.20			
1971	34.00			
1972	32.00			
1978	32.00			
1974	33.90			
1975	36.60			
1976	37.02			
1977	36.75			
1978	34.79			
1979	32.32			
1980	37.00			
1981	36.06	34.96	36.11	37.26
1982	36.25	36.68	38.43	41.97
1983	36.43	39.50	42.70	50.31
1984	36.62	43.46	48.61	61.04
1985	36.80	46.77	52.75	66.99
1986	36.98	50.20	56.93	72.81
1987	37.16	53.59	60.94	78.31
1988	37.33	57.00	64.78	83.48
1989	37.51	60.42	68.34	88.17
1990	37.68	63.98	72.32	93.38

Figure 3.1 (Cont.) Cuba's nickel production (thousand metric tons)

nonproductive category. Fifty-one percent of the 1980 population lived in urban areas, and the average household size was 5.1 persons.

Economy

In his August inauguration speech, President Jorge Blanco told the nation that it was in a state of financial bankruptcy and outlined an austerity program designed to reflect a sinking economy. The prime culprits in this decline have been a decline in the price of the primary Dominican exports coupled with spiraling oil prices.

Between 1968 and 1974, the GDP of the Dominican Republic grew at an average annual rate of 11 percent, one of the highest growth rates in the world. Growth slowed somewhat between 1974 and 1978, and fell to 5.3 percent in 1979 due to the double shock of hurricane David and tropical storm Frederick and a 50 percent increase in the cost of oil imports.

Gross national product in the Dominican Republic totaled $6.2 billion in 1980 and per capita GNP was $1,043. Growth rates in agriculture were slower than in industry and services during the 1960-1980 period. Agriculture is still a very important sector in the economy. Agriculture contributed 16.7 percent of the 1980 GDP; industry, 26.7 percent; services, 52.3 percent; and natural resources, 4.3 percent. The labor force of the Dominican Republic numbered 1.5 million people in 1980, and the inflation rate in that year was 16.6 percent.

The most important crop in the agricultural sector is sugar; in 1980, sugar and sugar byproducts earned 34 percent of total export earnings. The dominance of sugar also extends to the manufacturing sector where most manufacturing centers on the processing of sugar. Other important crops include coffee, cocoa, tobacco, and bananas. Crops such as rice, potatoes, maize and beans are grown for domestic consumption.

Another sector of the country's economy subject to the vagaries of world markets is the minerals industry. The principal commodities in this sector are gold, silver, and bauxite--all export commodities. Rapidly rising gold and silver prices in 1980 increased the earnings of those commodities, even though export volume had declined from the previous year. The reduction in the prices of these two commodities in the 1981-1982 period severely curtailed revenue earned from exports. Earnings from bauxite exports also declined, the result of a worldwide recession and the resultant reduced demand for aluminum.

Two other important elements of the economy are tourism and the government's participation in the economy. The Dominican Republic has long been a well-visited tourist site, but the government is seeking to attract a larger share of Caribbean-bound tourists. To that end, a cabinet-level Secretariat of State for Tourism was formed in 1979, and the Central Bank has made funds available for the development of the north coast for tourism purposes. The government's involvement in the economy extends even further: some twenty-six state enterprises are controlled under the umbrella of the Corporacion Dominicana de Empresas Estatales (Corde). These enterprises range in activity from the manufacturing of cars to the sale of insurance. Gold extraction, sugar production and processing, and the utilities are all government controlled.

The need to import virtually all its petroleum needs and the continuing upward pressure of oil prices prior to 1981 have caused severe trade imbalances. The oil price effects were somewhat mitigated by the agreement between Mexico and Venezuela to provide concessional financing for 30 percent of the petroleum bills of their Caribbean and Central American customers. Unfortunately, this relief has been offset by tumbling commodity prices so that the reduced or stabilized import costs are counterbalanced by severely depressed levels of export earnings.

The major exports from the Dominican Republic include sugar (23 percent), coffee (18 percent), gold and silver (15 percent), ferronickel (14 percent), cocoa (9 percent), and tobacco (6 percent). These exports were purchased by the United States (including Puerto Rico--59 percent), Switzerland (14 percent), Venezuela (6 percent), the Netherlands (5 percent), and Spain (5 percent). Petroleum products (23 percent), machinery (15 percent), metals (9 percent), cereals and food oils (8 percent), and motor vehicles purchased from the United States (44 percent), Venezuela (18 percent), Netherlands Antilles (7 percent), and Japan (7 percent) comprise the principal imports and import partners of the Dominican Republic.

Mineral Commodities

In addition to the production of gold, silver, and bauxite, the Dominican Republic produces cement, copper, gypsum, ferroalloys, lime, mercury, and nickel; some petroleum refining is also carried out. Gold and silver are exported in a combination called dore--84 percent silver and 16 percent gold. Production of these commodities is for the most part dominated by foreigners: Alcoa has the major bauxite concession; Falconbridge of Canada operates the major ferronickel mine. Soufriere of France conducts other local mineral operations. The country's sole oil refining is 50 percent Shell-owned; and, prior to being bought out by the government in 1979, foreigners owned 54 percent of Rosario Dominicana, the country's major producer of gold and silver.

Forecasts

Our forecasts of the population of the Dominican Republic suggest that it will increase from 5.9 million in 1980 to 7.5 million in 1990 and 9.3 million in the year 2000 (see Table 3.12). This represents increases of 27 percent between 1980 and 1990 and 23 percent between 1990 and 2000. The number of people in the "productive" category will rise from its 1980 level of 53 percent to reach 61 percent in the year 2000. Much as in 1980, the 0-4 age group will be the dominant grouping in the year 2000, with fully 12 percent of the population falling into that category. Average household size will decline by one person over the life of the forecast period: from 5.1 in 1980 to 4.5 in 1990 and 4.1 in the year 2000. The population of the Dominican Republic will acquire a decidedly urban flavor as we get closer to the year 2000. In 1980, 51 percent of the population resided in urban areas but in 1990 and 2000, 60 percent and 66 percent, respectively, of the population will reside in urban areas.

The economy of the Dominican Republic should experience 80 percent growth between 1980 and 1990 and 70 percent between 1990 and 2000 as measured by GNP. Gross national product will total $10.9 billion in 1990 and $18.4 billion in the year 2000 in contrast to a GNP of $6.2 billion in 1980 (see Table 3.13). The assumed growth rates (4.8 percent from 1980 to 1985 and 5.4 percent from 1985 to 2000) compare favorably with historical

52

TABLE 3.12
GLOBESCAN medium growth demographic projections
for Dominican Republic

Year	Population (Thousands)	Household Size	Households (Thousands)	Urban Population (Thousands)	Rural Population (Thousands)
1980	5947.0	5.1	1157.0	3033.0	2914.0
1981	6096.4	5.1	1203.2	3165.6	2930.8
1982	6249.5	5.0	1251.3	3304.0	2945.5
1983	6406.5	4.9	1301.2	3448.5	2958.0
1984	6567.4	4.9	1353.2	3599.3	2968.1
1985	6732.4	4.8	1407.2	3756.7	2975.7
1986	6886.3	4.7	1459.8	3898.7	2987.5
1987	7043.6	4.7	1514.3	4046.1	2997.5
1988	7204.6	4.6	1570.9	4199.1	3005.5
1989	7369.2	4.5	1629.5	4357.8	3011.4
1990	7537.6	4.5	1690.4	4522.6	3015.0
1991	7701.4	4.4	1744.7	4675.0	3026.4
1992	7868.7	4.4	1800.9	4832.5	3036.1
1993	8039.6	4.3	1858.8	4995.4	3044.2
1994	8214.2	4.3	1918.6	5163.7	3050.5
1995	8392.7	4.2	1980.3	5337.7	3054.9
1996	8562.5	4.2	2033.0	5496.2	3066.3
1997	8735.8	4.2	2087.2	5659.3	3076.4
1998	8912.6	4.2	2142.8	5827.3	3085.2
1999	9092.9	4.1	2199.9	6000.3	3092.6
2000	9276.9	4.1	2258.5	6178.4	3098.5

Population by age and sex

1985 (Thousands)				2000 (Thousands)		
Males	Females	Total	Age	Males	Females	Total
508.6	492.1	1000.7	0-04	602.4	581.1	1183.5
453.3	442.7	896.0	5-09	563.2	547.1	1110.2
443.5	432.8	876.3	10-14	516.0	505.2	1021.2
412.2	404.0	816.2	15-19	479.4	473.8	953.3
350.6	345.3	695.9	20-24	431.0	430.2	861.2
281.3	277.3	558.6	25-29	419.5	419.5	839.0
223.4	219.3	443.2	30-34	387.2	389.7	776.8
170.8	168.4	339.2	35-39	327.7	331.5	659.2
134.0	132.3	266.3	40-44	261.4	264.5	525.9
107.3	106.8	214.1	45-49	205.5	207.7	413.2
89.6	90.6	180.1	50-54	153.9	156.7	310.5
71.7	73.2	144.9	55-59	116.8	120.3	237.1
54.7	57.4	112.1	60-64	88.8	93.6	182.4
39.6	41.3	80.9	65-69	68.3	74.3	142.6
26.6	28.0	54.6	70-74	47.7	53.4	101.1
25.0	28.4	53.3	75+	47.4	56.9	104.3
3392.0	3340.4	6732.4	TOTAL	4716.3	4705.3	9421.5

TABLE 3.13
GLOBESCAN economic projections for Dominican Republic

Year	GNP in 1980 US$ (Millions)	Per Capita Income	Labor Force (Thousands)	Dependency Ratio (Per 100)
1980	6200.0	947.7	1592.2	89.4
1981	6581.3	981.3	1651.6	87.1
1982	6986.0	1016.1	1713.3	84.9
1983	7415.7	1052.2	1777.2	82.7
1984	7871.8	1089.5	1843.5	80.6
1985	8355.9	1128.2	1912.3	78.6
1986	8807.1	1161.4	1975.0	77.0
1987	9282.7	1195.6	2039.7	75.4
1988	9783.9	1230.7	2106.5	73.9
1989	10312.3	1267.0	2175.6	72.4
1990	10869.1	1304.2	2246.8	71.0
1991	11456.1	1344.0	2308.2	70.2
1992	12074.7	1385.0	2371.2	69.5
1993	12726.7	1427.2	2436.0	68.7
1994	13414.0	1470.7	2502.5	68.0
1995	14138.3	1515.6	2570.8	67.3
1996	14901.8	1564.1	2637.2	66.5
1997	15706.5	1614.2	2705.4	65.8
1998	16554.6	1665.9	2775.3	65.1
1999	17448.6	1719.3	2847.0	64.3
2000	18390.8	1774.4	2920.6	63.6

Income distribution--population with incomes above:

Year	Poverty Line (Thousands)	$1000 (Thousands)	$2000 (Thousands)	$5000 (Thousands)	$10000 (Thousands)
1980	5640.4	1626.2	761.5	282.8	217.4
1981	5792.9	1741.7	796.0	291.8	226.1
1982	5949.6	1865.4	832.1	301.0	235.2
1983	6110.5	1997.9	869.9	310.6	244.7
1984	6275.8	2139.9	909.4	320.5	254.5
1985	6445.5	2291.9	950.7	330.7	264.7
1986	6602.9	2425.4	993.6	347.6	273.7
1987	6764.2	2566.6	1038.6	365.5	283.0
1988	6929.4	2716.1	1085.6	384.2	292.6
1989	7098.7	2874.4	1134.6	403.9	302.5
1990	7272.1	3041.8	1186.0	424.6	312.8
1991	7440.8	3215.4	1284.3	462.0	322.8
1992	7613.4	3399.0	1390.9	502.6	333.1
1993	7789.9	3593.0	1506.3	546.9	343.7
1994	7970.6	3798.1	1631.2	595.0	354.7
1995	8155.5	4014.9	1766.6	647.4	366.0
1996	8331.4	4265.2	1885.8	690.7	376.8
1997	8511.1	4531.1	2013.2	737.0	387.8
1998	8694.7	4813.6	2149.1	786.3	399.2
1999	8882.2	5113.7	2294.2	839.0	410.9
2000	9073.8	5432.5	2449.1	895.1	423.0

Dominican growth rates (i.e., 5.4 percent in 1980). Per capita income will also record significant gains. With GNP growth outstripping population growth, per capita income will be $1,310 in 1990 and $1,802 in the year 2000, increases of 38 percent and 90 percent, respectively, over the 1980 level. The labor force will expand from its 1980 level to reach 2.2 million in 1990 and 2.9 million in the year 2000, and the dependency ratio will decline to 71/100 in 1990 and 63.3/100 in the year 2000.

EL SALVADOR

El Salvador, comprising 8,260 square miles (21,393 square kilometers), is the only Central American country that does not have coastlines touching both the Pacific Ocean and the Caribbean Sea. El Salvador is bounded by Guatemala, Honduras, the Pacific Ocean and, across the Gulf of Fonseca, Nicaragua. The predominantly Roman Catholic population is approximately 89 percent Mestizo, 10 percent Indian, and 1 percent Caucasian and is almost exclusively Spanish-speaking.

El Salvador has been the scene of many revolutions and military-dominated administrations. The constitution of 1962 provided for an elected president (serving a five-year term), a Legislative Assembly of fifty-four members (each serving a two-year term), and a judicial branch. Citing the inability of the government headed by General Carlos Humberto Romero to control the violence of both left- and right-wing factions, a group of officers led by Colonel Jaime Abdul Gutierrez and Colonel Adolfo Arnoldo Majano Ramos overthrew the Humberto regime in 1979. The country was subsequently put under the rulership of a five-man junta (three members of which were civilian) that promised social and economic reforms and a transition to democracy.

The junta was accused by the far left of being a U.S. puppet while the far right opposed the reform measures; both attempted to overthrow the government. The violence in the country escalated almost to the point of a full-fledged civil war. The leftists received arms and other aid from external sources; the Salvadoran army received arms and aid from the United States to put down the leftists; and charges circulated that the army was guilty of atrocities against its political opponents. The junta, headed by the formerly exiled Jose Napoleon Duarte, held elections in 1982 for the Constituent Assembly; the leftists did not participate. None of the participating parties won a majority of Constituent Assembly seats, and a Government of National Unity was formed to govern pending presidential elections. This government consists of representatives of the three major parties and is headed by Alvaro Magana. Roberto d'Aubuisson, a rightist who had been accused of complicity in many of the atrocities committed in El Salvador, was elected speaker of the Constituent Assembly.

Demography

The population of El Salvador numbered 4.8 million in 1980. The population is disproportionately young with 18 percent under the age of five. Forty-eight percent of the population are either younger than fifteen years of age or older than sixty-five years of age, indicating a relatively high dependency ratio. Indicative of the agrarian orientation of the Salvadoran populace, almost 59 percent of the population live in rural areas. The average household size in 1975 was 5.1 persons.

Economy

Over the period 1970-1979, Salvadoran GNP grew by 1.4 percent per year and, in 1980, totaled $2.69 million. The labor force size was 1.5 million and, of that total, 51 percent were employed in agriculture, 22 percent in industry, and 27 percent in services. Twenty-eight percent of Salvadoran GDP resulted from activity in the agricultural sector, while 22 percent and 50 percent of the GDP issued from the industrial and service sectors, respectively. The average annual inflation rate over the 1970-1979 period was 10.8 percent but jumped to 17.4 percent from 1979 to 1980.

Ranked among the world's top six coffee producers, El Salvador is heavily dependent on coffee exports for hard currency. In an economy where the agricultural sector is of paramount importance, coffee accounts for 40 percent of total employment and between 60 and 65 percent of export earnings. Other important agricultural commodities are cotton, sugar (export crops), maize, beans, and sorghum (domestic consumption).

The Salvadoran agricultural sector historically has been dominated by a group of wealthy landowners and businessmen loosely referred to as the "fourteen families." Prior to the introduction of land reform measures, approximately 75 percent of all arable Salvadoran land was owned by 8 percent of the farms. Furthermore, a 1975 survey of Salvadoran income distribution showed that the richest 5 percent of Salvadorans earned two-fifths of the national income while the poorest 20 percent received 2 percent. It was this gross maldistribution of income and productive resources that brought about the downfall of the Humberto Romero government and prompted the new junta to institute a program of land reform.

The Salvadoran land redistribution plan was broken up into three phases. Under Phase 1, all farms larger than 1,235 acres were expropriated (the original owners were compensated) and converted to peasant cooperatives. Phase 2 provided for farms larger than 247 acres to be similarly expropriated and converted to cooperatives. Phase 3 permitted peasants to purchase up to seventeen acres of land if they had been working on that land either as renters or sharecroppers. Phase 1 of the program is currently being carried out but Phases 2 and 3 have had indifferent success. Eighty-five percent of the families would have benefited under the Phase 2 and Phase 3 proposals, to the detriment of the landowners, and, as a result, a substantial amount of pressure was applied to defeat those two phases. The end result was that the Assembly voted to abandon Phase 2, and Phase 3 was suspended. As of this date, limited activity has resumed on Phase 3 proposals.

One of the benefits that El Salvador gained from becoming a member of CACM was the expansion of its industrial sector. The widening of the effective market caused Salvadoran industry to increase production to the extent that El Salvador became the most industrialized of the CACM countries. Salvadoran industrial production includes foodstuffs, textiles, clothing, and other consumer goods.

The continuing violence in El Salvador has made the country a less than desirable site for investment by either the foreign or domestic private sector. Rising oil prices and falling coffee prices have combined to place the Salvadoran economy in dire straits, and foreign commercial banks are in no mood to extend additional credit. The country has been forced to look to the United States and other international lending institutions to tide it over.

The most important Salvadoran exports are coffee and cotton. Coffee accounted for 61 percent of export earnings in 1979 while cotton accounted for 10 percent. The countries to which Salvadoran goods were exported include the United States (32 percent), Federal Republic of Germany (18 percent), Guatemala (13 percent), and the Netherlands (9 percent). El Salvador's most important imports are chemicals (20 percent); mining, construction, and industrial machinery (11 percent); foodstuffs (9 percent); motor vehicles (8 percent); crude petroleum (8 percent); and iron, steel, and metal products (8 percent). These goods are bought from the United States (29 percent), Guatemala (14 percent), Japan (11 percent), and Venezuela (9 percent).

Forecasts

Population growth in El Salvador will be relatively steady over the life of the forecast period (see Table 3.14). Population will increase by 36 percent between 1980 and 1990 and 34 percent between 1990 and 2000, and will number 6.5 million in 1990 and 8.7 million in the year 2000. The most populous age group will still be the 0-4 category, accounting for about 15 percent of the population, but those in the nonproductive category (below fifteen and above sixty-five years of age) will decline to 44.7 percent of the population by the year 2000. Average household size will decline slightly--from 5.1 in 1980 to 4.9 in 1990 and 4.7 in the year 2000-- but the number of households will almost double--from 944.3 in 1980 to 1,857.4 in the year 2000. The distinctly rural composition of the Salvadoran population will erode slightly, as the urban portion of the population increases to 45.5 percent in 1990 and 52.5 percent in the year 2000.

Salvadoran GNP could experience reasonable growth between 1980 and 2000 but per capita GNP will grow at a much slower rate. Gross national product will amount to $4.4 billion in 1990 and $7.5 billion in 2000 (see Table 3.15), while per capita income will be $642 in 1990 and $811 in the year 2000. Total growth for GNP will be 180 percent over the forecast period, in contrast to a growth of only 60 percent for per capita income. The labor force will double by the year 2000, as it grows from 1.5 million in 1980 to 2.1 million in 1990 and 2.9 million in the year 2000. The dependency ratio will decline from 93.3/100 in 1980 to 89.2/100 in 1990 and 81.1/100 in the year 2000.

GRENADA

Grenada, a former member of the now-defunct West Indies Federation and the Windward Islands Associated States, is the last link in the chain referred to as the Windward Islands, and is located 90 miles north of Trinidad and 150 miles southwest of Barbados. The State of Grenada consists of Grenada (the main island) plus the Grenadines, a group of small islands stretching between Grenada and St. Vincent. The largest of the Grenadine Islands is called Carriacon Island. The majority of the country's population is of African descent with the remainder being either mulatto, East Indian, or Caucasian. The official language is English but, reflecting

TABLE 3.14
GLOBESCAN medium growth demographic projections
for El Salvador

Year	Population (Thousands)	Household Size	Households (Thousands)	Urban Population (Thousands)	Rural Population (Thousands)
1980	4797.0	5.1	944.3	1971.6	2825.4
1981	4943.5	5.1	976.1	2050.2	2893.3
1982	5094.6	5.0	1008.9	2132.1	2962.5
1983	5250.2	5.0	1042.9	2217.1	3033.0
1984	5410.6	5.0	1078.0	2305.6	3105.0
1985	5575.8	5.0	1114.3	2397.6	3178.2
1986	5751.8	5.0	1153.6	2502.5	3249.3
1987	5933.3	5.0	1194.2	2611.9	3321.4
1988	6120.6	5.0	1236.3	2726.2	3394.4
1989	6313.7	4.9	1279.9	2845.4	3468.3
1990	6513.0	4.9	1325.0	2969.9	3543.0
1991	6708.9	4.9	1370.3	3101.1	3607.9
1992	6910.8	4.9	1417.3	3238.0	3672.8
1993	7118.7	4.9	1465.8	3381.0	3737.8
1994	7333.0	4.8	1516.0	3530.3	3802.7
1995	7553.6	4.8	1567.9	3686.2	3867.4
1996	7773.3	4.8	1621.9	3850.7	3922.6
1997	7999.5	4.8	1677.8	4022.6	3976.9
1998	8232.2	4.7	1735.7	4202.2	4030.0
1999	8471.6	4.7	1795.5	4389.7	4081.9
2000	8718.1	4.7	1857.4	4585.7	4132.4

Population by age and sex

1985 (Thousands)				2000 (Thousands)		
Males	Females	Total	Age	Males	Females	Total
498.8	481.0	979.9	0-04	677.7	652.9	1330.6
412.4	400.7	813.1	5-09	601.7	582.7	1184.4
350.9	342.1	693.1	10-14	539.7	523.1	1062.7
299.2	293.1	592.3	15-19	482.7	470.4	953.1
255.2	250.5	505.7	20-24	401.6	394.4	796.0
214.0	209.6	423.6	25-29	339.6	335.9	675.6
171.1	167.1	338.2	30-34	287.4	286.5	573.9
133.9	131.5	265.4	35-39	243.9	243.9	487.8
107.9	107.2	215.1	40-44	203.5	202.9	406.4
88.2	88.6	176.8	45-49	161.0	160.4	321.5
77.6	79.3	156.9	50-54	123.7	124.5	248.2
65.8	68.9	134.7	55-59	96.7	99.4	196.2
47.8	51.8	99.6	60-64	75.4	79.5	154.9
33.3	38.0	71.3	65-69	61.3	67.0	128.2
24.8	29.7	54.5	70-74	45.7	52.2	97.9
23.4	32.4	55.8	75+	44.0	56.8	100.7
2804.3	2771.5	5575.8	TOTAL	4385.5	4332.6	8718.1

TABLE 3.15
GLOBESCAN economic projections for El Salvador

Year	GNP in 1980 US$ (Millions)	Per Capita Income	Labor Force (Thousands)	Dependency Ratio (Per 100)
1980	2690.0	528.8	1674.2	93.3
1981	2820.5	538.0	1728.2	93.0
1982	2957.3	547.4	1783.9	92.7
1983	3100.7	556.9	1841.4	92.4
1984	3251.1	566.6	1900.8	92.0
1985	3408.7	576.5	1962.1	91.7
1986	3592.8	589.0	2029.4	91.2
1987	3786.8	601.9	2098.9	90.7
1988	3991.3	614.9	2170.8	90.2
1989	4206.8	628.3	2245.2	89.7
1990	4434.0	642.0	2322.2	89.2
1991	4673.5	656.9	2400.3	88.6
1992	4925.8	672.1	2481.0	87.9
1993	5191.8	687.7	2564.4	87.3
1994	5472.2	703.7	2650.7	86.6
1995	5767.7	720.0	2739.8	86.0
1996	6079.1	737.5	2834.6	85.0
1997	6407.4	755.3	2932.6	84.0
1998	6753.4	773.6	3034.0	83.0
1999	7118.1	792.3	3139.0	82.1
2000	7502.5	811.5	3247.6	81.1

Income distribution--population with incomes above:

Year	Poverty Line (Thousands)	$1000 (Thousands)	$2000 (Thousands)	$5000 (Thousands)	$10000 (Thousands)
1980	4089.6	675.7	229.7	114.2	
1981	4227.6	709.7	238.0	120.9	
1982	4370.2	745.3	246.7	128.1	
1983	4517.6	782.7	255.6	135.6	
1984	4670.0	822.0	264.8	143.6	
1985	4827.6	863.3	274.4	152.1	
1986	4997.6	929.9	295.4	161.0	
1987	5173.6	1001.7	318.0	170.5	
1988	5355.8	1079.0	342.3	180.4	
1989	5544.4	1162.3	368.5	191.0	
1990	5739.7	1252.0	396.7	202.2	
1991	5932.0	1333.2	433.9	212.3	
1992	6130.7	1419.8	474.7	222.9	
1993	6336.1	1511.9	519.4	234.0	
1994	6548.4	1610.0	568.2	245.7	
1995	6767.8	1714.5	621.6	257.9	
1996	6986.5	1822.5	668.6	269.8	39.2
1997	7212.3	1937.4	719.2	282.3	47.8
1998	7445.3	2059.6	773.6	295.4	58.2
1999	7685.9	2189.4	832.1	309.0	70.9
2000	7934.2	2327.4	895.0	323.3	86.4

former French ownership of the island, a French patois is also spoken. The capital of Grenada is St. George's and it is located on the main island. Subsequent to the dissolution of the West Indies Federation in 1962, England attempted to form another federation between Barbados and the smaller Caribbean islands. The failure of this venture forced Britain to rule the smaller islands (Grenada, St. Vincent, St. Lucia, Dominica, Antigua, and St. Kitts-Nevis-Anguilla) under Associated Statehood status. Associated Statehood status was a step below full statehood in that even though the country had full autonomy in domestic affairs, Britain was still responsible for its defense and external affairs. Grenada was an Associated State from 1967 until 1974, at which time it sought, and was granted, independence under the leadership of Prime Minister Eric Gairy. The Grenadian constitution was suspended in 1979 after a successful coup by the New Jewel Movement, led by Maurice Bishop, overthrew the government of Prime Minister Eric Gairy. The Bishop government then began to forge ties with Cuba and the Soviet Union to strengthen its socialist orientation.

In mid-October 1983, the island erupted in violence. Bishop and three members of the cabinet were executed by troops of the People's Revolutionary Army. This led to a U.S. decision, with the support of Jamaica, Barbados and five members of the Organization of Eastern Caribbean States, to invade the island and restore order. This mission was accomplished by the end of October, and Governor-General Sir Paul Scoon assumed control of the administration of the government. Day-to-day government was later turned over to a nine-member "advisory council" appointed by Scoon until elections could be held.

Demography

The Grenadian population numbered 111,000 in 1980 and, of that total, 30 percent were concentrated around the capital while the remainder were distributed evenly throughout Grenada. Overall, almost 48 percent of the Grenadian population lived in urban areas in 1980. Over 56 percent of the Grenadian population are either younger than fifteen or older than sixty-five, primarily due to a high rate of emigration among skilled Grenadians who, for the most part, fall into the twenty to sixty-four years of age category. The average Grenadian household size in 1980 was 5.6 persons.

Economy

A feature of the Grenadian economy, and one that has served to insulate it from the dislocations common to most agricultural economies, is the lack of dominance of any single crop. This feature ensures that even if the price of one commodity is depressed, the economy still functions reasonably well with the revenue derived from the other crops. The major export crops in the Grenadian economy are nutmeg, cocoa, bananas, and mace. Of lesser importance, but contributors nonetheless, are sugarcane, coconuts, citrus fruits, and cotton.

Industry exists on a very small scale with rum distilleries (six of them) being the most prominent entrant. Tourism has played an increasingly important role in the economy, but its growth was slowed by the attainment of independence and again by the coup. The completion of the international jetport at Point Salinas should provide some stimulus to the tourist industry.

Grenada is a member of both the Eastern Caribbean Common Market and CARICOM, but has not benefited immensely from membership in either organization (the leftward tilt of the present administration has not served to improve economic relations with countries such as Trinidad and Tobago and Barbados). Trade with both CARICOM members and the rest of the world has resulted in consistent trade deficits, a condition that the present administration is trying to dispel by seeking trade with Communist bloc nations. The principal Grenadian exports are cocoa (46 percent), nutmeg (21 percent), bananas (18 percent), and mace (4 percent); the export partners are the United Kingdom (41 percent), the Federal Republic of Germany (22 percent), the Netherlands (10 percent), and Belgium (6 percent). Food, fuel, machinery, and construction materials, imported primarily from the United Kingdom and the Federal Republic of Germany, comprise the principal Grenadian imports.

Forecasts

The Grenadian population, as illustrated in Table 3.16, will increase from 111,000 in 1980 to 141,300 in 1990 and 171,400 in the year 2000-- increases of 27 percent from 1980 to 1990 and 21 percent from 1990 to 2000. Sixty-five percent of the 1980 population could be classified as nonproductive, but only about 37 percent of the population will be thus classified in the year 2000. The average household size will also decline sharply over the forecast period--from 5.6 in 1980 to 4.4 in 1990 and 3.7 in the year 2000--but, predictably, the number of households will increase-- from 19,800 in 1980, to 32,200 in 1990, and 45,700 in the year 2000. The rural population will decline considerably throughout the period.

Grenadian GNP will increase by 46.5 percent over the 1980 level to reach $117.2 million in 1990 and by another 61 percent to reach $198.2 million in the year 2000 (see Table 3.17). Per capita income will increase at a slower rate: from $677 in 1980 to $779 in 1990 and $1,087 in the year 2000. A doubling in the labor force over the forecast period will result in a sharp decline in the dependency ratio--from 106.7/100 in 1980 to 60/100 in the year 2000.

GUATEMALA

Guatemala has a land area of 108,780 square kilometers (42,000 square miles) and is bounded by Belize, the Caribbean Sea, Honduras, El Salvador, the Pacific Ocean, and Mexico. The Guatemalan Pacific coast extends for over 200 miles while its Caribbean exposure is seventy miles. The population is half Indians and half Ladinos--persons of Spanish-Indian descent--and, even though Spanish is the official language, approximately twenty Indian languages are spoken.

Guatemala is ruled under a constitution, adopted in 1965, that provides for a president and vice-president--elected on the same ballot and serving for four years--and a Legislative Assembly. Continued violence has given many subsequent leaders the excuse to rule outside the confines of the constitution. Over the last thirty years, leadership of Guatemala has

TABLE 3.16
GLOBESCAN medium growth demographic projections
for Grenada

Year	Population (Thousands)	Household Size	Households (Thousands)	Urban Population (Thousands)	Rural Population (Thousands)
1980	111.0	5.6	19892.5	53.1	57942.0
1981	113.8	5.4	20945.8	56.4	57423.5
1982	116.6	5.3	22054.8	59.9	56769.8
1983	119.5	5.1	23222.6	63.6	55969.8
1984	122.5	5.0	24452.3	67.5	55011.8
1985	125.6	4.9	25747.0	71.7	53883.3
1986	128.6	4.8	26936.0	75.9	52643.3
1987	131.6	4.7	28179.9	80.4	51225.3
1988	134.8	4.6	29481.3	85.2	49616.3
1989	138.0	4.5	30842.8	90.2	47802.4
1990	141.3	4.4	32267.1	95.5	45768.9
1991	144.2	4.3	33506.6	100.6	43668.9
1992	147.3	4.2	34793.7	105.9	41362.3
1993	150.3	4.2	36130.3	111.5	38836.3
1994	153.5	4.1	37518.2	117.4	36077.1
1995	156.7	4.0	38959.3	123.7	33070.3
1996	159.6	4.0	40234.1	129.6	29965.3
1997	162.4	3.9	41550.5	135.8	26626.9
1998	165.4	3.9	42910.0	142.3	23042.3
1999	168.3	3.8	44314.0	149.1	19198.3
2000	171.4	3.7	45763.9	156.3	15080.7

Population by age and sex

Males	Females	Total	Age	Males	Females	Total
\multicolumn — 1985 (Thousands)				2000 (Thousands)		
8.8	9.1	18.0	0-04	9.1	9.4	18.5
8.7	8.4	17.1	5-09	9.3	9.7	19.0
8.7	8.2	16.9	10-14	9.3	9.7	19.0
8.4	8.2	16.6	15-19	8.6	9.0	17.6
7.6	7.1	14.7	20-24	8.5	8.4	16.8
5.9	5.1	11.0	25-29	8.5	8.1	16.5
3.1	3.1	6.1	30-34	8.1	8.0	16.2
2.3	2.3	4.5	35-39	7.3	6.9	14.2
1.4	1.7	3.1	40-44	5.6	5.0	10.6
1.1	1.4	2.5	45-49	2.9	3.0	5.9
1.1	1.7	2.7	50-54	2.1	2.2	4.3
1.3	1.5	2.9	55-59	1.2	1.6	2.8
1.3	1.6	2.9	60-64	.9	1.3	2.2
1.0	1.3	2.3	65-69	.8	1.4	2.3
.7	1.0	1.7	70-74	.9	1.2	2.1
1.1	1.6	2.7	75+	1.3	2.0	3.3
62.5	63.1	125.6	TOTAL	84.5	86.8	171.4

TABLE 3.17
GLOBESCAN economic projections for Grenada

Year	GNP in 1980 US$ (Millions)	Per Capita Income	Labor Force (Thousands)	Dependency Ratio (Per 100)
1980	80.0	677.5	27314.0	106.7
1981	81.9	676.8	28545.8	102.6
1982	83.9	676.1	29833.2	98.6
1983	85.9	675.4	31178.6	94.8
1984	88.1	674.8	32584.7	91.1
1985	90.1	674.1	34054.2	87.6
1986	94.9	694.0	35280.9	85.3
1987	100.1	714.5	36551.7	83.1
1988	105.5	735.6	37868.4	80.9
1989	111.2	757.3	39232.4	78.8
1990	117.2	779.6	40645.6	76.8
1991	123.5	804.8	41907.2	75.0
1992	130.2	830.9	43208.0	73.3
1993	137.2	857.7	44549.1	71.6
1994	144.6	885.4	45931.9	69.9
1995	152.4	914.0	47357.6	68.3
1996	160.6	946.4	48703.3	66.6
1997	169.3	979.8	50087.3	64.9
1998	178.5	1014.4	51510.6	63.2
1999	188.1	1050.3	52974.4	61.6
2000	198.2	1087.4	54479.8	60.0

Income distribution--population with incomes above:

Year	Poverty Line (Thousands)	$1000 (Thousands)	$2000 (Thousands)	$5000 (Thousands)	$10000 (Thousands)
1980	101.5	18.7	8.9	4.1	1.4
1981	104.1	19.2	9.1	4.2	1.4
1982	106.7	19.7	9.3	4.3	1.5
1983	109.4	20.1	9.5	4.5	1.5
1984	112.1	20.6	9.8	4.6	1.6
1985	114.9	21.1	10.0	4.7	1.7
1986	118.0	22.9	10.7	4.9	1.8
1987	121.3	24.8	11.4	5.1	2.0
1988	124.6	26.8	12.2	5.3	2.2
1989	128.0	29.0	13.1	5.5	2.4
1990	131.5	31.4	13.9	5.7	2.6
1991	134.7	33.7	14.7	5.9	2.8
1992	138.0	36.3	15.6	6.1	3.0
1993	141.3	39.0	16.4	6.3	3.2
1994	144.7	42.0	17.3	6.5	3.4
1995	148.2	45.1	18.3	6.7	3.6
1996	151.2	48.2	19.2	6.9	3.8
1997	154.3	51.6	20.1	7.1	4.0
1998	157.4	55.1	21.0	7.3	4.2
1999	160.5	59.0	22.0	7.5	4.5
2000	163.8	63.0	23.1	7.8	4.7

proved to be the proverbial siren song for Guatemalan Army generals. The roll call is as follows: Col. Jacobo Arbenz Guzman overthrown by Col. Carlos Castillo Armas in 1954; Col. Armas assassinated in 1957; General Miguel Ydigoras Fuentes deposed in a 1963 coup; General Romeo Lucas Garcia deposed by coup in 1982; two members of the three-man junta set up after the coup that deposed Garcia were forced to resign (their ministries were surrounded by soldiers loyal to the third member during the negotiations for their resignations) by the third member, General Rios Montt. Finally, General Mejia Victores seized power in August 1983. Presidential elections are now scheduled for 1985.

An ongoing battle between the government--regardless of who is in power--and a leftist faction, which has gained widespread support among the Indian population of Guatemala, has caused severe economic and political disruptions. The government's harsh methods of battling the insurgents have led to charges of genocide. Contraventions of basic human rights by Guatemalan armed forces led the Carter administration to withold U.S. assistance.

Demography

The Guatemalan population numbered 7.3 million in 1980; 3.7 million of that total were males and 3.6 million, females. The largest segment of the population was the 0-4 age group, which contained 17 percent of the total population. Persons who were fourteen years of age and younger and persons who were sixty-five years of age and older comprised 46.8 percent of the population. Almost the entire Indian population lives in rural areas and, when combined with the Ladinos living in rural areas, rural inhabitants account for over 61 percent of the total population. The average household size in Guatemala is 4.8 persons.

Economy

The GNP in Guatemala was $7.8 billion in 1980 and GNP per capita was $1,073. Agriculture contributed 25.5 percent of the GNP, and industry contributed 16.4 percent. The labor force was 2.2 million in 1980, of which total 56 percent were employed in agriculture, 21 percent in industry, and 23 percent in services. The average annual inflation rate for 1979-1980 (based on consumer prices) was 10.7 percent.

As coffee prices go, so goes the Guatemalan economy. Coffee is the most important crop in the agricultural sector, accounting for 30 percent of Guatemala's export earnings and 1 percent of the GNP. The record coffee prices of 1977 resulted in Guatemala attaining its highest levels yet of foreign reserves, but with the subsequent declines in price, reserve levels and economic growth have declined.

The agricultural sector as a whole contributes over 25 percent of export earnings and 67 percent of the GNP. Besides coffee, other important commodities are cotton, sugar, bananas, beef, chicle, and oils.

Sectors other than the hitherto dominant agricultural sector are making increasingly larger contributions to the Guatemalan economy; for example, manufacturing, construction and utilities contribute approximately 20 percent of the GDP. The major products manufactured in Guatemala are processed foods, textiles, rubber and chemicals, nonmetallic minerals, paper, and pharmaceuticals. The mining sector gained added importance with the opening of a nickel plant in 1977, but production at the plant was suspended temporarily in 1981 due to low world nickel prices.

Like most Third World countries, Guatemala is faced with fluctuating world prices for its exports, compared to steadily rising prices for its imports. Guatemala recorded a trade balance of $13.9 million in 1970 (prior to the first oil shock), but this had become a -$91.8 million balance in 1975. The positive trade balance in 1970 was aided by the reaction of Guatemalan industry to the formation of CACM in 1961; almost all of Guatemala's manufactured goods go to other CACM members.

Coffee is the largest export (approximately 48 percent), followed by cotton (approximately 13 percent), and sugar (approximately 4 percent). Guatemalan exports reach the United States (29 percent), the Federal Republic of Germany (12 percent), El Salvador (11 percent), Japan (7 percent), Costa Rica (6 percent), the Netherlands (5 percent), and Italy (5 percent). The major Guatemalan imports are machinery and transport equipment (31 percent), basic manufactures (20 percent), chemicals and chemical products (20 percent), and fuel and lubricants (13 percent). Countries importing to Guatemala include the United States (30 percent), Japan (11 percent), El Salvador (9 percent), Federal Republic of Germany (8 percent), and Venezuela (7 percent).

Mineral Commodities

Guatemala possesses extensive nickel reserves in the Lake Izabal region, and exploitation of these reserves commenced in 1978. In addition to nickel production, Exmibal (which has as its principal owner Inco of Canada) also extracts lead, copper, antimony, tungsten, clay, feldspar, limestone, and marble from sites in Guatemala. In April 1980, Guatemalan crude oil was sold on the spot market for the first time; the 120,000-barrel sale earned $4 million to the seller, Basic Resources International. About 20 percent of its domestic oil consumption is now produced by Guatemala, and extensive petroleum exploration is continuing.

Forecasts

The Guatemalan population, which numbered 7.3 million in 1980, will increase to 9.6 million in 1990 and 12.6 million in the year 2000 (see Table 3.18). There will be a reduction in the persons in the nonproductive category (below fifteen and above sixty-five) to 43 percent of the population. There will be very little reduction in the size of Guatemalan households by 2000 to 4.5 in 1990, and 4.3 in the year 2000, but the number of households will almost double from its 1980 level. The rural population will increase between 1980 and 2000, but its share of the population will decline to 55.7 percent in 1990 and 48.4 percent in the year 2000.

Guatemala's GNP could amount to $13.2 billion in 1990 and $22.3 billion in the year 2000 in comparison with $7.8 billion in 1980 (see Table 3.19), using the World Bank growth rate assumptions. Per capita income would then increase from $1,008 in 1980 to $1,281 in 1990 and $1,655 in the year 2000. The labor force will number 3.1 million in 1990 and 4.1 million in 2000, while the dependency ratio will decline to 81.2/100 and 75.9/100 in the same years.

TABLE 3.18
GLOBESCAN medium growth demographic projections
for Guatemala

Year	Population (Thousands)	Household Size	Households (Thousands)	Urban Population (Thousands)	Rural Population (Thousands)
1980	7262.0	4.8	1525.6	2824.9	4437.1
1981	7474.9	4.7	1578.6	2944.2	4530.7
1982	7694.0	4.7	1633.3	3068.5	4625.5
1983	7919.5	4.7	1690.0	3198.0	4721.5
1984	8151.7	4.7	1748.6	3333.0	4818.7
1985	8390.7	4.6	1809.3	3473.7	4916.9
1986	8627.6	4.6	1868.4	3620.5	5007.1
1987	8871.3	4.6	1929.5	3773.5	5097.7
1988	9121.8	4.6	1992.6	3933.0	5188.8
1989	9379.4	4.6	2057.8	4099.2	5280.2
1990	9644.3	4.5	2125.1	4272.4	5371.9
1991	9910.4	4.5	2195.1	4457.6	5452.8
1992	10183.8	4.5	2267.4	4650.7	5533.0
1993	10464.7	4.5	2342.1	4852.3	5612.5
1994	10753.5	4.4	2419.2	5062.6	5690.9
1995	11050.2	4.4	2498.9	5282.0	5768.2
1996	11350.6	4.4	2577.3	5509.2	5841.3
1997	11659.1	4.4	2658.2	5746.2	5912.9
1998	11976.1	4.4	2741.7	5993.4	5982.7
1999	12301.7	4.4	2827.8	6251.3	6050.4
2000	12636.1	4.3	2916.5	6520.2	6115.9

Population by age and sex

Males	Females	Total	Age	Males	Females	Total
\multicolumn{3}{}{1985 (Thousands)}				\multicolumn{3}{}{2000 (Thousands)}		
696.8	674.5	1371.3	0-04	949.8	919.7	1869.5
605.7	587.0	1192.6	5-09	834.5	807.7	1642.2
539.2	521.2	1060.4	10-14	743.7	721.5	1465.2
453.3	437.9	891.2	15-19	667.7	649.4	1317.2
395.2	382.2	777.4	20-24	586.7	572.3	1159.0
329.1	318.6	647.7	25-29	519.2	506.8	1026.0
277.7	268.6	546.3	30-34	432.9	423.3	856.1
219.3	213.3	432.7	35-39	375.3	367.4	742.6
174.0	169.9	343.8	40-44	310.6	304.1	614.7
144.5	141.9	286.4	45-49	259.3	253.7	513.0
123.8	123.1	246.9	50-54	200.7	198.4	399.1
102.7	103.8	206.5	55-59	154.2	154.3	308.5
73.8	76.8	150.5	60-64	121.8	124.0	245.8
49.9	52.5	102.5	65-69	96.1	100.4	196.5
32.8	35.5	68.3	70-74	69.6	74.9	144.5
31.1	35.0	66.1	75+	63.3	72.8	136.1
4248.9	4141.7	8390.7	TOTAL	6385.4	6250.7	12636.1

66

TABLE 3.19
GLOBESCAN economic projections for Guatemala

Year	GNP in 1980 US$ (Millions)	Per Capita Income	Labor Force (Thousands)	Dependency Ratio (Per 100)
1980	7790.0	1008.3	2309.3	88.3
1981	8206.8	1032.0	2384.7	87.6
1982	8645.8	1056.3	2462.5	87.0
1983	9108.4	1081.1	2542.8	86.4
1984	9595.7	1106.5	2625.8	85.8
1985	10109.0	1132.5	2711.5	85.2
1986	10654.9	1160.9	2800.5	84.4
1987	11230.3	1190.0	2892.5	83.6
1988	11836.7	1219.8	2987.5	82.8
1989	12475.9	1250.3	3085.6	82.0
1990	13149.6	1281.7	3186.9	81.2
1991	13859.7	1314.6	3285.0	80.6
1992	14608.1	1348.4	3386.2	80.0
1993	15397.0	1383.0	3490.5	79.5
1994	16228.4	1418.6	3598.0	78.9
1995	17104.7	1455.0	3708.8	78.4
1996	18028.4	1493.0	3820.1	77.9
1997	19001.9	1532.0	3934.6	77.4
1998	20028.0	1572.0	4052.7	76.9
1999	21109.5	1613.0	4174.2	76.4
2000	22249.5	1655.1	4299.5	75.9

Income distribution--population with incomes above:

Year	Poverty Line (Thousands)	$1000 (Thousands)	$2000 (Thousands)	$5000 (Thousands)	$10000 (Thousands)
1980	6917.3	2054.1	974.9	354.7	292.0
1981	7127.7	2176.8	1015.1	366.4	302.8
1982	7344.5	2306.9	1056.8	378.5	314.1
1983	7567.9	2444.8	1100.3	391.0	325.7
1984	7798.1	2590.9	1145.6	403.8	337.7
1985	8035.3	2745.7	1192.7	417.1	350.3
1986	8270.6	2898.5	1239.5	448.0	362.8
1987	8512.8	3059.8	1288.2	481.1	375.7
1988	8762.2	3230.0	1338.7	516.6	389.1
1989	9018.8	3409.8	1391.3	554.8	403.0
1990	9282.9	3599.5	1445.9	595.8	417.4
1991	9547.8	3786.0	1558.5	641.5	431.8
1992	9820.3	3982.1	1679.9	690.8	446.6
1993	10100.6	4188.5	1810.7	743.9	462.0
1994	10388.8	4405.5	1951.7	801.0	477.9
1995	10685.3	4633.7	2103.7	862.5	494.3
1996	10984.8	4889.7	2239.1	917.5	510.8
1997	11292.7	5159.8	2383.3	976.0	527.8
1998	11609.3	5444.8	2536.7	1038.2	545.4
1999	11934.7	5745.6	2700.0	1104.4	563.6
2000	12269.3	6062.9	2873.8	1174.8	582.4

GUYANA

Guyana is located on the southern flank of South America and is bordered by Venezuela to the northwest and west, Brazil to the west and south, Suriname to the east, and the Atlantic Ocean to the northeast. The former British colony has a land area of 215,000 square kilometers (83,000 square miles), but most of its 880,000 inhabitants live along a 63-mile coastal stretch. The dominant races in the country are East Indian and Negro, supplemented by inhabitants of mixed descent.

Guyana became an independent country in 1966 and declared itself a "cooperative" republic in 1970. The country is ruled by an executive president, Linden Forbes Sampson Burnham, and prime minister, Dr. Ptolemy Reid. Some 80 percent of Guyana's productive capacity is state-controlled, reflecting the regime's avowed commitment to socialism.

Demography

The 1980 population was evenly distributed between males and females, but 47.9 percent of the population were 14 or younger, or 65 and older. Only 21.9 percent of the population live in urban areas. The average household size is five persons.

Economy

The main factors in the economy of Guyana are agriculture and mining, and both industries are controlled, to one extent or the other, by the government. Prior to 1970, bauxite, gold and diamonds were mined either by expatriates or small local investors (in the case of diamond and gold). In 1971, after joint ownership talks between the government and the local Alcan subsidiary broke down, the bauxite operations in Demerara were nationalized. The holdings of Reynolds Metals in Guyana were subsequently nationalized in 1975, and the two nationalized entities were combined and called Guymine. Both Reynolds and Alcan were compensated for the expropriation of their holdings. The sugar holdings of the British-based Demerara Sugar Company were nationalized in 1975 and Booker McConnell in 1976 and were joined to form a state corporation, Guysuco.

Other industries that play a role in the Guyanese economy include rice, shrimp, and timber. The planting and reaping of rice crops are solely in the hands of private individuals, but the distribution of the end product is purely government controlled.

Guyana is a founding member of CARICOM, but, unlike Trinidad and Tobago, cannot export its principal commodity--bauxite--to group members. Deteriorating trade conditions forced the government to impose import restrictions not only on extraregional goods, but also on goods originating within the community. The restrictions, originally imposed in early 1977, have not prevented the country from racking up balance-of-payments deficits of $87.3 million in 1980 and $174 million in 1981, however.

Bauxite and alumina account for approximately 44 percent of Guyana's exports with sugar accounting for 31 percent and rice accounting for 11 percent. The United Kingdom receives approximately 28 percent of Guyana's exports; the United States, 21 percent; Trinidad and Tobago, 8 percent; Canada, 7 percent; Norway, 6 percent; and Jamaica, 5 percent.

All of Guyana's petroleum needs are fulfilled by importing oil, and the major beneficiary is Trindad and Tobago. Fully 24 percent of imports into Guyana fall into the fuel and lubricant category. Other major imports are capital goods (22 percent), food (16 percent), other consumer goods (10 percent), machinery and transport equipment (9 percent), and chemicals (6 percent). Guyana's principal import partners are Trinidad and Tobago (25 percent), the United States (24 percent), and the United Kingdom (20 percent). Guyana has attempted to foster trade relations with the Soviet Union and Eastern Europe, but this trade does not constitute a substantial percentage of imports and exports at present.

Mineral Commodities

The largest component of the Guyana mineral industry is bauxite which accounts for approximately 44 percent of the country's foreign exchange earnings. Guyana is the world's fifth-largest producer of bauxite and, prior to 1980, held a virtual monopoly on the production of calcined bauxite. Guyana's share of the calcined bauxite market fell to 60 percent by 1980, primarily due to production shortfalls and increased calcining capacity in other countries. In addition to bauxite, small quantities of gold and diamonds are mined in Guyana.

Forecasts

The population of Guyana will number 1.1 million in 1990 and 1.2 million in the year 2000 (see Table 3.20). The urban-rural population split will show a slight change. By the year 2000, when 30 percent of the populace will be urban residents. Average household size will decline to 3.9 persons by 2000, a reduction of one from 1980 levels.

Gross national product in Guyana could total $904 million in 1990 and $1.53 billion in the year 2000, according to our forecasts (see Table 3.21). Per capita income would then reach $769.5 in 1990 and $1,129 in 2000. The rise in the labor force from 275,100 in 1980 to 456,000 in 1990 will require substantial growth in the economy to provide jobs for the new entrants to the labor force.

Bauxite production in Guyana attained its highest level in 1970, but by 1980 it had fallen by more than 50 percent. A trend impact analysis of future production suggests further declines but on a more moderate scale-- 26 percent over the 1981-1990 period. The TIA forecast is illustrated in Figure 3.2.

The events that will have an impact on Guyana's bauxite production are listed in Table 3.22. The one with the most negative probable impact is the substitution of graphite-epoxy and/or Kevlar for aluminum in airframe manufacture (.35 by 1975; .75 by 1990). Airlines are interested in weight reduction, and the defense establishment is interested in radar-absorption-- features in which both alternative materials are superior.

Energy costs are extremely important in the operation of refineries, and the higher the cost of refining bauxite, the lower the demand for the end product (which will of necessity carry a high price). A 50 percent increase in energy costs (.10 by 1985; .40 by 1990) would have a negative impact on Guyana's bauxite production.

The strength of a cartel lies in its ability to limit production and raise prices. Formation of a bauxite cartel (.10 by 1985; .20 by 1990), of

TABLE 3.20
GLOBESCAN medium growth demographic projections
for Guyana

Year	Population (Thousands)	Household Size	Households (Thousands)	Urban Population (Thousands)	Rural Population (Thousands)
1980	883.0	5.0	178.0	193.4	689.6
1981	902.2	4.9	184.8	198.3	703.9
1982	921.8	4.8	191.7	203.3	718.5
1983	941.9	4.7	199.0	208.5	733.3
1984	962.3	4.7	206.5	213.8	748.5
1985	983.3	4.6	214.3	219.3	764.0
1986	1000.4	4.5	221.1	226.0	774.4
1987	1017.8	4.5	228.1	233.0	784.9
1988	1035.6	4.4	235.4	240.1	795.4
1989	1053.6	4.3	242.8	247.5	806.1
1990	1072.0	4.3	250.5	255.1	816.8
1991	1088.5	4.2	256.9	264.3	824.2
1992	1105.2	4.2	263.5	273.8	831.4
1993	1122.2	4.2	270.2	283.6	838.6
1994	1139.5	4.1	277.1	293.8	845.7
1995	1157.0	4.1	284.1	304.3	852.7
1996	1172.4	4.0	291.2	316.6	855.9
1997	1188.1	4.0	298.4	329.4	858.7
1998	1203.9	3.9	305.7	342.6	861.3
1999	1220.0	3.9	313.3	356.5	863.5
2000	1236.2	3.9	321.1	370.9	865.3

Population by age and sex

Males	Females	Total	Age	Males	Females	Total
	1985 (Thousands)				2000 (Thousands)	
65.2	63.1	128.4	0-04	59.2	57.3	116.6
62.0	60.3	122.3	5-09	60.5	59.1	119.6
56.2	54.8	111.0	10-14	61.9	61.0	123.0
57.5	56.9	114.5	15-19	62.5	62.3	124.8
53.5	53.0	106.5	20-24	59.6	59.6	119.2
46.6	47.1	93.7	25-29	53.6	53.9	107.5
36.1	36.5	72.5	30-34	54.6	55.9	110.5
25.6	26.8	52.4	35-39	50.6	51.9	102.4
17.9	19.1	36.9	40-44	43.9	46.0	89.9
14.9	15.1	30.0	45-49	33.7	35.3	69.0
13.7	15.0	28.7	50-54	23.5	25.6	49.1
11.5	12.9	24.4	55-59	15.9	17.9	33.8
10.2	10.7	20.9	60-64	12.6	13.7	26.4
7.9	8.5	16.3	65-69	10.8	12.9	23.7
6.3	6.2	12.5	70-74	8.0	10.0	18.0
5.4	6.9	12.4	75+	10.0	12.6	22.6
490.5	492.8	983.3	TOTAL	620.9	635.1	1255.9

TABLE 3.21
GLOBESCAN economic projections for Guyana

Year	GNP in 1980 US$ (Millions)	Per Capita Income	Labor Force (Thousands)	Dependency Ratio (Per 100)
1980	550.0	568.1	223.4	78.2
1981	555.5	561.5	230.6	76.4
1982	561.1	555.1	238.0	74.6
1983	566.7	548.7	245.7	72.8
1984	572.3	542.4	253.6	71.1
1985	578.1	536.2	261.8	69.4
1986	589.6	537.5	268.4	68.3
1987	601.4	538.9	275.3	67.2
1988	613.4	540.2	282.3	66.1
1989	625.7	541.6	289.5	65.1
1990	638.2	543.0	296.9	64.0
1991	654.2	548.1	304.3	62.6
1992	670.5	553.3	312.0	61.2
1993	687.3	558.5	319.8	59.8
1994	704.5	563.8	327.7	58.5
1995	722.1	569.2	335.9	57.2
1996	743.7	578.5	343.5	55.9
1997	766.1	588.1	351.2	54.6
1998	789.0	597.7	359.1	53.3
1999	812.7	607.6	367.2	52.1
2000	837.1	617.6	375.4	50.9

Income distribution--population with incomes above:

Year	Poverty Line (Thousands)	$1000 (Thousands)	$2000 (Thousands)	$5000 (Thousands)	$10000 (Thousands)
1980	729.9	125.6	71.8	38.0	25.7
1981	751.1	129.6	75.8	39.1	26.8
1982	772.8	133.8	80.0	40.3	28.0
1983	795.2	138.1	84.4	41.4	29.1
1984	818.3	142.6	89.1	42.7	30.4
1985	842.0	147.2	94.0	43.9	31.7
1986	866.5	159.2	98.9	45.1	32.9
1987	891.8	172.2	103.9	46.3	34.1
1988	917.8	186.3	109.3	47.5	35.4
1989	944.5	201.5	114.9	48.7	36.8
1990	972.0	218.0	120.8	50.0	38.2
1991	996.6	231.7	126.0	51.2	39.4
1992	1021.8	246.2	131.3	52.4	40.7
1993	1047.6	261.7	136.9	53.6	42.0
1994	1074.1	278.1	142.7	54.9	43.4
1995	1101.2	295.5	148.7	56.2	44.8
1996	1120.5	315.1	154.0	57.3	46.1
1997	1140.2	335.9	159.4	58.5	47.4
1998	1160.3	358.2	165.1	59.7	48.7
1999	1180.7	381.9	170.9	60.9	50.1
2000	1201.4	407.2	177.0	62.2	51.5

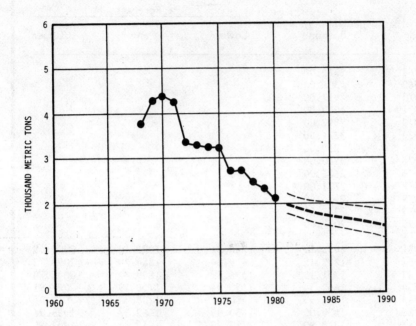

Figure 3.2 Forecast of Guyana's bauxite production

(Continued)

72

		Forecast		
Year	History/Baseline	Lower	Center	Upper
1968	3772.00			
1969	4306.00			
1970	4417.00			
1971	4234.00			
1972	3342.00			
1973	3276.00			
1974	3250.00			
1975	3250.00			
1976	2686.00			
1977	2731.00			
1978	2425.00			
1979	2312.00			
1980	2077.00			
1981	1995.10	1786.71	1995.10	2203.48
1982	1869.12	1674.64	1884.70	2098.22
1983	1751.10	1596.12	1809.77	2045.70
1984	1640.54	1535.24	1756.19	2027.91
1985	1536.95	1480.79	1708.32	2010.45
1986	1439.90	1430.09	1662.37	1986.21
1987	1348.99	1393.39	1619.01	1957.99
1988	1263.81	1335.54	1573.96	1923.84
1989	1184.01	1294.18	1525.00	1992.29
1990	1109.25	1229.85	1473.09	1934.06

Trend Impact Analysis

Baseline Curve No. = 2   Confidence Percentiles = 25 and 75

Figure 3.2 (Cont.) Guyana's bauxite production (thousand metric tons)

TABLE 3.22
Events that will have an impact on Guyana's bauxite production

Event No.	Year/ Probability	Years to First Impact	Years to Maximum Impact	Maximum Impact	Years to Steady State Impact	Steady State Impact	Relative Impact
3	1985 0.35 1990 0.75	2	3	-10.0%	3	-10.0%	-294.

Graphite-epoxy and/or kevlar replacing aluminum as the primary material in airframe manufacture.

4	1985 0.10 1990 0.40	2	4	-15.0%	4	-15.0%	-132.

Fifty percent increase in energy costs.

5	1985 0.10 1990 0.20	1	1	10.0%	1	10.0%	-120.

Formation of a strong bauxite cartel.

2	1985 0.10 1990 0.25	1	2	5.0%	2	5.0%	58.2

Widespread use of aluminum engine blocks by automobile engine manufacturers.

12	1985 0.20 1990 0.45	2	4	10.0%	4	10.0%	149.

Major infusion of capital for modernization and purchase of spare parts.

7	1985 0.20 1990 0.30	3	5	15.0%	5	15.0%	155.

Integration of bauxite production on a regional basis in the Caribbean as per CARICOM proposal regarding Jamaica, Guyana, and Trinidad and Tobago.

1	1985 0.05 1990 0.10	2	4	50.0%	4	50.0%	181.

Privatization of the Guyanese bauxite industry.

13	1985 0.50 1990 0.75	1	2	5.0%	2	5.0%	244.

Relaxation of foreign exchange controls.

9	1985 0.20 1990 0.50	1	2	20.0%	2	20.0%	465.

Construction of an aluminum smelter.

8	1985 0.20 1990 0.50	1	3	25.0%	3	25.0%	512.

New supply arrangements concluded with U.S. companies.

11	1985 0.40 1990 0.75	2	3	20.0%	3	20.0%	650.

Change in regime.

74

which Guyana would conceivably be a member, would serve to lower the production levels of member nations. But no bauxite cartel can be deemed strong without Australia and Brazil as members and, at present, neither of them is so inclined.

In attempting to don the mantle of socialism, the Guyana government has implemented policies that have been detrimental to the country as a whole and the bauxite industry in particular. By cultivating relations with Communist governments, Guyana has invited U.S. displeasure which has in turn attempted to block loans from international organizations to Guyana. A change in regime (.40 by 1985; .75 by 1990) could improve relations with the United States, making it easier to obtain funds for investment in the bauxite sector.

One result of the Guyanese nationalization of the bauxite industry was the loss of Western markets and a significant decline in foreign exchange earnings. Without the foreign exchange, spare parts and modernizing equipment could not be bought, resulting in long-term declines in production. If new supply agreements could be arranged with U.S. buyers (.20 by 1985; .50 by 1990), bauxite production would increase markedly.

Construction of an aluminum smelter (.20 by 1985; .50 by 1990) would have a positive effect on bauxite production. Production would be geared to the needs of the smelter in addition to the export of ore, and the volume of ore exports should not be affected.

HAITI

Haiti, long notorious as the poorest country in the Western Hemisphere, is located on the western one-third of Hispaniola, the island it shares with the Dominican Republic. The land area of Haiti measures 27,749 square kilometers (10,714 square miles), but approximately two-thirds of the total are arid, mountainous land, unsuitable for most productive purposes. The official language of Haiti is French, but the dominant language among the predominantly black populace is Creole.

Second only to the United States in the Western Hemisphere in terms of the length of its independence, Haiti has had a long and troubled history. Twenty-two dictators ruled the country between 1843 and 1915, but political and economic turmoil still persisted--so much so that the United States occupied Haiti in 1915 to protect U.S. lives and property. The zenith in turmoil was reached in 1957 when six different governments held power within the space of one year. Francois Duvalier was elected president in 1957 and became president for life in 1964. On Duvalier's death in 1971, his son, Jean-Claude "Baby Doc" Duvalier became president. The government of the elder Duvalier was notorious for its human rights violations, carried out, for the most part, by the Tonton Macoutes, the much-feared Haitian secret police. The constitution of 1964 vests executive authority in the president, and an amendment to the constitution allows the president to choose his successor. Opposition political activity is not allowed in Haiti.

Demography

The total population of Haiti in 1980 was 5.8 million, making it one of the most densely populated countries in the world. The poor economic conditions in Haiti have forced working-age persons to flee to the Bahamas, the Dominican Republic and the United States and are a contributing factor to the small size, less than 53 percent of the total population, of the productive age groups. A vast majority of the population (75 percent) resides in rural areas, and the average household size is 4.9 persons.

Economy

As is true for most of the other countries in the region, the Haitian economy is heavily dependent on the agricultural sector. Gross national product totaled $1.3 billion in 1980, and approximately 40 percent of that total resulted from activity in the agricultural sector, while manufacturing contributed 12 percent; government, 11 percent; and commerce, 10 percent. All the major sectors experienced negative or very little growth in the 1960-1970 period, but they all grew between 2.2 and 8.3 percent in the 1970-1979 period. The labor force numbered 2.3 million in 1980, but the government estimates that 14 percent of that total is unemployed and 65 percent underemployed. Unemployment in urban areas is even higher-- as high as 50 percent in the Port-au-Prince area. Migration from the rural areas to the urban areas is of the same magnitude as rural migration to the Bahamas and other countries, as the rural residents seek release from their subsistence existence.

Agriculture employs approximately 74 percent of the labor force. Only 30 percent of the land is considered suitable for cultivation, but more than 40 percent is actually worked, suggesting that many farmers cultivate marginal land. Primitive farming techniques and small plot sizes exacerbate productivity problems. The principal agricultural products are coffee, sugar, essential oils, sisal, meat, and grain, with coffee ranking highest in importance. Forty percent of export revenues is generated by coffee sales abroad, and coffee export taxes are the government's single largest source of income. Sugar, which used to be a major export earner, is currently being imported into Haiti as more and more of the sugarcane crop are diverted to rum production or is eaten in the fields.

An increasing percentage of export earnings flows from the manufacture of light industrial goods, as U.S. companies send U.S.-made components to Haiti for assembly and return to the United States. This activity has resulted in the creation of 60,000 new jobs over the past ten years, and stems from the cheap Haitian labor rates--the current minimum is $2.64 per day--and U.S. laws that allow manufactures with 35 percent value added in Haiti to enter the United States duty-free.

Increasing oil imports and declining export earnings have combined to deal Haiti trade deficits of $12.4 million in 1970, $68.4 million in 1975, and $183 million in 1980. The current Duvalier government has been accused of selling Haitian labor to the Dominican Republic to mitigate balance-of-payment problems.

The United States historically has been Haiti's most important trade partner, purchasing about 70 percent of its exports and accounting for 53 percent of its imports. Other important export partners are France (13 percent), Italy (7 percent), and Belgium (6 percent). Haiti exports coffee (35 percent) and bauxite (11 percent) while importing machinery and transport equipment (26 percent), foodstuffs (24 percent), basic manufactures (18 percent), fuels (9 percent), and chemicals (6 percent).

Mineral Commodities

Reynolds Haitian Mines Inc. has mined bauxite in Haiti for over forty years, but because of a decline in the quality and quantity of Haitian reserves, it announced it would close its facility in 1982. Haiti also contains deposits of copper, gold, and marble, but not in large enough quantities to warrant commercial exploitation.

Forecasts

Our projections for Haiti suggest that the population will grow to 7.5 million in 1990 and 9.6 million in the year 2000 (see Table 3.23). This represents increases of 29 percent between 1980 and 1990 and 28 percent between 1990 and 2000. There will be a substantial change (17 percent) in the number of people in the nonproductive categories, suggesting that unless the economy grows at a rate that will provide jobs for these people, the pressure for emigration (legal or illegal) will remain high. The average household size will show virtually no change over the forecast period—4.9 in 1980 and 4.7 in the year 2000—but the number of households will increase from 1.2 million to 2 million. The urban population will increase at a faster rate than the rural population over the forecast period— 162 percent as against 34 percent—but the rural population will still constitute a majority (61 percent) of the population in the year 2000.

The Haitian GNP could increase by 61 percent between 1980 and 1990—from $1.3 billion to $2.2 billion—and 69 percent between 1990 and 2000 ($3.7 billion in the year 2000; see Table 3.24), but, because of population increases, per capita GNP will experience much smaller gains. From $225 in 1980, GNP per capita will only rise to $281 in 1990 and $369 in the year 2000. An increase in the labor force, from 2.3 million in 1980 to 2.9 million in 1990 and 3.9 million in the year 2000, will place extreme pressure on the economy in new job requirements. The dependency ratio will decline from 88.1/100 in 1980 to 86/100 in 1990 and 83.1/100 in the year 2000.

HONDURAS

Honduras is bounded to the north and northeast by the Caribbean Sea, to the east and south by Nicaragua, to the northwest by El Salvador, and to the west and northwest by Guatemala; it has a relatively large exposure to the Gulf of Fonseca on the southwestern flank. The second-largest country in Central America, Honduras has a land area of 109,560 square kilometers (42,300 square miles). The population is comprised of Mestizos (90 percent), Negroes, Indians, and Caucasians. Spanish is the dominant language.

Unlike its neighbors—Guatemala, El Salvador, and Nicaragua— Honduras has not been racked by serious revolutionary activity. This is attributable to early attempts at agrarian reform by Honduran administrations, as well as a more even distribution of income than in neighboring states. Honduras has been ruled by the military for most of its recent history, but a move to reinstate civilian government was started by General Melger who ruled between 1975 and 1978. The movement came to fruition in January 1982 with the inauguration of Robert Suazo Cordova as president after free elections were held in 1981.

TABLE 3.23
GLOBESCAN medium growth demographic projections
for Haiti

Year	Population (Thousands)	Household Size	Households (Thousands)	Urban Population (Thousands)	Rural Population (Thousands)
1980	5809.0	4.9	1185.5	1446.4	4362.6
1981	5958.0	4.9	1218.1	1518.8	4439.2
1982	6110.8	4.9	1251.5	1594.7	4516.1
1983	6267.5	4.9	1285.9	1674.4	4593.1
1984	6428.2	4.9	1321.2	1758.2	4670.1
1985	6593.1	4.9	1357.5	1846.1	4747.0
1986	6761.8	4.8	1395.0	1938.4	4823.4
1987	6934.9	4.8	1433.5	2035.4	4899.4
1988	7112.3	4.8	1473.2	2137.3	4975.1
1989	7294.4	4.8	1513.9	2244.2	5050.1
1990	7481.0	4.8	1555.7	2356.5	5124.5
1991	7672.8	4.8	1598.1	2472.6	5200.2
1992	7869.5	4.8	1641.6	2594.5	5275.1
1993	8071.3	4.8	1686.4	2722.3	5349.0
1994	8278.2	4.8	1732.3	2856.4	5421.8
1995	8490.5	4.8	1779.5	2997.1	5493.3
1996	8706.7	4.8	1828.3	3140.2	5566.6
1997	8928.5	4.8	1878.5	3290.0	5638.4
1998	9155.9	4.7	1930.1	3447.0	5708.8
1999	9389.0	4.7	1983.0	3611.5	5777.5
2000	9628.2	4.7	2037.5	3783.9	5844.3

Population by age and sex

1985 (Thousands)				2000 (Thousands)		
Males	Females	Total	Age	Males	Females	Total
566.2	552.1	1118.2	0-04	782.1	758.9	1541.0
462.9	456.2	919.1	5-09	675.8	656.5	1332.2
400.1	393.8	793.9	10-14	590.9	573.9	1164.8
350.6	346.4	696.9	15-19	510.1	495.6	1005.8
297.4	296.1	593.5	20-24	429.5	421.7	851.2
246.3	248.4	494.8	25-29	368.9	363.3	732.2
200.4	204.6	405.0	30-34	319.3	317.0	636.3
162.4	171.7	334.2	35-39	268.5	268.6	537.1
133.4	145.6	278.9	40-44	220.4	223.0	443.4
111.5	125.2	236.7	45-49	176.4	181.1	357.5
93.8	106.4	200.3	50-54	139.2	149.2	288.4
75.2	87.8	163.0	55-59	109.7	122.9	232.5
59.0	70.4	129.4	60-64	86.0	100.6	186.6
43.5	54.0	97.5	65-69	65.4	78.4	143.8
30.0	37.7	67.7	70-74	44.4	55.6	100.0
27.3	36.7	64.1	75+	42.3	57.4	99.8
3259.9	3333.2	6593.1	TOTAL	4828.9	4823.7	9652.6

TABLE 3.24
GLOBESCAN economic projections for Haiti

Year	GNP in 1980 US$ (Millions)	Per Capita Income	Labor Force (Thousands)	Dependency Ratio (Per 100)
1980	1340.0	224.9	2300.0	88.1
1981	1399.0	228.9	2362.6	87.8
1982	1460.5	233.0	2427.0	87.5
1983	1524.8	237.2	2493.1	87.2
1984	1591.9	241.4	2561.0	86.9
1985	1661.9	245.8	2630.7	86.6
1986	1751.7	252.5	2700.5	86.5
1987	1846.2	259.5	2772.0	86.4
1988	1945.9	266.6	2845.5	86.2
1989	2051.0	274.0	2921.0	86.1
1990	2161.8	281.5	2998.4	86.0
1991	2278.5	289.2	3078.7	85.8
1992	2401.5	297.2	3161.2	85.6
1993	2531.2	305.3	3245.9	85.4
1994	2667.9	313.7	3332.8	85.3
1995	2812.0	322.4	3422.1	85.1
1996	2963.8	331.3	3517.3	84.7
1997	3123.9	340.4	3615.2	84.3
1998	3292.6	349.8	3715.7	83.9
1999	3470.4	359.5	3819.1	83.5
2000	3657.8	369.5	3925.4	83.1

Income distribution--population with incomes above:

Year	Poverty Line (Thousands)	$1000 (Thousands)	$2000 (Thousands)	$5000 (Thousands)	$10000 (Thousands)
1980	2581.8	288.4	241.2	99.9	
1981	2777.4	302.5	248.5	104.5	
1982	2987.9	317.4	256.1	109.4	
1983	3214.4	333.0	263.8	114.4	
1984	3458.0	349.4	271.8	119.7	
1985	3720.0	366.5	280.0	125.3	
1986	3893.8	399.9	290.3	135.9	
1987	4075.6	436.2	300.9	147.4	
1988	4266.0	475.9	312.0	160.0	
1989	4465.2	519.2	323.4	173.5	
1990	4673.7	566.4	335.3	188.3	
1991	4876.3	605.1	346.7	200.2	
1992	5087.6	646.4	358.6	212.9	
1993	5308.1	690.6	370.8	226.5	
1994	5538.1	737.7	383.5	240.8	
1995	5778.1	788.1	396.6	256.1	
1996	6016.3	832.3	409.4	269.4	30.0
1997	6264.3	879.0	422.6	283.3	41.0
1998	6522.5	928.3	436.2	298.0	56.0
1999	6791.4	980.4	450.2	313.4	76.5
2000	7071.3	1035.4	464.7	329.7	104.5

Demography

The Honduran population in 1980 comprised 1.9 million males and 1.8 million females, for a grand total of 3.7 million persons. Of the total population, 48 percent were fourteen years or younger, 39 percent were between twenty and sixty-four years of age, and 3 percent were sixty-five or older; thus, 55 percent of the 1980 population could be classified as nonproductive. The majority of Hondurans, indeed, over 64 percent, live in rural areas; the average household size (for both the urban and rural populace) was 5.4 persons.

Economy

Gross national product in Honduras amounted to $2.1 billion in 1980 while GNP per capita was $561. Gross domestic product grew at an annual average of 5.3 percent from 1960 to 1970 and 3.5 percent from 1970 to 1979, but growth in the major sectors did not all conform to this pattern. The growth of GDP in agriculture was much higher in the 1960-1970 time period than in the 1970-1979 period (5.7 percent to 1.3 percent), while the other sectors experienced relatively even growth over the two periods. Sectoral contributions to GDP are as follows: 32 percent from agriculture; 26 percent from industry (17 percent from manufacturing); and 42 percent from services. The labor force totaled 790,000 in 1980; and 63 percent of that total were employed in agriculture, 14 percent in industry, and 23 percent in services. The inflation rate in Honduras in 1980, based on consumer prices, was 15.6 percent.

Agriculture is the mainstay of the Honduran economy: bananas, coffee, meat, lumber, sugar, tobacco, and cotton are produced for export, while corn, beans, and rice are produced for domestic consumption. The level of production of locally consumed grain in 1980 was disappointing, and $32 million worth of grain had to be imported to make up the shortfall. Sixty-three percent of total exports are accounted for by four main export products, and even though 1980 production levels of these crops were lower than the previous year's, total revenue exceeded that of the prior year. The lower production levels were ascribed to various crop diseases as well as inclement weather. The Honduran government plays a very active role in the workings of the economy, but nowhere is the involvement more apparent than in the agricultural sector. The Instituto Hondureno del Cafe was established in 1970 with the stated intention of coordinating the development of coffee, while the Fondo Cafetelero Hondureno was set up to direct coffee earnings into crop diversification. The banana and forestry industries are also closely aligned with government development agencies.

The Honduran economy has a fairly diverse manufacturing sector that, although presently dominated by light industries and assembly plants, is branching out into areas such as chemicals, plastics and cement. Mining and commerce have enjoyed some growth, and tourism has increased significantly.

Even before the first oil shock, Honduras ran a persistent trade deficit; the rise in oil prices has thus added considerably to the pressure. The trade deficit was $41.6 million in 1970, but it had increased to $99.6 million by 1975 and $212.2 million by 1980. Expenditures on petroleum imports amounted to $171 million in 1980. Honduras is a member of the CACM but has not benefited as much as some of the other members. Honduras regularly records a deficit in trade with other CACM members, but the deficit is steadily being narrowed; it has indeed declined from $48 million in 1978 to $17 million in 1980.

The major Honduran exports are coffee (35 percent); bananas (24 percent); wood (7 percent); frozen beef (2 percent); and lead, zinc, and silver (5 percent). The major purchasing countries are the United States (57 percent), FRG (13 percent), the Netherlands (5 percent), and Guatemala (4 percent). Honduras buys machinery and transport equipment (39 percent), basic manufactures (26 percent), chemicals (19 percent), food and live animals (9 percent), and crude petroleum (7 percent). Its imports come from the United States (42 percent), Japan (9 percent), Guatemala (6 percent), Venezuela (6 percent), and Costa Rica (4 percent).

Honduras, like many other Third World countries, has been forced to borrow heavily from external sources to pay for petroleum purchases and to finance internal development. Honduras had a total debt of $102 million in 1970 and annual debt service of $7 million. This figure ballooned to $892 million in debt in 1980 and $1.4 billion in 1982, with service payments of $94.7 million in 1980 and $220 million in 1982. The 1980 debt was in excess of 43 percent of Honduran GNP.

It is expected, however, that the El Cajon hydroelectric project will substantially reduce fuel importation for energy purposes. This hopefully will reduce future borrowing requirements.

Mineral Commodities

Silver, gold, lead, mercury, and tin are mined for export, while deposits of copper and iron ore have been discovered. In addition, there are cement manufacturing and petroleum refining operations.

Forecasts

The total population of Honduras will increase by 38 percent between 1980 and 1990 to reach 5.1 million people (see Table 3.25). There will be a further increase of 36 percent between 1990 and 2000 when the population will number 6.9 million. Males and females will continue to supply roughly equal numbers to the total population, but the number of people in the dependent category will drop to 45 percent. Average household size will decline from 5.4 in 1980 to 4.8 in the year 2000 while, in the same time period, the urban population will rise from 36 percent to 51 percent of the total population.

From the 1980 level of $2.1 billion, Honduras' GNP, based on World Bank growth assumptions, could attain levels of $3.3 billion in 1990 and $5.6 billion in the year 2000 (see Table 3.26). The forecast is based on the assumption that economic growth will rebound from 2.5 percent in 1980 and zero growth in 1981 but will not reach the 7.8 percent average that was maintained in the 1976-1979 period. With GNP increasing at a faster rate than population, per capita income gains will amount to $234 over the life of the forecast period. The labor force, which numbered 790,000 in 1980, will gain 351,600 from 1980 to 1990 and 492,400 from 1990 to 2000 for a grand total of 844,000 new entrants over the life of the forecast period.

TABLE 3.25
GLOBESCAN medium growth demographic projections
for Honduras

Year	Population (Thousands)	Household Size	Households (Thousands)	Urban Population (Thousands)	Rural Population (Thousands)
1980	3691.0	5.4	686.1	1314.0	2377.0
1981	3817.1	5.4	711.1	1386.0	2431.1
1982	3947.5	5.4	737.0	1462.0	2485.5
1983	4082.4	5.3	763.9	1542.2	2540.3
1984	4221.9	5.3	791.7	1626.7	2595.2
1985	4366.2	5.3	820.6	1715.9	2650.3
1986	4502.0	5.3	851.7	1803.9	2698.1
1987	4642.1	5.3	884.0	1896.5	2745.6
1988	4786.5	5.2	917.6	1993.8	2792.8
1989	4935.5	5.2	952.4	2096.0	2839.4
1990	5089.0	5.1	988.6	2203.5	2885.5
1991	5245.6	5.1	1026.9	2310.9	2934.7
1992	5407.0	5.1	1066.7	2423.4	2983.6
1993	5573.3	5.0	1108.1	2541.4	3031.9
1994	5744.8	5.0	1151.1	2665.2	3079.6
1995	5921.5	5.0	1195.7	2794.9	3126.5
1996	6109.6	4.9	1241.0	2928.7	3180.9
1997	6303.7	4.9	1288.0	3068.9	3234.8
1998	6504.0	4.9	1336.8	3215.9	3288.1
1999	6710.6	4.8	1387.5	3369.8	3340.8
2000	6923.8	4.8	1440.0	3531.1	3392.7

Population by age and sex

Males	Females	Total	Age	Males	Females	Total
	1985 (Thousands)				2000 (Thousands)	
402.8	397.1	799.9	0-04	577.5	567.4	1144.9
340.8	339.2	680.0	5-09	479.5	473.3	952.8
290.0	288.1	578.1	10-14	416.6	413.4	829.9
239.1	236.8	475.9	15-19	383.9	382.5	766.4
194.1	191.4	385.4	20-24	329.2	330.8	660.0
154.8	153.3	308.1	25-29	278.5	280.3	558.8
124.4	123.5	247.9	30-34	227.6	229.0	456.7
96.3	96.0	192.3	35-39	183.6	184.1	367.7
81.3	81.0	162.4	40-44	145.5	146.4	291.9
68.1	69.0	137.1	45-49	115.7	116.8	232.4
56.5	57.8	114.2	50-54	87.7	89.4	177.0
45.7	47.3	93.0	55-59	71.7	73.7	145.4
35.7	37.5	73.2	60-64	57.0	60.4	117.4
25.8	27.4	53.3	65-69	43.4	47.2	90.7
16.5	18.4	34.9	70-74	30.6	34.2	64.8
13.6	16.9	30.5	75+	30.5	36.5	66.9
2185.5	2180.7	4366.2	TOTAL	3458.4	3465.4	6923.8

82

TABLE 3.26
GLOBESCAN economic projections for Honduras

Year	GNP in 1980 US$ (Millions)	Per Capita Income	Labor Force (Thousands)	Dependency Ratio (Per 100)
1980	2070.0	524.4	790.0	102.3
1981	2155.9	528.1	819.3	101.7
1982	2245.4	531.8	849.8	101.1
1983	2338.6	535.6	881.3	100.6
1984	2435.6	539.4	914.1	100.0
1985	2536.7	543.2	948.0	99.4
1986	2673.7	555.3	983.9	98.1
1987	2818.0	567.6	1021.2	96.8
1988	2970.2	580.2	1059.9	95.5
1989	3130.6	593.1	1100.0	94.3
1990	3299.7	606.2	1141.6	93.0
1991	3477.8	619.9	1184.0	91.8
1992	3665.6	633.9	1228.0	90.6
1993	3863.6	648.2	1273.5	89.5
1994	4072.2	662.8	1320.8	88.3
1995	4292.1	677.7	1369.8	87.2
1996	4523.9	692.3	1419.0	86.4
1997	4768.2	707.2	1469.9	85.7
1998	5025.7	722.5	1522.7	84.9
1999	5297.1	738.0	1577.3	84.2
2000	5583.1	754.0	1634.0	83.5

Income distribution--population with incomes above:

Year	Poverty Line (Thousands)	$1000 (Thousands)	$2000 (Thousands)	$5000 (Thousands)	$10000 (Thousands)
1980	2697.7	541.0	256.2	153.3	96.6
1981	2803.2	561.6	268.9	159.0	100.7
1982	2912.8	582.9	282.2	164.8	105.0
1983	3026.7	605.0	296.1	170.9	109.4
1984	3145.1	628.0	310.7	177.2	114.1
1985	3268.1	651.9	326.1	183.7	118.9
1986	3402.0	695.2	348.6	190.6	124.7
1987	3541.3	741.4	372.6	197.7	130.7
1988	3686.3	790.6	398.3	205.1	137.1
1989	3837.3	843.2	425.8	212.7	143.7
1990	3994.5	899.2	455.2	220.6	150.6
1991	4141.8	954.5	483.1	228.8	158.0
1992	4294.5	1013.2	512.7	237.4	165.7
1993	4452.8	1075.5	544.2	246.2	173.8
1994	4617.0	1141.6	577.6	255.3	182.4
1995	4787.2	1211.8	613.0	264.8	191.3
1996	4962.3	1279.0	647.0	274.8	200.3
1997	5143.8	1349.9	682.8	285.1	209.8
1998	5331.9	1424.7	720.7	295.7	219.7
1999	5526.9	1503.7	760.6	306.8	230.1
2000	5729.0	1587.1	802.7	318.3	241.0

JAMAICA

Jamaica is located south of the eastern portion of Cuba and has an area of 10,900 square kilometers. The country is a former British colony that gained independence in 1962. The present Jamaican government is a market-oriented, Western-leaning administration, headed by Prime Minister Edward Seaga. The Seaga administration replaced the "democratic socialist" government of Norman Manley in a move that was viewed with favor by the Jamaican and American private sectors and the Reagan administration. Seaga's government was apparently strengthened in December 1983 when his conservative Labor Party gained full control of parliament by sweeping the elections that were boycotted by the socialist opposition.

Demography

In 1980, the Jamaican population numbered 2.1 million, almost equally divided between males and females. Approximately half of the population resides in urban areas and a like number falls into the dependent categories. The average household size in 1975 was 4.3.

Economy

The Jamaican economy experienced rapid growth during the 1960s and early 1970s, but the GDP in 1980 represented the seventh straight year of a decline. The new administration has formulated a strategy based on private-sector investment and increased exports and this, combined with significant aid from the United States and the IMF, seems to have put the economy back on the growth path. The economy registered a real economic growth rate of 1.8 in 1981, a reduction of 23.3 percent in the rate of inflation, and a reduction of 1.5 percent in the unemployment rate.

The main sectors of the Jamaican economy are the bauxite and alumina sector (which is geared to production for export), agriculture (principally banana and sugar), tourism, and manufacturing.

Income distribution in Jamaica is heavily skewed to the most affluent members of the society. For instance, the richest 30 percent of the households receive 72.7 percent of the income and the richest 10 percent of the households receive 43.8 percent of the income. In contrast, the poorest 50 percent of the population receive only 12.8 percent of the income.

Over the past decade, Jamaica has experienced widening trade imbalances. The doubling in the value of its imports between 1970 and 1975 reflects increased energy costs. Jamaica's most important trading partner is the United States, receiving 46 percent, 45 percent, and 37 percent of Jamaica's exports in 1978, 1979, and 1980, respectively, and the United States accounted for 38 percent, 32 percent, and 31 percent, respectively, of Jamaica's imports in those same years. The present administration has pledged to increase exports and thus reverse the trend toward even more negative trade balances.

The most important foreign exchange earners in the Jamaican economy are bauxite and alumina exports. Fuels, minerals and metals, as a group, comprise 22 percent of all Jamaican exports. Other primary commodities (e.g., sugar) account for 46 percent of exports, while textile and clothing and transport equipment and machinery each account for 1 percent of exports. The remaining 30 percent of imports are concentrated in other manufacturing applications. Jamaican imports are principally food (22 percent), machinery and transport equipment (24 percent), and other manufactures (35 percent).

Since 1971, Jamaica has borrowed heavily to finance trade and budget deficits. Borrowings in 1975 exceeded 1970 figures by 179.6 percent while 1980 borrowing increased by 88.2 percent. There is a trend toward smaller public budgets in Jamaica (the 1981-1982 budget realized a real 10.7 percent decline over the 1980 budget) and this, coupled with the pledge to increase exports, should lead to reduced borrowings in the long run. Slow export growth, low demand for aluminum abroad, and increased borrowing by Jamaica have all combined to cause a larger proportion of Jamaica's export earnings to go toward debt servicing. In 1970, 5.6 percent of export earnings went to servicing the debt; this percentage increased to 10.6 in 1975 and registered 19.6 in 1980. Jamaica experienced a net outflow of reserves in the 1970s, but the tide was stemmed in 1981--due largely to the more than $1 billion the country received from the IMF and Western governments. Reserves in 1980 had declined by 16.4 percent from 1975 levels which had in turn declined 9.8 percent from 1970 levels. Reserves were at the same levels in 1981 as they were in 1970.

Current data are not available on the extent of U.S. direct investment in Jamaica, but it is expected to grow in the near future based on the Jamaican government's receptivity and the recent support offered by the Reagan administration. The latest available data (1977) reveal that U.S. investment in Jamaica earned returns of 12.1 percent.

Mineral Commodities

Jamaica is one of the major world producers of bauxite and alumina and also possesses significant bauxite reserves. Over 70 percent of the country's export earnings are derived from sales of these two commodities abroad, and together they contribute about 10 percent to the gross domestic product. Bauxite production fell as a result of production levies imposed by the Manley government, but with the reduction of those levies in 1979, production in 1980 rose to the highest levels yet since 1974. At present the Jamaican government is part-owner of four of the five operating bauxite and alumina plants in that country.

In addition to bauxite and alumina, Jamaican mineral production includes cement, petroleum products, gypsum, lime, sand and gravel, clay, salt, and stone. Some portion of each of these minerals is exported-- primarily to other Caribbean and Latin American countries.

Forecasts

Our forecasts suggest that the population of Jamaica in 1990 will exceed the 1980 population by 21.6 percent, while the growth between 1990 and 2000 will be 15.3 percent (see Table 3.27) the total population will be 2.6 million in 1990 and 3 million in the year 2000. The number of households will increase by 49 percent between 1980 and 1990 and by 29.3 percent between 1990 and 2000. Notwithstanding moderate total population growth, the urban population will almost double by 2000 while the rural population will increase slightly until 1990 and then decline to

TABLE 3.27
GLOBESCAN medium growth demographic projections
for Jamaica

Year	Population (Thousands)	Household Size	Households (Thousands)	Urban Population (Thousands)	Rural Population (Thousands)
1980	2188.0	4.3	514.8	1089.6	1098.4
1981	2224.6	4.2	535.4	1125.1	1099.5
1982	2261.9	4.1	556.9	1161.8	1100.1
1983	2299.8	4.0	579.1	1199.6	1100.2
1984	2338.3	3.9	602.3	1238.7	1099.6
1985	2377.5	3.8	626.4	1279.1	1098.4
1986	2410.5	3.7	646.8	1314.7	1095.8
1987	2444.0	3.7	667.9	1351.3	1092.8
1988	2478.0	3.6	689.6	1388.9	1089.1
1989	2512.5	3.5	712.1	1427.6	1084.9
1990	2547.4	3.5	735.3	1467.3	1080.1
1991	2578.4	3.4	753.2	1502.8	1075.6
1992	2609.8	3.4	771.5	1539.2	1070.7
1993	2641.6	3.3	790.3	1576.4	1065.2
1994	2673.8	3.3	809.6	1614.5	1059.3
1995	2706.4	3.3	829.3	1653.6	1052.8
1996	2729.0	3.2	845.4	1684.0	1045.0
1997	2751.9	3.2	861.9	1715.0	1036.9
1998	2774.9	3.2	878.3	1746.6	1028.3
1999	2798.2	3.1	895.9	1778.7	1019.4
2000	2821.6	3.1	913.4	1811.5	1010.1

Population by age and sex

Males	Females	Total	Age	Males	Females	Total
	1985 (Thousands)				2000 (Thousands)	
152.8	148.9	301.7	0-04	136.4	133.0	269.4
141.2	138.6	279.8	5-09	136.6	135.4	271.9
138.7	136.4	275.2	10-14	143.3	143.3	286.6
147.1	146.2	293.3	15-19	143.0	144.4	287.5
141.6	142.0	283.7	20-24	132.2	134.4	266.6
111.9	112.0	223.9	25-29	128.6	131.6	260.3
62.7	69.9	132.6	30-34	136.0	140.9	277.0
43.7	51.8	95.5	35-39	131.5	137.1	268.6
37.0	42.2	79.2	40-44	104.5	108.0	212.5
33.9	37.9	71.8	45-49	57.6	66.8	124.4
32.4	38.6	71.0	50-54	39.2	48.8	88.0
31.9	36.4	68.3	55-59	32.2	38.9	71.0
27.3	31.0	58.3	60-64	28.1	33.8	61.9
24.1	28.1	52.2	65-69	24.9	32.7	57.5
18.9	21.1	40.0	70-74	21.7	27.9	49.7
22.0	29.1	51.1	75+	28.4	39.5	67.9
1167.3	1210.1	2377.5	TOTAL	1424.3	1496.5	2920.8

1980 levels by 2000. The growth in urban population may well exacerbate the present urban crime problem and will severely test the government's ability to provide the requisite housing.

By the year 2000 the Jamaican population will be substantially older --that is, a larger percentage of the population will be over fifteen years of age than was the case in 1985. This also means, however, that more people will fall into the sixty-five-and-over age bracket than was the case in 1985.

The Jamaican GNP will likely exceed $5 billion by the year 2000 (see Table 3.28) after registering increases of 43 percent between 1980 and 1990 and 69 percent between 1990 and 2000. Over the entire period, it is expected that GNP will increase at a faster rate than does the population size, resulting in, with a few exceptions, constant increases in per capita income. As a whole, Jamaica should be better off in 1990 than it was in 1980 and even better off by the year 2000. The labor force will increase 36 percent from 1980 to 1990 and by 25 percent between 1990 and 2000.

A trend impact analysis of Jamaica suggests that bauxite production will increase by 18 percent over the 1981-1990 period (see Figure 3.3). This departs somewhat from the recent history of Jamaican bauxite production which grew at an annual average of 3.7 percent and was as high as 13.3 percent between 1968 and 1974. With the onset of the world economic crisis in 1974 and increased levies on bauxite by the Jamaican government, output fell drastically between 1974 and 1975 and remained at pre-1970 levels up until 1980.

The events that we expect will have an impact on Jamaica's bauxite production are listed in Table 3.29. The event with the strongest negative impact is alternative material substitution. Airlines are increasingly concerned about reducing the weight of their aircraft in an effort to improve fuel efficiency. Kevlar has been authorized for use in certain portions of aircraft, while Lear has just completed an experimental graphite-epoxy aircraft. Both of these materials combine strength with lightness, and as such, pose a marked threat to the aluminum domination of the airframe market. Added to this is the fact that the defense establishment is interested in materials that can absorb rather than reflect radar waves, and the chances become greater (.35 by 1985; .75 by 1990) that aluminum will be replaced by one of these alternative materials.

The second most negative event affecting Jamaica's bauxite production is a possible loss of foreign expertise. This loss of expertise could result from nationalization of the bauxite industry and would leave the operation of the industry in the hands of relatively unskilled Jamaican nationals. The probability of such an event occurring is perhaps .10 by 1985 and .50 by 1990.

The process of refining bauxite to produce aluminum is very energy intensive, and energy costs are a prime determinant of the final cost of aluminum. A 50 percent increase in energy prices would have a negative impact on the amount of bauxite refined and, thus, on the amount of bauxite produced. With the likelihood of continued volatility in the Mideast--the prime source of crude oil--an oil embargo or regionwide conflict could cause the price of oil to increase by 50 percent. The likelihood of such an event occurring is .20 by 1985 and .50 by 1990.

The event that would have the most positive impact on Jamaica's bauxite production stems from the Reagan administration's decision to make Jamaica the centerpiece of its Caribbean Basin Initiative. As a

TABLE 3.28
GLOBESCAN economic projections for Jamaica

Year	GNP in 1980 US$ (Millions)	Per Capita Income	Labor Force (Thousands)	Dependency Ratio (Per 100)
1980	2250.0	927.6	741.7	85.0
1981	2358.0	956.1	764.7	82.4
1982	2471.2	985.5	788.4	79.8
1983	2589.8	1015.7	812.8	77.3
1984	2714.1	1047.0	838.0	74.9
1985	2844.4	1079.1	863.9	72.6
1986	2998.0	1119.2	885.3	71.1
1987	3159.9	1160.8	907.2	69.7
1988	3330.5	1203.9	929.7	68.3
1989	3510.4	1248.7	952.7	66.9
1990	3699.9	1295.1	976.2	65.6
1991	3899.7	1346.2	997.5	64.2
1992	4110.3	1399.4	1019.3	63.0
1993	4332.3	1454.7	1041.5	61.7
1994	4566.2	1512.2	1064.3	60.5
1995	4812.8	1571.9	1087.5	59.3
1996	5072.7	1638.3	1109.6	57.8
1997	5346.6	1707.6	1132.2	56.4
1998	5635.3	1779.7	1155.2	55.0
1999	5939.6	1854.9	1178.8	53.6
2000	6260.3	1933.3	1202.8	52.3

Income distribution--population with incomes above:

Year	Poverty Line (Thousands)	$1000 (Thousands)	$2000 (Thousands)	$5000 (Thousands)	$10000 (Thousands)
1980	1888.3	596.1	294.5	106.2	88.4
1981	1929.9	627.1	304.4	108.4	90.8
1982	1972.5	659.7	314.7	110.7	93.2
1983	2015.9	694.0	325.3	113.1	95.7
1984	2060.3	730.1	336.3	115.5	98.2
1985	2105.7	768.1	347.7	117.9	100.9
1986	2150.1	807.8	371.3	127.5	103.4
1987	2195.5	849.6	396.4	137.8	106.0
1988	2241.8	893.5	423.3	148.9	108.7
1989	2289.0	939.7	452.0	161.0	111.4
1990	2337.3	988.3	482.7	174.0	114.2
1991	2379.1	1033.8	512.1	187.7	116.7
1992	2421.6	1081.3	543.4	202.5	119.2
1993	2464.9	1131.1	576.5	218.4	121.8
1994	2509.1	1183.1	611.6	235.7	124.4
1995	2553.8	1237.6	648.9	254.2	127.1
1996	2590.1	1296.0	689.7	268.7	129.4
1997	2626.8	1357.3	733.1	284.1	131.8
1998	2664.1	1421.4	779.2	300.1	134.2
1999	2701.9	1488.6	828.1	317.2	136.7
2000	2740.2	1559.0	880.2	335.2	139.2

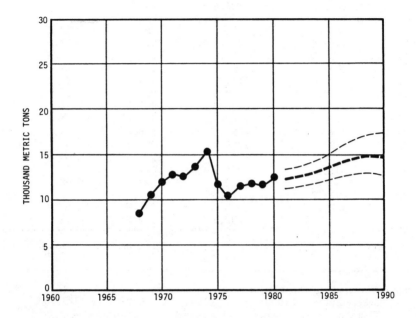

Figure 3.3 Forecast of Jamaican bauxite production

		Trend Impact Analysis		
Baseline Curve No. = 6		Confidence Percentiles = 25 and 75		

Year	History/ Baseline	Forecast		
		Lower	Center	Upper
1968	8525.00			
1969	10499.00			
1970	12009.00			
1971	12767.00			
1972	12543.00			
1973	13600.00			
1974	15328.00			
1975	11571.00			
1976	10296.00			
1977	11433.00			
1978	11777.00			
1979	11505.00			
1980	12261.00			
1981	12118.30	11154.08	12203.13	13265.71
1982	12189.90	11360.81	12435.73	13563.95
1983	12262.28	11546.56	12668.98	13853.45
1984	12335.45	11767.93	13007.73	14344.72
1985	12409.42	12106.78	13513.86	15133.46
1986	12484.21	12414.86	13994.80	15882.81
1987	12559.83	12631.35	14361.11	16467.99
1988	12636.29	12747.52	14631.77	16952.77
1989	12713.61	12647.14	14706.47	17202.99
1990	12791.80	12349.24	14598.65	17218.42

Figure 3.3 (Cont.) Jamaican bauxite production (thousand metric tons)

TABLE 3.29
Events that will have an impact on Jamaican bauxite production

Event No.	Year/ Probability	Years to First Impact	Years to Maximum Impact	Maximum Impact	Years to Steady State Impact	Steady State Impact	Relative Impact
3	1985 0.35 1990 0.75	2	3	-10.0%	3	-10.0%	-2890.

Graphite-epoxy and/or kevlar replacing aluminum as the primary material in airframe manufacture.

| 10 | 1985 0.10
1990 0.50 | 1 | 5 | -25.0% | 7 | -20.0% | -2490. |

A loss of foreign expertise.

| 4 | 1985 0.20
1990 0.50 | 2 | 4 | -15.0% | 4 | -15.0% | -2290. |

Renewed trade between Cuba and the U.S.

| 7 | 1985 0.10
1990 0.20 | 1 | 1 | -10.0% | 1 | -10.0% | -1130. |

Formation of strong bauxite cartel.

| 1 | 1985 0.05
1990 0.25 | 2 | 3 | -10.0% | 3 | -10.0% | -576. |

Restrictive government regulation and taxation of bauxite enterprises.

| 2 | 1985 0.10
1990 0.25 | 1 | 2 | -5.0% | 2 | -5.0% | -561. |

Widespread use of aluminum engine blocks by automobile engine manufacturers.

| 9 | 1985 0.20
1990 0.30 | 3 | 5 | -15.0% | 5 | -15.0% | -157. |

Integration of bauxite production on a regional basis in the Caribbean as per CARICOM proposal regarding Jamaica, Guyana, and Trinidad and Tobago.

| 6 | 1985 0.50
1990 0.60 | 1 | 3 | 5.0% | 5 | 10.0% | 3080 |

Reversal of shift from Jamaica to Australia as premier supplier of bauxite to the U.S.

| 11 | 1985 0.70
1990 0.80 | 0 | 1 | 10.0% | 2 | 5.0% | 4190 |

Purchase of Jamaican bauxite for U.S. strategic reserves.

| 8 | 1985 0.35
1990 0.60 | 2 | 4 | 20.0% | 4 | 20.0% | 4840 |

Five percent annual growth rate in U.S. economy.

| 5 | 1985 0.70
1990 0.80 | 2 | 4 | 15.0% | 4 | 15.0% | 6750 |

New investment in bauxite industry by U.S. aluminum companies.

consequence of the regime change in Jamaica, and the administration's response to that change, U.S. aluminum companies have already tentatively decided to inject significant new investments into the bauxite industry. The probability of new investment is thus quite high (.70 by 1985; .80 by 1990).

The bulk of Jamaican bauxite is purchased by the United States, so Jamaican production has often been affected by U.S. economic trends. A return to a 5 percent economic growth rate in the United States would undoubtedly cause an increased demand for industrial goods, including aluminum; that should, in turn, lead to an increase in Jamaican bauxite production. The probability of this event has been pegged at .35 by 1985 and .60 by 1990.

One of the effects of the bauxite levy imposed by the Manley government was to cause the United States to rely more on Australia, and less on Jamaica, as a source for bauxite. The Caribbean Basin Initiative will have another positive effect on Jamaican bauxite production, as U.S. companies reverse the process and once again come to rely on Jamaican bauxite. The probability of a reversal of the shift is moderately high (.50 by 1985; .60 by 1990).

Jamaican bauxite production is depressed due to a worldwide slump. Because bauxite is the biggest Jamaican foreign reserve earner, this hurts the government's aim of having exports lead the economy to recovery. In an attempt to help Jamaica over this hurdle, the Reagan administration has proposed purchasing 1.6 million tons of Jamaican bauxite for the U.S. strategic reserve. This likelihood (.70 by 1985; .80 by 1990) will have a positive effect on Jamaican bauxite production.

A second trend impact analysis was performed to observe what impacts the Caribbean Basin Initiative might have on Jamaican bauxite production. This was accomplished by omitting the events that were viewed as CBI-related (events 5, 6 and 11 of Table 3.29) and recalculating the TIA. The results are indicated in Figure 3.4. When compared to Figure 3.3, the second run affirms the importance of the CBI to future Jamaican bauxite production.

NICARAGUA

With a land area of 57,000 square miles (147,888 square kilometers), Nicaragua is the largest of the Central American countries. Bounded to the north by Honduras, to the south by Costa Rica, to the east by the Caribbean Sea, and to the west by the Pacific Ocean, Nicaragua is peopled by Mestizos (70 percent), Caucasians (17 percent), Negroes (9 percent), and Indians (4 percent). The official language is Spanish and is widely used by the predominantly Roman Catholic population. English is spoken in the areas along the Caribbean coast that have significant Negro populations (the Negroes living in Nicaragua are of Jamaican descent).

Until the ouster of Anastasio Somoza-Debayle in 1979, the Nicaraguan government was closely controlled by the Somoza family which, in addition to its political strength, had a substantial financial interest in the Nicaraguan economy. The Somoza dynasty began in 1936 when Anastasio Somoza Garcia, at that time the Commander of the Nicaraguan National Guard, assumed the presidency in 1936. Upon his assassination in 1956, his eldest son, Luis Somoza-Debayle, succeeded him and ruled until 1963 when

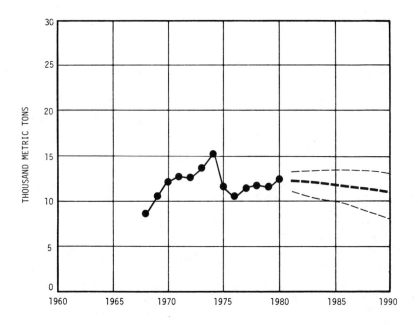

Figure 3.4 Jamaican bauxite production without CBI influence

a former foreign minister was elected president. The new president, Rene Schick, died before the completion of his term. In 1967, Anastasio Somoza-Debayle, youngest son of the senior Somoza, was elected president and, in 1972, was returned to office for another six-year term. The second Somoza term was never completed as he was forced to resign office in 1979 in the face of a devastating civil war and intense pressure from external forces. After fleeing to Miami initially, Debayle set up residence in Asuncion, Paraguay, where he was assassinated on September 17, 1979.

The organization that forced the ouster of Somoza was a revolutionary group calling itself the Sandinist National Liberation Front. Nicaragua was placed under the rulership of a five-man junta two days after the Somoza ouster. Two members of the junta were non-Sandinists and who subsequently resigned, charging that the power really rested with the nine-man Sandinist National Directorate. A forty-seven-member Advisory Committee was convened the following year with the intention of drafting a new constitution. The present three-man junta has very close economic and political ties with Cuba and Salvadoran guerrillas and widening contacts with the Soviet Union and other Communist nations.

Demography

When considered in terms of its large land area, Nicaragua, with a total population of 2.7 million people in 1980, is the least densely populated Central American country. The majority of the Nicaraguan populace, 53.3 percent, however, live in urban areas. Over 50 percent of the 1980 population were either fourteen years of age and younger or sixty-five years of age and older, and the average household size was 6.9 persons.

Economy

The Nicaraguan economy declined significantly during the 1979 revolution but has shown signs of improving since. Gross national product in 1980 totaled $1.93 billion, while GNP per capita was $706. Gross domestic product grew at a 7.2 percent annual rate in the 1960-1970 period, and by 2.6 percent between 1970 and 1979, but had a negative rate of -7.9 percent in 1978. All major sectors in the economy (agriculture, industry, and services) had annual growth rates between 5.7 and 11 percent from 1960 to 1970, but declined to between 1.3 and 4.2 percent in the 1970-1979 period. The average annual inflation rate was 12.2 percent between 1970 and 1979 but had skyrocketed to 35.3 percent in 1980.

The agricultural sector has historically contributed in excess of 75 percent of Nicaraguan export earnings, and its resurgence is clearly necessary if the country is to escape the crushing burden of debt that it now faces. Cotton, coffee, sugar, cattle and bananas (export commodities) and rice, corn, and beans (domestic consumption) are the main components of an agricultural sector that contributes 29 percent of GDP and employs 40 percent of the 874,600 labor force. Approximately 500,000 acres of cotton were planted annually prior to the war, but only 85,000 acres were planted in the 1979-1980 season. Government attempts to increase production resulted in 230,000 acres planted in 1980, but the industry was still plagued by uncertainty and shortages of labor; total output was 160 million pounds (compared to 260 million pounds before the disruptions).

The evident decline in the cotton industry was also evident in the other major export crops. Coffee production had increased from 64 million pounds in 1962 to 141 million pounds in the 1978-1979 season, but in the following year, production fell to 125 million pounds. Meat exports fell from 79 million pounds in 1979 to 42 million pounds in 1980 due to several hundred thousand head of cattle wandering across Nicaragua's borders and to wanton killing of cattle during the revolution.

Immediately following the establishment of the Sandinist-dominated junta, the government embarked on a wide-ranging expropriation endeavor, with much of the activity concentrated in the agricultural sector. Land owned by the Somoza family prior to the revolution--approximately 1.5 million acres--was expropriated as was unfarmed acreage and land belonging to somocistas--landowners associated with the former president. In addition, the shrimp and lobster packing plants and part of the fishing fleet were nationalized; the four largest gold mines were nationalized, as were domestically owned banks and the insurance industry. According to the 1980 Economic Recovery Plan, the government had gained a majority control in mining (95 percent), construction (70 percent), and services (55 percent) in addition to its minority participation in manufacturing and agriculture.

The industrial sector, comprised of the manufacturing, construction, utilities, and mining industries, is responsible for 20 percent of the GDP and employs 14 percent of the labor force. The largest segment in the industrial sector is manufacturing, providing 24 of the 28 percent that the industrial sector contributes to GDP. The major manufacturing activities are centered in the processing of agricultural commodities, but they also encompass production of beverages, textiles, refined petroleum, cement, and fabricated metals.

Nicaraguan exports declined sharply in 1980 when compared to the previous year's level, and the country recorded a negative trade balance. (In 1976, 1978, and 1979, Nicaragua had registered merchandise trade surpluses.) Imports into Nicaragua declined, in part, because of the lack of hard currency, and local industry began to suffer from shortages of spare parts that were no longer being imported. The trade balance deficit in 1980 amounted to $436.8 million. Nicaraguan exports then consisted of coffee (31 percent), cotton (23 percent), and meat (10 percent) and were bought by the United States (25 percent), FRG (14 percent), Japan (9 percent), Costa Rica (9 percent), El Salvador (6 percent), China (5 percent), and Guatemala (5 percent). The principal imports were industrial raw materials (40 percent), nondurable consumer goods (17 percent), industrial machinery (13 percent), durable consumer goods (8 percent), agricultural materials (6 percent), and fuel lubricants (5 percent); the principal import partners have been the United States (31 percent), Venezuela (12 percent), Guatemala (9 percent), Costa Rica (7 percent), Japan (7 percent), FRG (5 percent), and El Salvador (5 percent).

Mineral Commodities

Gold, silver, lead, and zinc are currently mined in Nicaragua and, in addition, exploitable reserves of gypsum and natural gas have been discovered. The four largest gold mines were nationalized after the revolution--the mines were owned by one Canadian and two American companies; negotiations are still ongoing to determine the level of compensation for the original owners.

Forecasts

Our demographic projections suggest that the Nicaraguan population will increase from 2.7 million in 1980 to 3.8 million in 1990 and 5.2 million in the year 2000 (see Table 3.30), increases of 39 percent from 1980 to 1990 and 36 percent from 1990 to 2000. The number of people in the nonproductive category will fall from 50 percent in 1980 to 46 percent in the year 2000. The urban population will increase from 53.3 percent of the population in 1980 to 59.7 percent in 1990 and 65.9 percent in the year 2000.

Economic projections are very risky at this point, but if World Bank growth assumptions prove reasonable, Nicaraguan GNP could surpass the $3 billion mark for the first time by 1990 and then exceed $5 billion by the year 2000 (see Table 3.31). The projected 1990 GNP would represent an increase of 60 percent over 1980 GNP, while GNP in the year 2000 would be 69 percent larger than its 1990 counterpart. The annual growth rates assumed for this forecast were 4.8 percent from 1980 to 1995 and 5.4 percent thereafter. This, when compared with the Nicaraguan experience of 7.2 percent in the decade of the 1960s and 5.8 percent from 1970 to 1977, assumes that post-1985 Nicaragua will have recovered from the effects of the war, and the major economic sectors will be contributing as before. Nicaraguan per capita income will then increase by 38 percent over the life of the forecast period--from $649 in 1980 to $898 in the year 2000--while, within the same period, the labor force will increase by 104 percent--from 874,600 in 1980 to 1.8 million in the year 2000. Admittedly, these projections may not be totally realistic in light of recent events. They must be taken as a fairly optimistic outlook on Nicaragua's prospects. The economy could obviously perform much more poorly if the instability and conflict continue.

PANAMA

Panama has a land area of 75,650 square kilometers (29,208 square miles) and is the thinnest piece of land separating the Caribbean Sea and Pacific Ocean; this feature was exploited in constructing the Panama Canal. The Panamanian population is comprised of 70 percent Mestizos, 14 percent Negroes, and 9 percent Caucasian, with the remaining 7 percent being Indian and other ethnic divisions. Although the official language is Spanish, approximately 14 percent of the population speak English, and many Panamanians are bilingual.

Panama is ruled by a president and vice-president (elected by the National Assembly) and the National Assembly of Community Representatives (popularly elected) which exercises legislative powers. President Aristides Royo was named president by General Omar Torrijos Herrera, the National Guard commandant, in 1978, but his power was subordinate to the general's. General Torrijos died in a plane crash in 1981, and the job of commandant of the National Guard passed on to General Ruben Dario Paredes who pressured President Royo to resign in 1982. Royo was replaced by his vice-president, Ricardo de la Espriella, who resigned without explanation in February 1984. Espriella was succeeded by his vice president, Jorge Illueca, a career diplomat who was then serving as president of the United Nations General Assembly. The leadership change

TABLE 3.30
GLOBESCAN medium growth demographic projections
for Nicaragua

Year	Population (Thousands)	Household Size	Households (Thousands)	Urban Population (Thousands)	Rural Population (Thousands)
1980	2733.0	6.9	396.1	1456.7	1276.3
1981	2826.0	6.9	410.8	1523.9	1302.1
1982	2922.1	6.9	426.1	1594.2	1327.9
1983	3021.5	6.8	441.9	1667.8	1353.7
1984	3124.3	6.8	458.3	1744.7	1379.5
1985	3230.5	6.8	475.3	1825.3	1405.3
1986	3337.1	6.8	492.8	1906.4	1430.8
1987	3447.2	6.7	510.9	1991.1	1456.1
1988	3560.9	6.7	529.7	2079.5	1481.4
1989	3678.4	6.7	549.2	2171.9	1506.5
1990	3799.8	6.7	569.4	2268.5	1531.3
1991	3921.9	6.6	590.9	2365.9	1555.9
1992	4048.0	6.6	613.3	2467.6	1580.3
1993	4178.1	6.6	636.5	2573.7	1604.4
1994	4312.4	6.5	660.5	2684.3	1628.1
1995	4451.0	6.5	685.5	2799.7	1651.3
1996	4586.8	6.5	710.8	2912.1	1674.7
1997	4726.7	6.4	736.9	3029.0	1697.7
1998	4870.8	6.4	764.1	3150.6	1720.2
1999	5019.4	6.3	792.3	3277.1	1742.3
2000	5172.5	6.3	821.5	3408.7	1763.8

Population by age and sex

1985 (Thousands)				2000 (Thousands)		
Males	Females	Total	Age	Males	Females	Total
308.3	298.4	606.7	0-04	437.8	422.8	860.6
252.1	246.6	498.7	5-09	385.4	375.9	761.3
213.5	209.0	422.5	10-14	336.2	329.8	666.0
176.4	172.0	348.4	15-19	288.1	283.9	572.0
147.6	145.6	293.1	20-24	240.0	238.8	478.7
121.5	121.6	243.1	25-29	202.0	201.9	403.9
101.2	102.0	203.2	30-34	165.2	165.1	330.3
73.6	74.1	147.7	35-39	137.3	138.8	276.0
56.2	58.6	114.9	40-44	112.2	115.0	227.2
43.6	47.9	91.5	45-49	92.3	95.3	187.6
35.4	39.0	74.5	50-54	65.6	68.1	133.7
27.3	31.8	59.1	55-59	48.4	52.6	101.0
20.9	25.3	46.3	60-64	35.4	41.2	76.7
14.7	22.7	37.3	65-69	26.3	31.2	57.5
9.5	13.1	22.5	70-74	17.5	22.3	39.8
8.6	12.4	21.0	75+	16.6	24.8	41.4
1610.2	1620.3	3230.5	TOTAL	2606.2	2607.5	5213.8

TABLE 3.31
GLOBESCAN economic projections for Nicaragua

Year	GNP in 1980 US$ (Millions)	Per Capita Income	Labor Force (Thousands)	Dependency Ratio (Per 100)
1980	1930.0	649.7	874.6	100.8
1981	2001.4	651.6	905.8	100.5
1982	2075.5	653.4	938.1	100.2
1983	2152.3	655.3	971.6	99.9
1984	2231.9	657.2	1006.3	99.5
1985	2314.5	659.1	1042.3	99.2
1986	2439.4	672.1	1081.1	98.5
1987	2571.2	685.3	1121.3	97.8
1988	2710.0	698.8	1163.0	97.1
1989	2856.4	712.6	1206.3	96.5
1990	3010.6	726.6	1251.2	95.8
1991	3173.2	741.7	1297.0	95.0
1992	3344.5	757.0	1344.5	94.3
1993	3525.1	772.7	1393.7	93.5
1994	3715.5	788.7	1444.7	92.8
1995	3916.1	805.0	1497.6	92.1
1996	4127.6	823.0	1552.2	91.0
1997	4350.5	841.3	1608.8	90.0
1998	4585.4	860.1	1667.4	89.0
1999	4833.0	879.3	1728.2	88.0
2000	5094.0	898.9	1791.2	87.1

Income distribution--population with incomes above:

Year	Poverty Line (Thousands)	$1000 (Thousands)	$2000 (Thousands)	$5000 (Thousands)	$10000 (Thousands)
1980	2449.1	420.7	238.3	113.5	65.5
1981	2533.9	438.0	247.4	117.5	68.1
1982	2621.6	456.1	256.9	121.7	70.8
1983	2712.4	474.9	266.7	126.0	73.5
1984	2806.3	494.5	277.0	130.4	76.4
1985	2903.5	514.8	287.6	135.1	79.4
1986	3011.5	552.4	304.3	140.5	83.7
1987	3123.7	592.8	322.0	146.2	88.3
1988	3239.9	636.1	340.8	152.1	93.1
1989	3360.6	682.5	360.6	158.2	98.1
1990	3485.7	732.4	381.6	164.5	103.5
1991	3610.8	779.4	402.1	170.9	108.6
1992	3740.3	829.4	423.7	177.5	114.0
1993	3874.5	882.6	446.5	184.3	119.6
1994	4013.6	939.3	470.4	191.5	125.5
1995	4157.6	999.5	495.7	198.9	131.8
1996	4299.1	1059.8	520.5	206.2	137.8
1997	4445.4	1123.6	546.5	213.7	144.1
1998	4596.5	1191.4	573.7	221.6	150.7
1999	4753.0	1263.2	602.4	229.7	157.6
2000	4914.8	1339.3	632.5	238.2	164.8

occurred just four months before what was to be Panama's first scheduled presidential elections in sixteen years.

Demography

The Panamanian population numbered 1.9 million in 1980. About 54.3 percent reside in urban areas. The Panamanian population structure compares favorably with that of other countries in the region, with 43.9 percent in the nonproductive age groups. Average household size in 1980 was 4.1 persons.

Economy

The economy of Panama has two main sectors--agriculture and a service-oriented sector centered on the Panama Canal. Much of the agricultural sector consists of subsistence farming; it supports over 30 percent of the population but makes a rather small contribution to the country's gross domestic product. The canal contributes about $300-$400 million to Panama's economy annually, and canal-related commercial activity, including shipping, has been very important. Panama is a growing center for international finance and banking operations. The government encourages foreign direct investment and has a liberal regulation policy toward foreign banks. There is no central bank in Panama.

The economy has grown rapidly in recent years. Inflation reached 15 percent in 1980 but has been declining since. Unemployment remains very high, and new job creation has not matched the number of labor force entrants each year. Panama's external debt increased substantially in 1979, but the rate of growth has now slowed considerably.

Panama's major export goods include bananas, sugar, coffee, cocoa, shrimp, fishmeal, meat and petroleum products. Unfortunately, large amounts of imported oil have accentuated persistent balance-of-trade/balance-of-payment difficulties. The government's efforts to exploit Panama's substantial hydroelectrical potential, however, should help reduce oil imports in the future. In 1981 total imports from the United States exceeded Panama's exports to the United States by more than $500 million. Total U.S. direct investment in Panama for 1980 exceeded $3 billion.

Mineral Commodities

Panama appears to have substantial reserves of copper, as well as limited amounts of manganese, iron and asbestos. As yet, the copper reserves have not been exploited economically, but the government reached agreement with a British firm, Rio Tinto Zinc Corporation, in 1980 to this end. The agreement joined the British firm with CODEMIN, the state-owned mining corporation, to form the Cerro Colorado Copper Enterprise in a project to begin to develop the large copper deposits.

Forecasts

The Panamanian population will, according to GLOBESCAN forecasts, increase from 1.9 million in 1980 to 2.4 million in 1990 and 2.9 million in the year 2000 (see Table 3.32). This represents increases of 24.5 percent between 1980 and 1990 and 20.9 percent between 1990 and

TABLE 3.32
GLOBESCAN medium growth demographic projections
for Panama

Year	Population (Thousands)	Household Size	Households (Thousands)	Urban Population (Thousands)	Rural Population (Thousands)
1980	1899.0	4.1	468.9	1031.2	867.8
1981	1942.6	4.0	483.8	1067.7	874.9
1982	1987.2	4.0	499.1	1105.6	881.6
1983	2032.8	3.9	515.0	1144.8	888.0
1984	2079.5	3.9	531.3	1185.4	894.1
1985	2127.2	3.9	548.2	1227.4	899.8
1986	2172.7	3.8	565.1	1267.7	905.0
1987	2219.1	3.8	582.7	1309.2	909.9
1988	2266.5	3.8	600.7	1352.2	914.4
1989	2314.9	3.7	619.3	1396.5	918.4
1990	2364.4	3.7	638.5	1442.3	922.1
1991	2411.5	3.7	656.8	1485.7	925.8
1992	2459.6	3.6	675.6	1530.4	929.2
1993	2508.6	3.6	695.0	1576.5	932.2
1994	2558.7	3.6	714.9	1623.9	934.7
1995	2609.7	3.5	735.5	1672.8	936.9
1996	2657.6	3.5	753.8	1718.7	939.0
1997	2706.5	3.5	772.7	1765.9	940.7
1998	2756.3	3.5	792.0	1814.3	942.0
1999	2807.0	3.5	811.8	1864.1	942.9
2000	2858.6	3.4	832.0	1915.3	943.3

Population by age and sex

1985 (Thousands)				2000 (Thousands)		
Males	Females	Total	Age	Males	Females	Total
140.6	135.4	275.9	0-04	162.2	156.5	318.7
134.1	131.0	265.2	5-09	154.1	150.0	304.0
128.1	124.6	252.7	10-14	145.4	141.9	287.3
118.2	113.6	231.8	15-19	137.1	134.1	271.2
103.9	99.5	203.4	20-24	131.1	129.9	261.1
89.8	86.4	176.3	25-29	124.5	123.2	247.7
76.9	73.5	150.4	30-34	114.1	111.9	226.0
62.0	58.5	120.5	35-39	99.9	97.8	197.6
51.1	48.4	99.5	40-44	85.9	84.6	170.5
41.0	39.4	80.4	45-49	72.9	71.3	144.3
34.8	34.2	69.0	50-54	57.8	56.1	113.9
28.6	28.1	56.7	55-59	46.2	45.6	91.8
24.2	23.8	48.1	60-64	35.5	36.0	71.4
19.7	19.4	39.1	65-69	27.9	29.6	57.5
14.3	14.8	29.1	70-74	20.2	22.0	42.3
13.7	15.6	29.3	75+	24.5	28.8	53.3
1080.9	1046.3	2127.2	TOTAL	1439.3	1419.3	2858.6

2000. Persons in the nonproductive categories (younger than fifteen and older than sixty-four) will comprise only 37 percent of the population, a favorable statistic when compared with neighboring states. Household size, which averaged 4.1 persons in 1980, will average 3.7 persons in 1990 and 3.4 persons in the year 2000. The urban component of the population will grow at a much faster rate than the rural component, resulting in the urban population representing 61 percent of the total population in 1990 and 67 percent in 2000, up from 54.3 percent in 1980.

Panamanian GNP could increase by 59 percent between 1980 and 1990, to total $5.1 billion, and by 69.2 percent between 1990 and 2000, amounting to $8.5 billion at the end of the forecast period (see Table 3.33). Per capita income would then increase by 27.7 percent between 1980 and 1990 and by 39.9 percent between 1990 and 2000, totaling $1,822 in 1990 and $2,551 in the year 2000. The increase in the labor force, from 1.1 million in 1980 to 1.8 million in the year 2000, when coupled with the lower population growth, results in a declining dependency ratio--78.5/100 in 1980, 66.4/100 in 1990, and 59.2/100 in the year 2000.

SURINAME

Suriname is a former Netherlands colony located on the Atlantic coast of South America. The population is a mix of African, Indian, Creole and descendants of various other nationalities, and while Dutch is the official language, English, Hindi, and Chinese also are spoken. Suriname has a land area of 142,700 square kilometers and was granted full independence from the Netherlands in November 1975, under a constitution that provided for a titular president, a prime minister, and a thirty-nine-member parliament. In 1980, the civilian government of Prime Minister Henck Arron was toppled by a military coup, but the leaders quickly turned control over to a civilian administration headed by Dr. Henck R. Chin A Sen. The Chin A Sen government was then replaced by a military regime headed by Colonel Daysi Bouterse in early 1982. The Bouterse regime executed several leading opponents in December 1982 for involvement in what was termed an attempted coup. Labor unrest and sabotage in 1983, in response to planned tax and price increases, led Bouterse to dismiss his civilian cabinet in early 1984 and cancel the increases.

Demography

The population of Suriname numbered 387,000 in 1980, with females outnumbering males by 11,000. Approximately 45 percent of the population live in urban areas with the majority concentrated in the capital city of Paramaribo. The population is very young, with 63 percent below twenty years of age, 82 percent below thirty-five, and only 11 percent above fifty-four. Accentuating the youthfulness of the population, and hence an unfavorable dependency ratio, is the fact that the average household size in 1975 was 6.9 persons.

Economy

During the period 1970-1977, Suriname's economy averaged 6.3 percent real annual growth, mainly due to export earnings realized from

TABLE 3.33
GLOBESCAN economic projections for Panama

Year	GNP in 1980 US$ (Millions)	Per Capita Income	Labor Force (Thousands)	Dependency Ratio (Per 100)
1980	3170.0	1427.3	1092.1	78.5
1981	3300.0	1452.4	1125.3	77.2
1982	3435.3	1478.0	1159.6	75.9
1983	3576.1	1504.1	1194.8	74.6
1984	3722.7	1530.6	1231.2	73.3
1985	3875.4	1557.6	1268.6	72.1
1986	4084.6	1607.4	1304.6	70.9
1987	4305.2	1658.8	1341.5	69.8
1988	4537.7	1711.8	1379.5	68.6
1989	4782.7	1766.5	1418.6	67.5
1990	5041.0	1822.9	1458.7	66.4
1991	5313.2	1883.8	1495.6	65.5
1992	5600.1	1946.7	1533.4	64.6
1993	5902.5	2011.7	1572.2	63.8
1994	6221.3	2078.9	1611.9	62.9
1995	6557.2	2148.3	1652.7	62.1
1996	6911.3	2223.5	1689.1	61.5
1997	7284.5	2301.2	1726.3	60.9
1998	7677.9	2381.7	1764.3	60.3
1999	8092.5	2465.0	1803.2	59.8
2000	8529.5	2551.1	1842.9	59.2

Income distribution--population with incomes above:

Year	Poverty Line (Thousands)	$1000 (Thousands)	$2000 (Thousands)	$5000 (Thousands)	$10000 (Thousands)
1980	1816.6	1066.8	356.4	91.8	57.9
1981	1859.7	1113.9	377.8	94.4	59.8
1982	1903.7	1163.0	400.5	97.0	61.8
1983	1948.8	1214.4	424.5	99.7	63.8
1984	1995.0	1268.0	450.0	102.5	65.8
1985	2042.2	1323.9	477.0	105.3	68.0
1986	2088.4	1391.1	518.6	115.0	70.8
1987	2135.6	1461.8	563.8	125.5	73.7
1988	2183.8	1536.0	613.0	137.0	76.8
1989	2233.1	1614.0	666.5	149.6	80.0
1990	2283.6	1695.9	-724.6	163.3	83.3
1991	2331.6	1763.0	787.7	176.8	86.4
1992	2380.6	1832.7	856.3	191.3	89.6
1993	2430.6	1905.2	930.9	207.0	93.0
1994	2481.7	1980.5	1012.0	224.1	96.5
1995	2533.9	2058.8	1100.2	242.5	100.1
1996	2582.9	2124.3	1180.0	258.5	103.5
1997	2632.8	2192.0	1265.7	275.6	107.1
1998	2683.8	2261.8	1357.5	293.8	110.8
1999	2735.7	2333.8	1456.1	313.1	114.6
2000	2788.6	2408.1	1561.7	333.8	118.5

bauxite and related materials sales abroad. In addition to export earnings, Suriname is the recipient of an aid package from the Netherlands which is worth $1.5 billion to be disbursed over the period 1975-1990. The aid package was intended to ease the transition from colonial to independent status and to keep the Suriname standard of living at a high enough level to encourage Surinamers living in the country to remain and those living in the Netherlands to return home. The package is now in jeopardy, however, due to negative feelings in the Dutch government stemming from the December executions in Suriname.

The mainstay of the Suriname economy is the mineral industry, but it is not the sole component. Prior to the discovery of bauxite, the economy was agriculture-based with coffee, sugar, cotton and cocoa as the main products. Other agricultural crops of note include rice, sugarcane, and citrus. Shrimping is an industry of growing importance, with the 1980 production of 3,416 metric tons (up from a 1979 total of 2,962 metric tons).

Income distribution in Suriname is fairly flat. From the poorest 10 percent to the eighth richest 10 percent, there is an average of 1 percent difference in the percentage of income accruing to each successive bloc. Fifty-eight percent of the income goes to the poorest 80 percent of the population, with the remaining 20 percent of the population sharing 42 percent of the income.

Even though its political, cultural and social ties are oriented toward the Netherlands, Suriname's economy is inextricably linked to the U.S. economy. The Suriname guilder (the local currency unit) is pegged to the U.S. dollar, and the major trading partner of Suriname is the United States. Suriname has consistently experienced deficits on current accounts, and severe balance-of-payments dislocations have been averted only by the steady inflow of aid funds from the Netherlands. The value of exports and imports doubled from 1970 to 1976 and almost doubled again by 1980. The trade balance, however, declined, due to the increasing cost of necessary imports.

The principal exports from Suriname are alumina (48 percent), bauxite (20 percent) and aluminum (16 percent). The United States takes 41 percent of Suriname's exports; the Netherlands, 24 percent; Norway, 8 percent; the United Kingdom, 7 percent; and Japan, 5 percent. The main imports are basic manufactures (27 percent), food and beverages (26 percent), investment goods (21 percent), and fuel and lubricants (21 percent); 31 percent of the imports are from the United States, 21 percent from the Netherlands, 14 percent from Trinidad and Tobago and 7 percent from Japan.

Mineral Commodities

Bauxite mining and processing is the dominant industry in the Suriname economy, accounting for 40 percent of the government's revenue and 30 percent of gross domestic product. The two firms involved in this industry are Suraco, a wholly owned subsidiary of Alcoa, and Billiton Maatschappij Suriname, N.V., owned by Royal Dutch Shell. Bauxite products are exported from Suriname in one of three stages: (1) bauxite ore, (2) alumina (processed bauxite), and (3) aluminum. Suriname is endowed with a hydroelectric facility (Afobaka) which supplies approximately 92 percent of its output to the bauxite-aluminum industry. In addition, Suriname produces copper, gold, iron and steel, lead, cement, and petroleum refinery products.

Forecasts

According to our projections, the 1990 population of Suriname will exceed 1980 levels by 38.3 percent, while the 2000 population will surpass the 1990 population by 29.2 percent (see Table 3.34). The total population in 1990 will be 536,700 and the population in 2000 will be 693,000. Household size, meanwhile, will have declined to 5.4 persons per household at the end of the forecast period. The urban areas will experience increases in the percentage of the population they support. The urban portion of the total population will be 48 percent in 1990 and 54 percent in 2000. By the year 2000, the population will be equally divided between men and women but will still be comparatively young.

Suriname's total GNP could reach U.S. $1.6 billion in 1990 and U.S. $2.8 billion in the year 2000 (see Table 3.35), based on a World Bank growth assumption. Per capita income would then increase by 18.9 percent from 1980 to 1990 (to $2527) and 30.9 percent from 1990 to 2000 (to $3310.5). The labor force will double by the year 2000 and it is doubtful, based on the high unemployment rates that accompanied the 6 percent growth rates of the 1970s, that the economy will be able to provide jobs for all the new entrants.

Suriname's bauxite production experienced rather heavy annual growth between 1969 and 1972 and then suffered a precipitous decline from 1973 to 1975. Production in 1980 was 4.6 million tons--just a little below the average production levels of the past six years. A trend impact analysis of bauxite production suggests that production levels are likely to deteriorate even further. Production levels in 1990 likely will drop 38 percent from 1980 levels. The forecast is illustrated graphically in Figure 3.5.

The future events that could have an impact on Suriname's bauxite production are listed in Table 3.36. The event having the most significant negative impact is the exhaustion of reserves in the Paramaribo area. A significant portion of Suriname's mine output comes from this area; thus, its removal as a source (.10 by 1985; .65 by 1990) would be a severe blow to Suriname's productive ability.

It seems reasonably likely that the government of Suriname will institute new mining and allocation laws, either in response to environmental concerns or to appease a political faction; such an event would inhibit the long-term productive capacity of the bauxite industry. Similarly, if bauxite-rich plots are allocated to farming, or land restoration agreements become a prerequisite to awarding mining claims, smaller portions of land would be mined, thus reducing bauxite output. The probability of such an event occurring was set at .50 by 1985 and .75 by 1990.

Construction of another aluminum smelter (.20 by 1985; .50 by 1990) would have a markedly positive effect on Suriname's bauxite production in that bauxite production would be geared to the needs of the smelter and would be at a higher level than production of ore for export. It is also likely that foreign buyers would still be willing to buy unrefined ore.

Suriname's capacity for bauxite production obviously would be greatly enhanced if the reserves in the western portion of the country were exploited (.10 by 1985; .40 by 1990). These reserves have remained unmined primarily because of the relative accessibility of the Paramaribo reserves.

104

TABLE 3.34
GLOBESCAN medium growth demographic projections
for Suriname

Year	Population (Thousands)	Household Size	Households (Thousands)	Urban Population (Thousands)	Rural Population (Thousands)
1980	388.0	6.9	56.3	173.8	214.2
1981	400.5	6.7	59.3	180.1	220.3
1982	413.4	6.6	62.5	186.7	226.7
1983	426.7	6.5	65.9	193.4	233.2
1984	440.4	6.3	69.4	200.5	239.9
1985	454.5	6.2	73.1	207.7	246.8
1986	469.9	6.1	76.5	216.4	253.5
1987	485.8	6.1	80.0	225.5	260.3
1988	502.2	6.0	83.6	234.9	267.3
1989	519.2	5.9	87.4	244.7	274.5
1990	536.7	5.9	91.4	255.0	281.8
1991	552.0	5.9	94.3	265.3	286.7
1992	567.6	5.8	97.4	276.1	291.5
1993	583.7	5.8	100.6	287.3	296.4
1994	600.2	5.8	103.8	299.0	301.3
1995	617.3	5.8	107.2	311.1	306.2
1996	631.8	5.7	111.1	323.0	308.8
1997	646.7	5.6	115.1	335.3	311.4
1998	661.9	5.6	119.2	348.1	313.8
1999	677.4	5.5	123.5	361.3	316.1
2000	693.4	5.4	128.0	375.1	318.3

Population by age and sex

Males	Females	Total	Age	Males	Females	Total
	1985 (Thousands)				2000 (Thousands)	
44.8	43.5	88.3	0-04	48.4	47.2	95.5
34.0	33.3	67.3	5-09	49.6	48.3	97.9
27.9	27.3	55.2	10-14	48.9	47.2	96.1
29.7	28.9	58.6	15-19	42.3	40.6	83.0
25.6	25.9	51.5	20-24	32.2	31.0	63.2
20.5	20.5	41.0	25-29	26.0	24.9	50.9
8.9	10.6	19.5	30-34	27.7	26.6	54.3
3.4	5.8	9.2	35-39	23.9	23.9	47.8
2.2	5.6	7.8	40-44	19.3	19.2	38.5
3.9	6.6	10.5	45-49	8.3	9.8	18.2
4.7	5.6	10.4	50-54	3.1	5.1	8.2
4.6	5.6	10.2	55-59	1.8	4.8	6.7
4.6	4.8	9.4	60-64	3.2	5.7	8.9
2.7	3.0	5.7	65-69	3.6	4.5	8.1
2.5	1.9	4.4	70-74	3.1	4.1	7.2
2.5	3.0	5.5	75+	4.1	4.9	9.0
222.5	232.0	454.5	TOTAL	345.5	347.9	693.4

TABLE 3.35
GLOBESCAN economic projections for Suriname

Year	GNP in 1980 US$ (Millions)	Per Capita Income	Labor Force (Thousands)	Dependency Ratio (Per 100)
1980	1000.0	2126.3	97.6	110.7
1981	1048.0	2158.9	101.9	108.3
1982	1098.3	2192.0	106.3	105.9
1983	1151.0	2225.7	111.0	103.6
1984	1206.3	2259.8	115.8	101.4
1985	1264.2	2294.5	120.9	99.2
1986	1332.4	2339.3	124.6	99.8
1987	1404.4	2385.0	128.4	100.4
1988	1480.2	2431.6	132.4	101.0
1989	1560.2	2479.1	136.5	101.6
1990	1644.4	2527.6	140.7	102.2
1991	1733.2	2590.6	145.4	101.2
1992	1826.8	2655.2	150.2	100.2
1993	1925.4	2721.4	155.2	99.2
1994	2029.4	2789.3	160.4	98.2
1995	2139.0	2858.9	165.8	97.3
1996	2254.5	2944.0	172.3	94.1
1997	2376.3	3031.6	179.1	91.1
1998	2504.6.	3121.9	186.2	88.2
1999	2639.8	3214.8	193.5	85.4
2000	2782.4	3310.5	201.1	82.7

Income distribution--population with incomes above:

Year	Poverty Line (Thousands)	$1000 (Thousands)	$2000 (Thousands)	$5000 (Thousands)	$10000 (Thousands)
1980	384.5	320.1	163.6	26.4	11.0
1981	396.9	334.7	170.2	28.8	11.9
1982	409.8	350.0	177.1	31.5	12.8
1983	423.1	365.9	184.2	34.5	13.8
1984	436.8	382.6	191.7	37.7	14.9
1985	450.9	400.1	199.4	41.3	16.1
1986	466.2	417.8	211.7	44.2	16.9
1987	482.0	436.2	224.7	47.4	17.7
1988	498.4	455.5	238.6	50.8	18.5
1989	515.3	475.6	253.2	54.4	19.4
1990	532.8	496.6	268.8	58.3	20.3
1991	548.0	513.7	287.4	62.1	21.0
1992	563.7	531.3	307.2	66.1	21.8
1993	579.7	549.6	328.4	70.3	22.7
1994	596.3	568.4	351.1	74.9	23.5
1995	613.3	587.9	375.3	79.8	24.4
1996	627.8	602.6	395.4	85.9	25.3
1997	642.7	617.5	416.7	92.6	26.2
1998	657.9	632.9	439.1	99.8	27.1
1999	673.5	648.6	462.7	107.6	28.1
2000	689.5	664.8	487.6	115.9	29.1

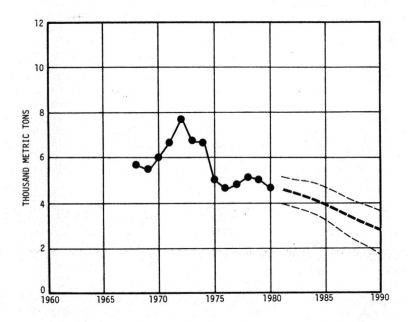

Figure 3.5 Forecast of Suriname's bauxite production

			Forecast	
	Trend Impact Analysis			
Baseline Curve No. = 5		Confidence Percentiles = 25 and 75		
Year	History/Baseline	Lower	Center	Upper
1968	5658.00			
1969	5458.00			
1970	6022.00			
1971	6718.00			
1972	7777.00			
1978	6686.00			
1974	6706.00			
1975	4928.00			
1976	4613.00			
1977	4805.00			
1978	5188.00			
1979	5010.00			
1980	4643.00			
1981	4596.76	3985.27	4573.77	5143.00
1982	4485.64	3850.59	4459.47	5037.23
1983	4379.77	3702.96	4335.97	4944.10
1984	4278.78	3493.71	4166.92	4811.42
1985	4182.34	3263.10	3983.68	4660.38
1986	4090.16	2882.97	3699.55	4411.96
1987	4001.95	2554.38	3450.01	4197.38
1988	3917.46	2269.71	3232.89	4021.36
1989	3836.47	2015.54	3037.53	3871.04
1990	3758.76	1767.06	2842.56	3715.59

Figure 3.5 (Cont.) Suriname's bauxite production (thousand metric tons)

TABLE 3.36
Events that will have an impact on bauxite production in Suriname

Event No.	Year/ Probability	Years to First Impact	Years to Maximum Impact	Maximum Impact	Years to Steady State Impact	Steady State Impact	Relative Impact
2	1985 0.10 1990 0.65	0	0	-25.0%	0	-25.0%	-2410
	Exhaustion of reserves in the vicinity of Paramaribo.						
9	1985 0.50 1990 0.75	2	3	-10.0%	3	-10.0%	-1160
	New mining and land allocation laws.						
1	1985 0.25 1990 0.50	3	5	-25.0%	5	-25.0%	-1040
	Nationalization of Suriname's bauxite industry and a loss of foreign expertise.						
6	1985 0.35 1990 0.75	2	3	-10.0%	3	-10.0%	-900
	Graphite-epoxy and/or kevlar supplanting aluminum as the premier material in airframe manufacture.						
7	1985 0.10 1990 0.40	2	4	-15.0%	4	-15.0%	-410
	Fifty percent increase in energy costs.						
9	1985 0.10 1990 0.20	1	1	-10.0%	1	-10.0%	-358
	Formation of a strong bauxite cartel.						
5	1985 0.10 1990 0.25	1	2	5.0%	2	5.0%	176
	Widespread use of aluminum engine blocks by automobile engine manufacturers.						
3	1985 0.10 1990 0.40	1	3	25.0%	3	25.0%	961
	Exploitation of reserves in the western portion of Suriname.						
4	1985 0.20 1990 0.50	1	2	20.0%	2	20.0%	1410
	Construction of an aluminum smelter.						

TRINIDAD AND TOBAGO

Trinidad and Tobago is a country comprising two islands located off the northeast coast of Venezuela and having a combined land area of 5,128 square kilometers (1,980 square miles). Trinidad is the larger and better developed of the two islands, having approximately 95 percent of both the land area and total population. The populace is primarily Negro (43 percent) and East Indian (40 percent) and speaks English exclusively. The dominant religion is Roman Catholicism, but Hinduism, Protestant Christianity, and Islam are also practiced.

Trinidad and Tobago is a stable, democratic country with a history of free and fair elections. A former British colony and member of the defunct W. I. Federation (Trinidad and Tobago hastened the collapse of the Federation by refusing to remain a member once Jamaica pulled out), it gained independence from Britain in 1962 and adopted a republican constitution in 1976. Dr. Eric Eustace Williams was designated colonial chief minister in 1956 and prime minister in 1962. He was subsequently returned to office following parliamentary elections in 1966, 1971, and 1976 and led the country until his death in office in 1981. George M. Chambers assumed the prime ministership upon Williams' death and was subsequently elected in his own right in elections held in 1981. The country is also served by a president (elected by parliament to serve for five years), a thirty-one-member Senate, and a thirty-six-member House of Representatives.

Demography

Trinidad and Tobago is basically a rural country with over 78 percent of its inhabitants residing outside of urban areas. The 1980 population consisted of 595,000 males and 575,000 females, and only 37 percent of the population could be classified in the nonproductive age groups. The average household size is about four.

Economy

The economy recorded phenomenal growth rates in 1979 and 1980, as increasing world oil prices drove the country's oil revenues ever higher and higher. Real GDP growth of 17 percent in 1979 and 10.1 percent in 1980 drove up per capita GDP, making Trinidad and Tobago one of the wealthiest countries in the hemisphere. Sectoral contributions to GDP in 1979 were as follows: agriculture 3 percent, industry 54 percent, and services 43 percent. The labor force of 452,000 is deployed 16 percent in agriculture, 36 percent in industry, and 48 percent in services. The inflation rate, which averaged 13 percent between 1970 and 1980, jumped to 17.5 percent in 1980, one of the unpleasant side effects of the booming economy. The government acted to stem the tide by imposing strict credit controls on consumer loans, and inflation subsided to 5 percent over the first half of 1981.

While rising oil prices have served to stagnate or even depress the economies of many countries in the world, it has been a boon to Trinidad and Tobago because of the country's significant crude petroleum and natural gas reserves. The major reason for the 17 percent economic growth in 1979 was a 95 percent increase in petroleum export prices, an

110

increase which served to increase revenue in the face of declining production. Other energy-related sectors also figure prominently in the economy and will probably make even more important contributions if new oil deposits are not found before the present reserves are depleted. Natural gas, asphalt, ammonia, petroleum refining, and potential applications for liquefied natural gas are on stream, or are soon to be introduced, in the economy.

A second unwanted side effect of the petroleum boom is the apparent neglect of the agricultural sector. From a net exporter of food twenty years ago, Trinidad and Tobago imported $350 million worth of foodstuffs in 1980; agriculture only contributed 2 percent of GDP in that year. The major cash crops--sugar, coffee, and cocoa--have been plagued by the outflow of labor from agriculture to petroleum where the salaries are higher and where there is more prestige associated with the job. Production of all three crops has declined drastically since 1975, with sugar recording a 40-year low with its 1981 total. A viable livestock industry is in place, however, and broiler and meat production is on the upswing.

The construction, manufacturing, and tourist industries are also experiencing growth, although productivity in manufacturing is chronically low. The government's attempt to mitigate the housing shortage aided the construction industry in increasing output by 44.6 percent from 1979 and 1980 and to add 21,000 new jobs in 1978 and 1979.

Trinidad and Tobago, in seeking to exploit its vast natural gas reserves, has drawn up a development strategy consisting of expansion into energy-related high-technology areas. Two facets of this multifaceted project already have been implemented--an ammonia plant and a steel mill have already commenced production--and the government has let contracts totaling $300 million for the construction of methanol and urea facilities. Feasibility studies are presently under way for the construction of an aluminum smelter and an LNG facility.

Oil imports historically have enabled balance-of-payments surpluses; in 1980, a $623 million surplus was recorded. Ninety-five percent of the exports are mineral fuels and lubricants that are mainly exported to the United States (61 percent) and the Netherlands (8 percent). Trinidad and Tobago imports mineral fuels and lubricants (41 percent), machinery and transportation equipment (22 percent), basic manufactures (15 percent), and food and live animals (9 percent); imports come principally from the United States (26 percent), Saudi Arabia (20 percent), the United Kingdom (11 percent), Japan (10 percent), and Canada (6 percent).

Mineral Commodities

Trinidad and Tobago's contribution to world petroleum production and reserves is quite modest, but this sector accounts for 50 percent of the country's GDP. In addition to its own crude production, Trinidad and Tobago imports crude oil, mostly from Saudi Arabia, for refining and transshipment. The government has full or majority ownership in all but two of the producing companies and the oil refinery owned by Texaco Trinidad, Inc. Other mineral industries include exploitation of the huge natural gas reserves and cement production.

Forecasts

The total population of Trinidad and Tobago is projected to rise to
1.3 million in 1990 and 1.5 million in the year 2000 (see Table 3.37),
increases of 14.5 percent over 1980 totals and 10 percent over 1990 totals.
The number of people in the nonproductive category will decline until it
represents 32 percent of the 2000 population. Household size will decline
slightly--from 4.0 in 1980 to 3.3 in the year 2000--and the rural population
will decline from 78.5 percent of the 1980 population to 68.8 percent of the
population in the year 2000.

Gross national product is projected to triple over the forecast period:
from $5.1 billion in 1980, it will increase to $9.1 billion in 1990 and
$16.9 billion in the year 2000 (see Table 3.38). Per capita income will then
also record phenomenal increases, rising from $4,105 in 1980 to $6,344 in
1990 and $10,618 in the year 2000. In line with the small increase in
population, the labor force will increase by only 38.5 percent between 1980
and 2000 (from 452,000 in 1980 to 626,300 in the year 2000), and the
dependency ratio will decline from 60.3/100 in 1980 to 47.5/100 in the year
2000.

Trinidad and Tobago experienced significant declines in crude oil
production growth in the 1968-1973 period but has fared much better since
then. Table 3.39 is a listing of the events that could have an impact on
Trinidad and Tobago's crude oil output. First, if the OPEC cartel were to
break up, the incentives of members to restrain production would diminish,
and they would increase production in an attempt to increase oil revenues.
This would result in a world oil supply glut. (The probabilities set for this
were .50 by 1985; .60 by 1990.) With buyers in a position of being able to
choose a seller, and with Trinidad and Tobago producing more than it can
sell, it would be forced to cut back production.

Second, a stronger government presence in the oil industry, mani-
fested in restrictive government regulation and taxation (.10 by 1985; .60
by 1990), would result in smaller profit margins for the oil industry. Oil
companies might also view it as the first step toward complete nationalization of the industry. The new effect is likely to be reduced investment in
oil facilities and a negative impact on oil production.

On the other hand, an oil embargo by the Arab members is not
unthinkable (.50 by 1985, .60 by 1990), given the present turmoil in the
Middle East, and such an event would have a favorable effect on Trinidad
and Tobago's crude oil production. With the Arab oil off the market,
buyers would be willing to buy all the oil that could be brought to the
market from other sources. Very much the same effect would result in the
event of a 50 percent cutback in Saudi oil production (.60 by 1985; .80 by
1990). With these event probabilities in mind, a trend impact analysis of
Trinidad and Tobago's crude oil production suggesting moderate production
increases is illustrated in Figure 3.6.

TABLE 3.37
GLOBESCAN medium growth demographic projections
for Trinidad and Tobago

Year	Population (Thousands)	Household Size	Households (Thousands)	Urban Population (Thousands)	Rural Population (Thousands)
1980	1170.0	4.0	294.0	251.6	918.5
1981	1186.6	3.9	303.3	257.7	928.9
1982	1203.4	3.8	312.9	263.9	939.4
1983	1220.4	3.8	322.8	270.4	950.1
1984	1237.7	3.7	333.1	276.9	960.8
1985	1255.2	3.7	343.6	283.7	971.6
1986	1271.7	3.6	352.3	292.1	979.6
1987	1288.4	3.6	361.2	300.7	987.7
1988	1305.4	3.5	370.3	309.7	995.7
1989	1322.5	3.5	379.7	318.8	1003.7
1990	1339.9	3.4	389.3	328.3	1011.6
1991	1355.0	3.4	395.5	339.2	1015.8
1992	1370.2	3.4	401.8	350.6	1019.7
1993	1385.7	3.4	408.2	362.3	1023.4
1994	1401.2	3.4	414.6	374.4	1026.9
1995	1417.0	3.4	421.2	386.8	1030.2
1996	1429.2	3.4	425.9	400.5	1028.7
1997	1441.5	3.3	430.7	414.6	1026.9
1998	1453.9	3.3	435.5	429.2	1024.7
1999	1466.4	3.3	440.3	444.3	1022.1
2000	1479.0	3.3	445.2	460.0	1019.0

Population by age and sex

1985 (Thousands)				2000 (Thousands)		
Males	Females	Total	Age	Males	Females	Total
61.7	59.6	121.3	0-04	60.7	58.2	118.9
56.9	56.4	113.2	5-09	63.4	61.7	125.2
63.3	61.5	124.8	10-14	63.1	61.9	125.0
72.2	70.5	142.7	15-19	59.5	58.7	118.2
72.9	70.4	143.4	20-24	54.9	55.5	110.4
62.9	61.4	124.4	25-29	60.7	60.4	121.1
51.1	44.5	95.6	30-34	68.9	69.0	137.9
39.2	36.6	75.8	35-39	69.4	68.8	138.2
32.3	31.5	63.8	40-44	59.6	59.8	119.4
25.3	26.5	51.8	45-49	48.0	43.0	91.0
24.0	24.4	48.4	50-54	36.2	34.9	71.0
23.7	21.3	45.0	55-59	28.9	29.5	58.4
17.6	18.1	35.7	60-64	21.6	24.0	45.6
14.2	14.7	29.0	65-69	19.0	20.9	39.9
10.0	10.5	20.4	70-74	16.6	16.5	33.1
8.9	11.1	19.9	75+	17.4	21.3	38.6
636.2	619.0	1255.2	TOTAL	748.0	744.2	1492.2

TABLE 3.38
GLOBESCAN economic projections for Trinidad and Tobago

Year	GNP in 1980 US$ (Millions)	Per Capita Income	Labor Force (Thousands)	Dependency Ratio (Per 100)
1980	5110.0	4105.5	452.0	60.3
1981	5385.9	4266.7	463.4	58.5
1982	5676.8	4434.3	475.0	56.8
1983	5983.3	4608.5	487.0	55.1
1984	6306.4	4789.5	499.2	53.5
1985	6647.0	4977.7	511.8	51.9
1986	7072.4	5225.1	520.6	51.3
1987	7525.0	5484.9	529.6	50.8
1988	8006.6	5757.6	538.7	50.2
1989	8519.0	6043.9	548.0	49.7
1990	9064.3	6344.3	557.4	49.2
1991	9644.4	6671.3	563.9	49.2
1992	10261.6	7015.1	570.5	49.2
1993	10918.3	7376.6	577.1	49.3
1994	11617.1	7756.8	583.9	49.3
1995	12360.6	8156.5	590.7	49.3
1996	13151.7	8598.3	597.6	49.0
1997	13993.4	9064.1	604.7	48.6
1998	14889.0	9555.0	611.8	48.2
1999	15841.9	10072.6	619.0	47.9
2000	16855.8	10618.2	626.3	47.5

Income distribution--population with incomes above:

Year	Poverty Line (Thousands)	$1000 (Thousands)	$2000 (Thousands)	$5000 (Thousands)	$10000 (Thousands)
1980	1156.2	976.3	701.0	273.2	135.4
1981	1173.1	1002.8	732.0	292.5	141.1
1982	1190.2	1030.2	764.4	313.2	147.1
1983	1207.6	1058.2	798.2	335.4	153.4
1984	1225.2	1087.0	833.5	359.2	159.9
1985	1243.1	1116.6	870.4	384.6	166.6
1986	1260.2	1143.2	907.2	414.1	175.5
1987	1277.5	1170.4	945.5	446.0	184.8
1988	1295.0	1198.2	985.5	480.2	194.7
1989	1312.8	1226.7	1027.1	517.1	205.1
1990	1330.8	1255.8	1070.5	556.8	216.0
1991	1346.6	1275.7	1103.3	597.3	237.6
1992	1362.5	1295.9	1137.2	640.7	261.4
1993	1378.6	1316.4	1172.0	687.3	287.6
1994	1394.9	1337.2	1207.9	737.3	316.4
1995	1411.4	1358.4	1245.0	790.9	348.2
1996	1424.3	1373.3	1268.9	839.8	382.6
1997	1437.3	1388.4	1293.2	891.8	420.5
1998	1450.5	1403.7	1318.0	947.0	462.1
1999	1463.8	1419.1	1343.3	1005.6	507.9
2000	1477.2	1434.7	1369.0	1067.8	558.2

TABLE 3.39
Events that will have an impact on crude oil production
in Trinidad and Tobago

Event No.	Year/ Probability	Years to First Impact	Years to Maximum Impact	Maximum Impact	Years to Steady State Impact	Steady State Impact	Relative Impact
7	1985 0.50 1990 0.60	0	1	-10.0%	1	-10.0%	-36600
	World oil supply glut due to the collapse of OPEC.						
6	1985 0.10 1990 0.60	2	3	-20.0%	3	-20.0%	-20100
	Restrictive government regulation and taxation of foreign oil enterprises.						
11	1985 0.10 1990 0.30	1	2	-25.0%	5	-15.0%	-19400
	Loss of foreign expertise.						
10	1985 0.10 1990 0.20	2	3	-20.0%	3	-20.0%	-12700
	Development of alternatie energy sources in the U.S.						
9	1985 0.20 1990 0.35	2	3	-10.0%	5	01.0%	-12200
	Increased energy conservation effort in the U.S.						
1	1985 0.05 1990 0.10	1	2	-10.0%	2	-10.0%	-3980
	Trinidad and Tobago joins OPEC.						
4	1985 0.25 1990 0.50	3	5	5.0%	5	5.0%	5340
	Maintenance of oil revenue levels in the face of falling prices caused by new oil finds in other parts of the world.						
8	1985 0.30 1990 0.50	1	1	10.0%	2	5.0%	14400
	Trinidad and Tobago increases aid to fellow CARICOM members in event of economic crisis.						
12	1985 0.10 1990 0.30	2	4	30.0%	4	30.0%	18900
	Major oil finds in Trinidad and Tobago.						
2	1985 0.60 1990 0.80	1	2	20.0%	4	10.0%	54800
	Mideast conflict forces fifty percent cutback in Saudi oil production.						
5	1985 0.50 1990 0.60	1	1	20.0%	2	15.0%	56600
	OAPEC embargo or major oil price increase.						

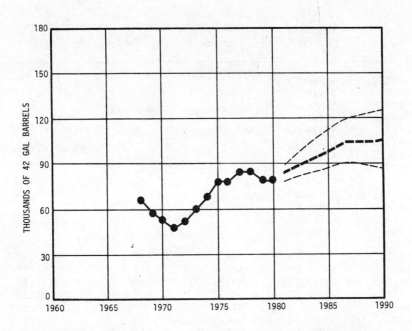

Figure 3.6 Forecast of Trinidad and Tobago's crude oil production

(Continued)

116

			Forecast	
Year	History/ Baseline	Lower	Center	Upper
1968	66904.00			
1969	57418.00			
1970	51047.00			
1971	47147.00			
1972	51719.00			
1973	60666.00			
1974	68131.00			
1975	78613.00			
1976	77673.00			
1977	83950.00			
1978	83773.00			
1979	78249.00			
1980	78000.00			
1981	83759.86	77901.62	83341.06	88675.26
1982	86008.05	81352.51	87728.21	95494.30
1983	88253.97	83934.15	91960.64	102153.86
1984	90497.63	85652.76	95520.25	107538.25
1985	92739.04	87485.21	98906.18	112596.60
1986	94978.18	90073.40	102861.37	118174.45
1987	97215.07	90584.87	104506.20	120567.96
1988	99449.71	89602.22	105018.89	121796.72
1989	101682.10	88005.06	105359.60	123321.17
1990	103912.25	87085.08	106302.23	125842.32

Trend Impact Analysis

Baseline Curve No. = 7   Confidence Percentiles = 25 and 75

Figure 3.6 (Cont.) Trinidad & Tobago's crude oil production (thousands of 42-gallon barrels)

4
Interrelationships Among Demographic, Economic, and Environmental Trends

The trends presented in Chapter 3 necessarily will have varying impacts on the different sectors of the countries considered. This chapter presents a series of analyses that focus on the impact of interactions among the demographic, economic, and environmental trends in each country. Topics addressed include the impact on:

- arable land per capita
- the balance between agricultural production and consumption
- income per capita growth
- energy consumption
- forest usage
- water availability
- pollution control and land restoration
- political instability
- tourism

Clearly, many of the Caribbean basin countries face challenges other than the ones listed above or discussed in Chapter 3. Drug trafficking and related criminal activities have been on the rise in many areas. There have been reports that pollution control near some Caribbean islands may be complicated by apparent illegal waste and toxic material dumping by organized crime elements from the United States. There is evidence, furthermore, of external subversion efforts including illegal arms shipments to insurgent groups and movements in several Caribbean basin countries that the governments in question have found difficult to control. Unfortunately, data limitations do not permit us to explore these challenges in any depth.

ARABLE LAND PER CAPITA

The Food and Agriculture Organization defines arable land as "land under temporary crops, temporary meadows for mowing or pasture, land under market and kitchen gardens, and land temporarily fallow or lying idle" and land under permanent crops as "land cultivated with crops that occupy the land for long periods and need not be replanted after each harvest."[1] (The latter definition excludes timberland.) For purposes of

expediency, both categories--arable land and land under permanent crops--
are combined in this study under the heading arable land.

The amount of arable land a country possesses or utilizes is an
important barometer of its ability to feed itself or to earn hard currency
through agricultural exports. In some Caribbean countries, the amount of
arable land (measured in hectares) has remained constant over the past
20 years while other countries have been consistently adding arable land to
their total arable land pool. For example, the Bahamas, Barbados, and
Grenada have experienced little or no gain in arable land over the past
20 years while Cuba, Guatemala, and Honduras have all gained considerable
amounts of arable land over the same period. It should be noted that the
countries experiencing little or no gain are small islands while, with the
exception of Cuba, the gainers are all mainland countries. A country's pool
of arable land could be increased through land reclamation projects,
irrigation of desert areas, or the conversion of timberland and forests to
agriculture. Arable land could be lost, on the other hand, due to natural
disasters (e.g., tidal waves) and construction.

It can be argued that as the Caribbean countries become more
technologically sophisticated, agricultural output per capita will increase,
even in the face of declining arable land per capita. Better methods of
fertilization and pest control and capital-intensive agriculture could
conceivably increase crop yield, but certain segments of such an approach
would be economically and politically unacceptable to the region's rulers.
One of the common denominators in the region is a high level of
unemployment, and to the extent that mechanization of the agriculture
industry would displace labor--with no alternative outlets to absorb
displaced individuals--it would not be viewed in the region as a viable
alternative. The amount of arable land a country possesses, then, is
inextricably linked to its agricultural output.

Table 4.1 presents projections of arable land per capita in the
pertinent countries, based on population projections. Data on arable land
for the pertinent countries were collected from the FAO Production
Yearbook. The data spanned 20 years, during which time some countries
added arable land at fast rates, others at slower rates and some not at all.
It was assumed that countries would continue adding arable land during the
forecast period at the same rate at which they added land over the period
covered by the data. In the cases where a country had not added any
arable land in the previous five-year period, it was assumed that that
country had exhausted its ability to add arable land to the pool. In
instances where a country had consistently added arable land over the
years but had recorded declines in the latest years, the last recorded figure
was used as the basis for the forecast. The forecasted arable land figure
was then divided by the population forecasts to yield forecasts of arable
land per capita.

Since population usually grows at a faster rate in this region than
additions are made to arable land, the tendency is for arable land per
capita to decline over time (see Table 4.2). All countries covered in this
analysis record declines in arable land per capita over the forecast period.
Furthermore, as the population increases, more and more of a country's
arable land is diverted to residential construction, which may lead to a
decline in agricultural production. If a country has an agriculture-based
economy, as do most of these countries, a lower arable land per capita
figure translates into a diminishing ability to feed the inhabitants--if

TABLE 4.1
Arable land per capita in the principal countries of the
Caribbean basin

Country	Arable Land Per Capita (Hectares)		
	1980	1990	2000
Bahamas	.07	.06	.05
Barbados	.13	.11	.11
Belize	.54	.47	.39
Costa Rica	.22	.18	.15
Cuba	.33	.30	.27
Dominican Republic	.21	.18	.16
El Salvador	.14	.11	.08
Grenada	.13	.10	.08
Guatemala	.25	.21	.17
Guyana	.43	.36	.32
Haiti	.15	.13	.11
Honduras	.48	.37	.29
Jamaica	.12	.11	.11
Nicaragua	.53	.38	.28
Panama	.30	.25	.20
Suriname	.10	.09	.08
Trinidad and Tobago	.14	.13	.12
Average	.22	.19	.15

production is for domestic consumption--or lessened earnings from foreign exports--if production is for export. To the extent that these countries need hard currency to satisfy their myriad import needs, lower foreign exchange earnings also amount to a diminishing ability to feed the populace.

The countries that show the smallest percentage decline in arable land per capita over the forecast period--Barbados, Cuba, Jamaica, and Trinidad and Tobago--accomplish this feat mostly by controlling population growth. Barbados' population will grow by only 18 percent over the life of the forecast period, Cuba's by 19 percent, Jamaica's by 28 percent, and Trinidad and Tobago's by 26 percent. Conversely, the countries experiencing the largest decline--El Salvador, Honduras, Nicaragua and Grenada--will experience population increases of 81 percent, 87 percent, 89 percent and 54 percent, respectively. Cuba's cause will be further helped by significant additions to its arable land pool, but the significant expected gains made in that category by Honduras will not be enough to offset the rapid population increase.

Of the countries listed in Table 4.1, the best example of a nonagricultural economy is the Bahamas. Arable land per capita among the

TABLE 4.2
Change in arable land per capita in the principal
countries of the Caribbean basin

Country	Percent Change in Arable Land Per Capita		
	1980-1990	1990-2000	1980-2000
Bahamas	-14.3	-16.7	-28.6
Barbados	-15.4	0	-15.4
Belize	-13.0	-17.0	-27.8
Costa Rica	-18.2	-16.7	-31.8
Cuba	-9.1	-10.0	-18.2
Dominican Republic	-14.3	-11.1	-23.8
El Salvador	-21.4	-27.3	-38.5
Grenada	-23.4	-20.0	-38.5
Guatemala	-16.0	-19.0	-32.0
Guyana	-16.3	-11.1	-25.6
Haiti	-13.3	-15.4	-25.7
Honduras	-22.9	-21.6	-39.6
Jamaica	-8.3	0	-8.3
Nicaragua	-28.3	-26.3	-47.2
Panama	-16.7	-12.0	-26.7
Suriname	-10.0	-11.1	-20.0
Trinidad and Tobago	-7.1	-7.7	-14.3
Average	-13.6	-21.1	-31.8

countries studied will average .22 hectares, .19 hectares, and .15 hectares in 1980, 1990, and 2000, respectively, but will only amount to .07 hectares, .06 hectares, and .05 hectares in the Bahamas. Obviously, agriculture will not surpass tourism and petroleum refining as the mainstays of the Bahamian economy.

Even though the decline of arable land per capita in Haiti compares favorably with declines in other countries, there is still cause for some concern regarding its agricultural output. Most of the good farmland in Haiti has long been placed under crops, and subsequent additions to the arable land pool have been of marginal quality. Output from these subpar lands will diminish much more rapidly than output from prime land, and, in addition, marginal land requires longer fallow periods. Agricultural output per capita in Haiti will decline at a faster rate than will arable land per capita unless methods of crop enhancement are introduced and accepted in Haiti.

THE BALANCE BETWEEN AGRICULTURAL PRODUCTION AND CONSUMPTION

The balance between agricultural production and consumption can determine how well the people eat, as well as foreign currency earnings and import expenditures. If a country produces more agricultural commodities than it consumes, the surplus product could conceivably be traded for hard currency--a positive impact on a country's trade balance. If, however, a country consumes more agricultural products than it produces, the agricultural product that is not produced domestically will have to be imported--an obvious negative effect on the trade balance plus a diversion of funds from expenditures with more long-term benefits.

In the case of the Caribbean basin countries, the agricultural production/consumption balance is not restricted to the value of the agricultural products; it also encompasses the kind of agricultural product. For instance, the major agricultural crops in the region are sugar, rice, citrus fruits, and bananas, but with the exception of rice, none of these products are staples of the regional diet. They are grown with an eye on the export market, thus guaranteeing that a sizeable portion of agricultural consumption will be filled from extra-regional sources. Meat and wheat, two agricultural necessities, are purchased from extra-regional sources or from countries in the region that produce these items for export.

The reasons why the Caribbean basin countries do not produce more basic agricultural commodities are myriad, but the most obvious is that they are producing the goods they know best how to produce and for which the climate and soil are particularly suitable. As colonial entities, these countries were geared to produce the crops that could not be produced in the mother countries, and even after independence, they tend to fulfill the same role. The foreign currency earned by these crops further militates against a switch to internally consumable crops. The main agricultural crop is, in most cases, the principal foreign-exchange earner. Without the foreign exchange thus acquired, the purchases needed to fuel economic growth cannot be made. If the earnings from agricultural sales abroad are enough to cover agricultural imports plus other essential imports, then the law of comparative advantage would appear to be working well. If, however, agricultural export sales do not cover agricultural imports, and other sectors of the economy are not earning significant surpluses, then both aspects of the production/consumption imbalance are evident; the country is producing a type of good that it cannot consume (imbalance A) and is consuming more--in terms of value--agricultural product than it is producing (imbalance B).

In order to determine the agricultural production/consumption balance in the pertinent countries over the forecast period, agricultural production and consumption first had to be forecasted and then ratioed. Future agricultural production was forecasted in the following manner: (a) determining what percentage of the last-reported GNP for each country was contributed by agriculture; (b) converting the percentage to a dollar figure; (c) obtaining the growth rate in agriculture for each of the countries over the decade of the seventies; (d) using (b) and (c) to forecast a dollar figure for agricultural production in 1980, 1990, and 2000. The forecasts are reported in Table 4.3 as the percentage of GNP attributable to agriculture in 1980, 1990, and 2000.

TABLE 4.3
Percentage of GNP attributable to agriculture
in the principal countries of the Caribbean basin

Country	Agriculture as a Percentage of GNP		
	1980	1990	2000
Bahamas	3.0	2.5	2.1
Barbados	10.0	6.9	4.1
Belize	24.0	21.6	16.8
Costa Rica	19.0	14.6	11.1
Cuba*	-	-	-
Dominican Republic	19.0	15.4	13.0
El Salvador	28.0	22.8	18.1
Grenada*	-	-	-
Guatemala	25.5	25.1	24.6
Guyana	17.7	18.3	16.6
Haiti	40.1	29.1	20.6
Honduras	32.0	21.1	13.1
Jamaica	7.0	4.8	3.2
Nicaragua	29.0	19.8	19.1
Panama	17.0	13.4	9.9
Suriname	7.6	6.6	5.5
Trinidad and Tobago	3.0	1.4	0.6

*Could not be forecast due to unavailability of adequate historical data.

The rationale for using the 1970s growth rate as the forecast vehicle for individual countries is simple. During the 1970s, agricultural earnings of the Caribbean basin countries fluctuated wildly; there were very good times, and there were very bad times. A coffee shortage in 1977 resulted in very high earnings for coffee exporters, but a glut in 1979 depressed coffee prices severely. The growth rate for the entire decade captures both effects, with the negatives and positives cancelling out each other until the true direction is revealed. We see nothing to indicate any major change in the agricultural fortunes of these countries. Surpluses on the international markets will continue to be rewarded with low prices while shortages will result in higher prices and earnings. The growth rate in agriculture in each of these countries will not vary much from the seventies' mold over the life of the forecast period.

All the countries that had an agricultural contribution to GNP of 10 percent or less in 1980 also had substantial alternative industries. The Bahamas (agriculture contributing 3 percent of GNP in 1980), Barbados (agriculture contributing 10 percent of GNP in 1980), Jamaica (agriculture contributing 7 percent of GNP in 1980), and Trinidad and Tobago (agriculture contributing 3 percent of GNP in 1980) all have significant tourist industries that, even though subject to economic conditions abroad and political conditions at home, will continue to grow. In addition, Barbados has a budding petroleum industry, the Bahamas are major petroleum refiners, Jamaica is a major bauxite producer, as is Suriname (7.6 percent of GNP contributed by agriculture in 1980), and Trinidad and Tobago is a producer of crude oil as well as a refiner.

Table 4.4 presents the probable changes in the contribution of agriculture to GNP between 1980 and 1990, 1990 and 2000, and 1980 and 2000. Except in the case of Guyana between 1980 and 1990, the agricultural contribution to GNP will decline in every instance. This does not necessarily indicate a wholesale decline in agriculture as an important sector. Rather, it is probably attributable to the growth, both in terms of value and importance, of other major sectors of the economy. Most of the political leaders and technocrats in the region have been alerted to the fact that agriculture, because of its price volatility, is not the appropriate vehicle for stable, long-term growth. They have seen what industrialization has done for the Western world, and they covet the results. The headlong rush to diversify away from agriculture and into the more stable manufacturing and service sectors will result in larger and larger shares of each country's GNP being provided by those faster-growing sectors. Thus, if agriculture were to maintain the growth rates of the seventies, this would not be enough to keep its contribution to GNP from declining.

TABLE 4.4
Change in agriculture's contribution to GNP in the principal countries of the Caribbean basin

Country	1980-1990	1990-2000	1980-2000
Bahamas	-16.7	-16.0	-30.0
Barbados	-31.0	-40.6	-59.0
Belize	-10.0	-22.2	-30.0
Costa Rica	-23.7	-23.4	-41.6
Cuba*	-	-	-
Dominican Republic	-18.9	-15.6	-31.6
El Salvador	-18.6	-20.6	-35.4
Grenada*	-	-	-
Guatemala	-1.6	-2.0	-3.5
Guyana	3.4	-9.3	-6.2
Haiti	-27.4	-29.2	-48.6
Honduras	-34.1	-37.9	-59.1
Jamaica	-31.4	-33.3	-54.3
Nicaragua	-31.7	-3.5	-34.1
Panama	-21.2	-26.1	-41.8
Suriname	-13.2	-16.7	-27.6
Trinidad and Tobago	-53.3	-57.1	-80.0

*Could not be forecast due to unavailability of adequate historical data.

Countries like Trinidad and Tobago (80 percent reduction in agriculture's contribution to GNP), Barbados (59 percent reduction) and Jamaica (54.3 percent reduction) are countries that have the infrastructure in place to further displace agriculture as a major player in the economy. The oddity here is the rapid decline in Honduran agriculture's contribution to GNP. The contribution will likely fall from 32 percent in 1980, to 21.1 percent in 1990, and 13.1 percent in the year 2000. Such a development suggests that the industrial and service sectors of the economy will experience tremendous growth, thus vindicating the government's attempt to diversify into areas such as chemicals, plastics, and cement.

The countries likely to experience relatively small changes in the importance of agriculture to the economy--Guatemala (3.5 percent reduction in agriculture's contribution to GNP), Guyana (6.2 percent reduction), and Grenada (17.8 percent reduction)--attain that distinction because agriculture grows at almost the same rate as does the rest of the economy. In the case of Guatemala, this translates to a high growth rate for agriculture, but in the case of Guyana and Grenada, it means slow growth in the rest of the economy. Grenada is primarily dependent on its agriculture and tourism, and to the extent that tourism is hurt by the political conditions in the country, it will become even more dependent on agriculture. The fact that the decline is sharper between 1990 and 2000 than it is between 1980 and 1990 seems to bear out that hypothesis. As Guyana's bauxite production continues its decline, agricultural production will grow in importance between 1980 and 1990--a reversal of the commonly accepted growth models. The rest of the economy will manage to grow at a rate faster than the agriculture growth rate, probably as a result of increased oil production between 1990 and 2000.

The next step in this process was to project agricultural consumption in 1980, 1990, and 2000, a somewhat more difficult task. The first problem faced was calculating agricultural consumption. The formula used for this calculation was:

$$AC = AP + AI - AE,$$

where:

AC is agricultural consumption
AP is agricultural production
AI is agricultural imports
AE is agricultural exports

Agricultural production, import, and export data for the decade of the seventies were collected for each country from several sources[2] and combined as above to determine historical agricultural consumption patterns. For each country, the calculated consumption was ratioed to the equivalent year's population, and the average of the ratios was taken. This ratio represented the average consumption per capita for each of the individual countries. Forecasts for agricultural consumption were thus made based on the premise that the countries would, at least, want to maintain the level of consumption that was obtained in the 1970s. If levels lower than the 1970s occurred in the 1980s and 1990s, it would be a disaster in light of the population increases. Our projection, then, is probably conservative--agricultural consumption may in fact be somewhat higher over the forecast period. Each country's expenditure on agricultural consumption was determined by multiplying its calculated agricultural consumption per capita figure by its population in 1980, 1990 and 2000.

The consumption figures were then ratioed with the previously calculated production figures to produce the production/consumption ratio presented in Table 4.5.

A production/consumption ratio of 1 indicates that the value of agricultural production in a country is equivalent to the value of its agricultural consumption. A value less than 1 indicates a negative imbalance in agricultural trade, while a value greater than 1 indicates a surplus in agricultural trade. The production/consumption ratio does not necessarily indicate the condition of a country's balance of payments. For instance, Trinidad and Tobago is the country with the second-lowest production/consumption ratio in 1990 and 2000, but it is the one most likely, because of its petroleum reserves and its relatively sophisticated industrial and service sectors, to register balance-of-trade surpluses in those years. In cases where agriculture is a significant foreign-exchange earner, however, if consumption exceeds production it is highly likely that that country will experience balance-of-payments problems in the pertinent years and over the life of the forecast period.

Costa Rica's very low production/consumption ratio is cause for some concern, especially in light of the fact that the country's agricultural production is such a large component of GNP. It will import a significant amount of agricultural products for internal consumption--goods the value of which far exceed domestic production and exceed agricultural exports

TABLE 4.5
Agriculture production/consumption ratio in the
principal countries of the Caribbean basin

Country	1980	1990	2000
Bahamas*	-	-	-
Barbados	.64	.59	.55
Belize	2.24	2.35	2.44
Costa Rica	.17	.17	.19
Cuba*	-	-	-
Dominican Republic	1.61	1.81	2.09
El Salvador	1.16	1.15	1.15
Grenada*	-	-	-
Guatemala	.44	.56	.70
Guyana	.45	.45	.46
Haiti	.73	.66	.62
Honduras	2.17	1.65	1.28
Jamaica	.63	.61	.62
Nicaragua	.30	.36	.43
Panama	1.82	1.84	1.91
Suriname	2.54	2.62	2.89
Trinidad and Tobago	.48	.36	.28

*Could not be calculated due to lack of historical data on agricultural trade or production.

even further. Costa Rica would seem to be a prime candidate for future severe balance-of-payment dislocations, and loans by the international monetary organizations and commercial lending institutions will be very much in demand.

More than half of the countries studied will experience increases in their production/consumption ratio over the life of the forecast period, while others stay very close to the levels they attained in 1980. Only Barbados and Trinidad and Tobago will experience any significant decline in their production/consumption ratio over the forecast period. The fact that the ratio will not decline (for all the countries) in tandem with the decreasing importance of agriculture to GNP, or the increasing consumption associated with increased population, suggests that the ratio of agricultural imports to agricultural consumption will stay fairly even over the forecast period. In other words, the increasing consumption will be offset by increasing production.

INCOME PER CAPITA GROWTH

As part of its demographic and economic forecasts, forecasts of income per capita were generated for all the pertinent countries. These forecasts are presented in Table 4.6. The most striking feature of the table is the disparity between the richest and poorest countries in a region that is considered poor overall. Income per capita is not a valid measure of the well-being of the citizens of a country because income distribution has a notorious tendency to be skewed toward the more affluent segments of a society, as the income distribution data in Chapter 3 suggest. Substantial growth in income per capita, however, will obviously have some positive effects on the country as a whole.

The highest per capita income of the countries studied is enjoyed by Trinidad and Tobago, and this will remain the case in the future. Haiti, on the other hand, has the reputation of being the poorest country in the Western Hemisphere; this too will continue. Countries such as El Salvador, Honduras, and Guyana fall far below the average income per capita and fail to surpass the $1,000 income per capita mark prior to the end of the forecast period. All of the countries studied are projected to experience a GNP growth rate that exceeded population growth, resulting in across-the-board increases in income per capita (see Table 4.7).

Increasing income per capita in combination with an increasing population size serves not only to widen the consumer market, but, theoretically, indicates that the larger market also has more funds to spend. This line of thinking presupposes that increased income per capita translates to increased disposable income. With an increased consumer base, domestic producers could expand production and attain economies of scale, resulting in lower unit cost that could be passed on to the domestic consumers as lower prices, but that would also serve to make exports more competitive on the world market. The perception of a larger market and higher disposable income could also serve to attract heretofore uninterested foreign investors with a potential for increases in the number of jobs provided and increased export earnings.

An increase in consumption resulting from steadily increasing purchasing power will benefit not only domestic producers; it is quite likely that imports will experience a larger increase than will consumption of domestically produced items. The country that stands to gain the most

TABLE 4.6
Growth in income per capita in the principal
countries of the Caribbean basin

Country	Income Per Capita (1980 US$)		
	1980	1990	2000
Bahamas	3,120.3	4,256.2	6,101.5
Barbados	2,716.3	3,625.1	5,697.6
Belize	928.4	1,084.7	1,446.9
Costa Rica	1,586.3	2,152.4	3,004.3
Cuba	844.4	1,114.5	1,447.4
Dominican Republic	947.7	1,304.2	1,774.4
El Salvador	528.8	642.0	811.5
Grenada	677.5	779.6	1,087.4
Guatemala	1,008.3	1,281.7	1,655.1
Guyana	568.1	543.0	617.6
Haiti	224.9	281.5	369.5
Honduras	524.4	606.2	754.0
Jamaica	927.6	1,295.1	1,933.3
Nicaragua	649.7	726.6	898.9
Panama	1,427.3	1,822.9	2,551.1
Suriname	2,126.3	2,527.6	3,310.5
Trinidad and Tobago	4,105.5	6,344.3	10,618.2

from any increased imports into the region is the United States; with few exceptions, the United States is the major trading partner of the Caribbean basin countries. (The most notable exception is, of course, Cuba.) Exposure to American tourists, news media, films, and television, and continuing contacts with friends and relatives now living in the United States, has created an insatiable appetite for U.S. goods. The proximity of the U.S. market to these countries further enhances the appeal of U.S. imports. The only cloud on the horizon, as far as the United States is concerned, is the growing importance of Brazil as a major player in regional exports.

Increases in income per capita in the Caribbean basin will come about as a result of growth in sectors of the economy other than agriculture. Except in a few cases (Guatemala, for instance), the growth in the agricultural sector will barely be enough to maintain its level of employment over the forecast period and will be woefully inadequate in absorbing significant amounts of the new entrants to the labor force. Since agriculture is unlikely to be able to provide rural labor force entrants with jobs and the faster-growing sectors will be located in urban areas, there will be a continuing trend of movement from rural areas to urban areas in the Caribbean basin. Higher income per capita will thus be reflected in a larger urban population.

Forecasts of rural and urban populations were generated for Chapter 3, and the percentage increases in the urban population of the

TABLE 4.7
Change in per capita income 1980-2000

	Percentage Change in GNP Per Capita		
Country	1980-1990	1990-2000	1980-2000
Bahamas	36.4	43.4	95.5
Barbados	33.5	57.2	109.8
Belize	16.8	33.4	55.8
Costa Rica	35.7	39.6	89.4
Cuba	32.0	29.9	71.4
Dominican Republic	37.6	36.1	87.2
El Salvador	21.4	26.4	53.5
Grenada	15.1	39.5	60.5
Guatemala	27.1	29.1	64.1
Guyana	-4.4	13.7	8.7
Haiti	25.2	31.3	64.3
Honduras	15.6	24.4	43.9
Jamaica	39.6	49.3	108.4
Nicaragua	11.8	23.7	38.4
Panama	27.7	39.9	78.7
Suriname	18.9	31.0	55.7
Trinidad and Tobago	54.5	67.4	158.6

countries under study are given in Table 4.8. Increase in urban population results not only from rural inhabitants moving to the city, it can also be a result of urban areas expanding and absorbing areas previously referred to as rural. It is not readily apparent which of these phenomena is the dominant one in urban population growth in the Caribbean basin countries, but past experience suggests that the former is more likely.

Rapid urbanization in countries such as the Dominican Republic, El Salvador, Grenada, Guatemala, Haiti, Honduras, Nicaragua, and Suriname will put extreme pressure on the respective governments to maintain the social and economic fabric of the urban areas in the face of rapid urban growth. Adequate housing, sewer facilities, transportation facilities, educational facilities, health facilities, and safety services (police, fire protection) are all areas that will require prompt government attention.

ENERGY CONSUMPTION

Chapter 3 details the impact that the high cost of imported energy has had on many of the countries of the Caribbean basin. Trinidad and Tobago is the sole net exporter of energy, and most of the region has suffered severe dislocations in its balance-of-payments picture as a result of the two oil-price shocks in the seventies. Unfortunately, the energy

TABLE 4.8
Forecasts of urban population growth in the
principal countries of the Caribbean basin

Country	Percentage Change in Urban Population		
	1980-1990	1990-2000	1980-2000
Bahamas	27.8	26.6	61.9
Barbados	23.5	25.2	54.6
Belize	38.2	36.7	88.8
Costa Rica	40.5	38.6	94.7
Cuba	16.0	18.1	37.1
Dominican Republic	49.1	36.6	103.7
El Salvador	50.6	54.4	132.6
Grenada	79.8	63.7	194.3
Guatemala	51.2	52.6	130.8
Guyana	31.9	45.4	91.8
Haiti	62.9	60.6	161.6
Honduras	67.7	60.2	168.7
Jamaica	34.7	23.5	66.6
Nicaragua	55.7	50.3	134.0
Panama	39.9	32.8	39.1
Suriname	46.7	47.1	115.8
Trinidad and Tobago	30.5	40.1	82.8

picture for the region through the year 2000 does not appear bright, without a drastic modification in the world energy pricing structure or a dramatic breakthrough in alternative energy sources or technology.

Moreover, trends in energy costs and consumption are closely related to other aspects of the region's economic and social prospects. Certainly the economic prospects for many of the Caribbean basin's poorer countries were not overly promising before the quadrupling of oil prices since 1973; but since most industrial countries reacted to the price increases by raising the prices of their own exported goods, most non-OPEC developing countries have suffered from both high-priced imported energy and high-priced manufactured and industrial goods from the North, while finding their own attempts to gain better prices for their agricultural and mineral commodities generally ineffective. Raising a country's GNP and a population's standard of living in such a situation is obviously a serious challenge. Energy consumption is closely tied to economic growth and the level of economic development attained. It also is related, though less directly, to population growth. These relationships will be explored in the remainder of this section, as we address two crucial questions: Given trends in economic performance, population growth and energy consumption, how much energy will each of the Caribbean basin countries require to attain the GNP forecasts described in Chapter 3? What is the probable severity of balance-of-payments difficulties, given the projected extent of continued dependence on external sources of energy? Noncommercial energy consumption, particularly in the form of fuelwood and its relation to trends in population growth, also will be explored in the next section.

There is a strong correlation between a country's level of industrialization and its energy consumption. Quite simply, the lower a country's dependence on agriculture for economic growth, the higher its energy usage. Moreover, as a country becomes more developed, its utilization of wood fuels, dung and charcoal declines, while the use of commercial sources such as imported oil increases. With this in mind, an initial effort to categorize the Caribbean basin countries according to the nature of their economies may be instructive. Given our analysis in Chapter 3, five distinct categories seem relevant:

- Industrialized countries--those for which the industrial sector is the largest sector in terms of percentage of gross domestic product.
- Oil exporters--countries that are net exporters of crude oil.
- Balanced growth economies--those in which the industrial sector is relatively developed but not dominant in terms of contribution to GDP.
- Primary exporters--minerals account for the bulk of total exports and are a major contributor to GDP.
- Agriculturally oriented economies--countries in which agricultural output clearly dominates GDP.[3]

For our purposes, Cuba was categorized as a primary exporter because of its nickel exports. Barbados and the Bahamas do not fit well into any of the categories but might be classified as balanced-growth economies.

Table 4.9 presents the resulting categorization for the seventeen principal Caribbean basin countries. Both commercial and noncommercial energy consumption is forecast for each of these countries. In each case, there are regions where noncommercial fuel use is the rule rather than the exception; hence, an estimate of the potential demand for these traditional fuels is necessary.

Commercial energy projections were made based on income elasticities of demand derived from a World Bank study[4] and the 1978 Brookhaven study prepared for USAID. Income elasticities of demand postulate a relationship between an increase in income (in this case GNP) and an increase in energy consumption. An income elasticity of demand greater than 1 indicates that for a given increase in income, expenditure on a particular good will increase at a rate faster than the increase in income. The income elasticities of demand assumed by the Lambertini World Bank study are especially appropriate for this study, as the assumed GNP growth rates are essentially the same as those used in our own GNP projections in Chapter 3. The Brookhaven study assumed different GNP growth rates but came up with much the same income elasticities of demand as did Lambertini. The Brookhaven elasticities are reproduced in Table 4.10.

In forecasting energy consumption for these countries, we initially calculated our own income elasticities of demand, using the period 1970-1979 as our historical base. But since some of the countries experienced negative real GNP growth over the period, quite a few of the income

TABLE 4.9
Categorization of Caribbean basin countries
by economic structure

Oil Exporters	Balanced Growth Countries	Primary Exporters	Agriculture Economies
Trinidad and Tobago	Bahamas Barbados Panama	Cuba Guyana Jamaica Suriname	Belize Costa Rica Dominican Republic El Salvador Grenada Guatemala Haiti Honduras Nicaragua

TABLE 4.10
Income elasticities of demand by type of commercial energy

	Oil Exporting	Balanced Economies and Primary Exporters	Agricultural Countries
Oil			
1980-1990	.85	1.04	.90
1990-2000	.82	.98	.96
Electricity			
1980-1990	1.09	1.52	1.70
1990-2000	1.03	1.43	1.60
Natural Gas			
1980-1990	.97	1.17	1.03
1990-2000	.94	1.13	1.06
Coal			
1980-1990	1.12	.98	1.57
1990-2000	1.30	1.08	1.68

Source: Palmedo et al., "Energy Needs, Uses and Resources in Developing Countries," 1978.

elasticities were negative. Negative income elasticities of demand could not be used to forecast energy consumption under our scenario, since we are postulating real GNP increases for all the countries, except Guyana between 1980 and 1990. The period prior to 1975 exhibited a closer relationship between GNP and energy consumption and that is the period used in both the World Bank and Brookhaven studies. It should be reiterated at this point that the energy consumption projections are based on the GNP projections and a calculated relationship between GNP and energy consumption. Obviously, if the GNP picture in these countries were modified, the energy projections would need revision.

Commercial energy projections encompassed commercial primary energy--oil, natural gas, coal, and primary electricity (hydropower)--and to that extent data on consumption of these energy forms in 1979 were collected from UN sources.[5] The historical data on energy consumption in the region indicate a disproportionate dependence on oil as the principal energy source; natural gas, coal and hydropower are used in very few of the countries.

The growth rates for the differing energy forms were determined by multiplying the assumed GNP growth rates by the income elasticities of demand for the separate categories. Since the income elasticities differed from category to category and from energy form to energy form, a wide variety of growth rates was developed. The projected growth rates were then multiplied by 1979 consumption data to project consumption of oil, natural gas, coal and primary electricity in 1980, 1990, and 2000, respectively.

Once the preliminary estimates were made, they were reduced by a price elasticity of demand of -.11. The price elasticity of demand (ratio of the change in price to the change in demand) indicates how demand for a good is affected by a given change in price. The price elasticity of demand used here is the same as used in the World Bank study and indicates a relatively inelastic demand for energy among these countries, that is, at best, an 11 percent reduction in demand. Reducing the preliminary forecast by the price elasticity of demand therefore makes allowances for reduced consumption due to severe price increases.

Projections for the energy forms were made in the units of measurement in which they were originally reported but were eventually converted to a common unit of measure for purposes of comparison and further analysis. The conversion factors are indicated in Table 4.11.

No totally adequate methodology for forecasting the consumption of traditional fuels exists. Following the approach utilized in the Brookhaven study, we have assumed a noncommercial energy consumption figure of 400 kilograms coal equivalent per capita per year. This corresponds to approximately 1 ton of wood per year per person and is based on an estimated energy budget coinciding with the minimum level of food and shelter requirement for survival in a rural agrarian setting. This lowest level of energy use is termed "subsistence" level. Obviously, in many areas the consumption of noncommercial energy would be above the subsistence level and, to that extent, our noncommercial projection is conservative.

The projected energy consumption of the Caribbean basin countries is presented in Table 4.12 and Figures 4.1 and 4.2. Oil will remain the dominant form of energy consumed in the region over the life of the forecast period. Total oil consumption will increase by 79 percent between 1980 and 1990 and 81 percent between 1990 and 2000. Other forms of

TABLE 4.11
Energy conversion units

Unit	Conversion Multiply by	Divide by	Unit
Metric tons of oil	7.33		Barrels of oil
Kilowatt hours	3413		British thermal units (Btu)
Btu		5,800,000	Barrels of oil
Terajoules		.0293076	Metric tons of coal equivalent (MTCE)
MTCE	.687623		Metric tons of oil equivalent
Annual oil consumption		365	Daily oil consumption

noncommercial energy, on the other hand, will increase by only 48 percent between 1980 and 1990 and 58 percent between 1990 and 2000.

Trinidad and Tobago, the only oil-exporting country, and the group of balanced-growth countries each consume a total amount of energy (especially oil) similar to all of the agriculture-oriented countries in 1980, even though the agriculture-oriented countries are much more numerous. Trinidad and Tobago, the Bahamas (balanced growth) and Panama (balanced growth) all import large amounts of crude for their refineries. Even though the refined products are reexported, the crude consumed is figured into their oil consumption. These countries will need to continue the large-scale consumption of crude to attain the levels of GNP specified in this study.

The countries most likely to have severe balance-of-payments dislocations as a result of increased energy imports are the group labeled agriculture-oriented countries. Even if the price of energy were to remain fixed out to the year 2000, the rapidly increasing energy needs of these countries would place a severe strain on their trade balances. For illustrative purposes it should be noted that while energy consumption in Trinidad and Tobago increases by 125 percent over the forecast period, balanced growth by 174 percent, and primary exporters by 84 percent, energy consumption in the agricultural countries will increase by 293 percent. If the commodity terms of trade remain turned against these countries, they will be hard pressed to purchase the energy needed to sustain the projected levels of growth.

TABLE 4.12
Projected energy consumption of Caribbean basin countries

Category	Energy Type	Thousand Barrels/Day Oil Equivalent		
		1980	1990	2000
Oil	Oil	218.7	335.3	513.0
importers	Other commercial	44.0	61.8	86.5
	Total commercial	262.7	397.1	599.5
	Noncommercial	6.5	7.4	8.2
	Total	269.2	404.5	607.7
Balanced	Oil	231.4	387.8	650.6
growth	Other commercial	.6	1.7	2.8
	Total commercial	232.0	389.5	653.4
	Noncommercial	13.3	16.2	19.4
	Total	245.3	405.7	672.8
Primary	Oil	137.5	200.8	290.8
exporters	Other commercial	3.5	7.2	13.4
	Total commercial	141.0	208.0	304.2
	Noncommercial	72.6	80.8	90.3
	Total	213.6	288.8	394.5
Agriculture-	Oil	85.9	282.9	734.9
oriented	Other commercial	4.7	7.9	21.1
countries	Total commercial	90.6	290.8	756.1
	Noncommercial	180.6	238.4	309.9
	Total	271.2	529.2	1,066.0
Total	Oil	673.5	1,206.8	2,189.3
	Other commercial	52.8	78.2	123.9
	Total commercial	726.3	1,285.0	2,313.2
	Noncommercial	273.0	342.8	427.8
	Total	999.3	1,627.8	2,741.0

Alternative energy sources do not provide much hope for the Caribbean basin countries. Guyana has extensive hydroelectric potential, but unless its border dispute with Venezuela is resolved favorably, it will be unable to raise the required capital; Suriname also possesses some untapped hydro potential. The big user of natural gas is presently Trinidad and Tobago, but with future energy finds in the region, and a larger industrial base, the potential for wider use of natural gas exists. Cuba is the only current consumer of coal, and that condition is likely to remain constant. Cuba is likely to step up its importation of Polish coal in order to compensate for declining oil allowances from the Soviet Union.

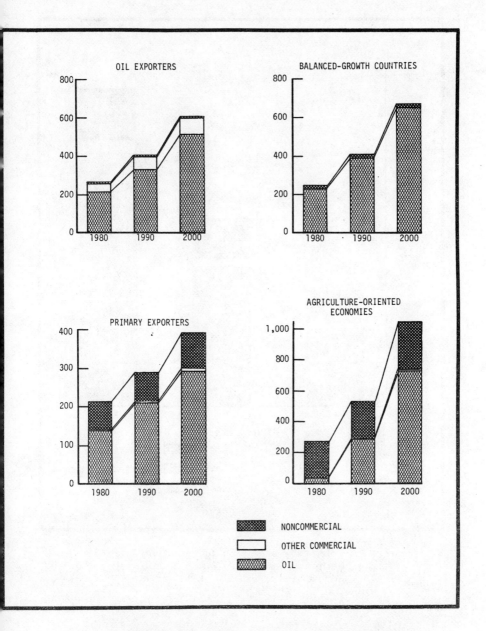

Figure 4.1   Daily energy consumption projections by Caribbean basin country groups (million barrels per day oil equivalent)

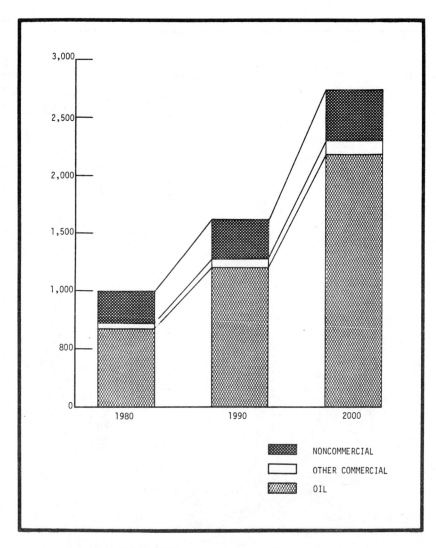

Figure 4.2   Total daily energy consumption projections for
Caribbean basin countries (million barrels per day
oil equivalent)

FOREST USAGE

One energy resource that is present in much of the region is virgin forest, but if in the future forests are exploited at current rates, they will be considerably depleted by the year 2000. Unfortunately, attempts by concerned citizens, countries, and organizations to stem the tide of declining forests tend to be viewed with suspicion by these countries--as attempts to keep them underdeveloped.

The noncommercial energy most widely used is of course fuelwood. Approximately 90 percent of worldwide fuelwood consumption occurs in developing countries, and this source generally accounts for 30-60 percent of all energy use in these countries.

Fuelwood consumption in the Caribbean basin has been particularly high and is expected to increase 60-90 percent by the year 2000. Indeed, increases in fuelwood consumption in the region will outdistance all other areas of the world, due to the current availability of fuelwood and the high population growth rates in comparison to other regions.

Moreover, several countries in the Caribbean basin already are facing forest depletion. For example, rapid population growth in Haiti has led to loss of over 90 percent of its original forested area. As a consequence, floods are unmoderated by forest buffers. There is extensive erosion. Siltation is threatening the irrigation and hydroelectric systems, and the soil is rapidly losing its fertility.

The continuing use of wood as a fuel will be buffeted by two opposite factors during the forecast period. The large-scale movement of population from rural to urban areas suggests the use of more conventional fuels, and less fuelwood, as distribution becomes less of a deterrent. This is counterbalanced, however, by the potential for increasing energy prices and the inability of these countries to import large quantities of oil at high prices. A reduction in the number of people living in the rural areas would reduce the pressure on the forests to provide fuelwood; high energy prices would force larger and larger segments of the population to burn wood in lieu of petroleum (where possible). Countries with oil and gas reserves and petroleum refineries (Guatemala, Panama, the Bahamas, Barbados, and Trinidad and Tobago) will obviously experience less fuel-oriented deforestation. Countries that possess significant indigenous Indian populations and make no attempt to integrate them into the mainstream of modern life will experience accelerated fuel-related deforestation from that constituency.

Economic growth in and of itself will dictate that large expanses of forest be cut down to fuel the growth machine. Many of these countries have thriving export markets for their forestry products, and as tropical forests in other parts of the world become denuded, the Caribbean region will gain importance as a supplier. As these countries become more technologically advanced they will construct pulp factories and produce paper products. The forestry industry will thus be supplying its traditional market plus fulfilling these new sources of demand.

Population growth will also place major strains on the ability of the forests to maintain their place in nature. Population increases will dictate that additional housing be constructed to absorb the growing number of families. Furthermore, land has to be cleared so that these new houses can be built, and the nature of the logging industry guarantees that the two activities will not be occurring in the same location. The construction of roads to serve the logging facilities, as well as roads to serve the new communities, will also result in the destruction of forests.

A second principal cause of the loss of forests in the region is conversion of forested areas to use for agriculture. Lack of employment opportunities and inequality of land distribution force "slash and burn" farmers to clear large areas of forest for planting. The continuous cropping practiced by these farmers quickly drains the soil of its nutrients thus reducing agricultural output in short order. This causes the farmer to move on to other locations where the cycle is repeated.

The Caribbean countries under study will not of course be affected equally by the onrushing tide of slash and burn farmers. Indeed, the countries can be readily categorized in terms of the likelihood of severe deforestation through agriculture incursion, based on their additions to arable land over the past 20 years (see Table 4.13). In our arable land per capita forecast, we hypothesized that the rates of addition to the arable land pool would be much the same for the forecast period as they were for the two decades directly preceding that period. Since most of the addition to arable land is as a result of clearing forests, we extend the previous hypothesis to suggest the rate at which forests will be cleared for agricultural purposes.

In Honduras, the widespread use of slash and burn techniques has already consumed more than 2.2 million hectares, some 30 percent of the total forested area. The intense cultivation that has followed in each new area has often destroyed the regenerative capacity of the soil, making it infertile and incapable of being farmed economically.

Of the other countries likely to have a high incidence of agriculture encroachment into forested areas, Guatemala and Haiti appear to have the highest probability. Guatemala is expected to have the highest agriculture growth rate of the countries studied, adding 360,000 hectares to its arable land pool by the year 2000--most of that coming as a result of clearing

TABLE 4.13
The effect of incursion of agriculture into forested areas
for Caribbean basin countries

Countries Most Likely To Experience Rapid Deforestation Through Agricultural Expansion	Countries Least Likely To Experience Deforestation
Cuba	Bahamas
Dominican Republic	Barbados
Guatemala	Belize
Haiti	Costa Rica
Honduras	El Salvador
Suriname	Grenada
	Guyana
	Jamaica
	Nicaragua
	Trinidad and Tobago

forests. Haiti is projected to add 182,000 hectares to its arable land pool by 2000, but because most of the land being added is less than marginal, the length of time that crops can be supported is open to question, suggesting that the actual amount of forest cleared could exceed the projected figure by up to 50 percent.

WATER AVAILABILITY

Because of the scarcity of data on water utilization or water resources in the Caribbean basin countries, it is difficult to generate a numerical forecast of consumption and reserves and, hence, water availability. Instead, we will try to identify and analyze the effects of economic and population growth on the region's usage.

The various uses for water are domestic use, industrial use, crop irrigation, and energy production. The Global 2000 report presents forecasts of future per capita use of drinking water in several of the countries, but these numbers possibly only represent consumption from official reservoirs.[6]

Domestic use includes drinking, cooking, bathing, etc., and these functions will vary depending on the level of urbanization in a country. For instance, in the urban areas, bathing and flushing of toilets will use up much more water than equivalent practices do in rural areas. Simply put, the rural toilet is generally an outhouse with no running water, and many rural baths take place in the neighborhood creek or stream.

Due to problems associated with transportation and distribution--problems that are both logistical and financial--residents in urban areas in developing countries have had better access to sanitary drinking water than residents in rural areas. Increased population in all the Caribbean basin countries indicates higher utilization of water for purposes of domestic consumption. With most of the population growth occurring in urban areas, however, it is likely that higher percentages of the population of these countries will have access to potable water. Water consumption (for domestic use) will thus rise dramatically over the forecast period, stemming from the double pressures of increasing population and increasing urbanization.

Rapid urbanization will not only require significant investment in housing but will also require substantial investment in water provision and sewage facilities. To the extent that water provision is a governmental responsibility in these countries, the fiscal health of the governments, or their ability to raise capital in the international markets or from multilateral lending institutions, will determine the extent to which the additional service will be provided, and the quality of the service.

Historically, water usage for industrial purposes has represented a relatively small portion of the total water used in most of these countries. The reason for this, of course, is the low level of industrialization. In the primary exporting countries like Suriname and Guyana, water usage has played a very important part in stripping overburden from the bauxite. In the refining and chemical industries in Trinidad and Tobago, water also plays an important role.

The increasing contribution that industry will make to the GNP of the Caribbean basin countries, however, also suggests increased water consumption. Adequate water supply facilities will be a prerequisite to many forms of foreign investment and because of the intense competition in the region for foreign investors, few of the countries will choose to eliminate themselves from investment consideration due to nonprovision of such a basic service.

With the exception of the Bahamas, crop irrigation is a very important form of water usage in all the Caribbean basin countries. Even though no reliable figures are available, it clearly appears that the use of water for crop irrigation far outstrips other uses. Even though the contribution of agriculture to GNP will decline in real terms (for the most part) over the life of the forecast period, the amount of water used for irrigation will not decline much, if at all. As less fertile land becomes exploited, or as the land being farmed becomes less fertile, Caribbean basin farmers will be forced to increase fertilizer and water usage to maintain yields.

Water's utility in energy provision is confined mainly to the cooling of turbines in electric generating facilities. The generation of electricity in the region has been below par for the most part; most countries are subject to intermittent power outages. In order to remain competitive, however, and to attain the specified levels of GNP, the Caribbean basin countries must attract foreign investors. At minimum this requires adequate utilities. Some expansion of the electricity supply systems is thus in order. More efficient systems may require less water for cooling, but it is also likely that the greater number of plants required to satisfy the increased power needs will increase the total amount of water used in power generation.

Most of the mainland Caribbean basin countries have adequate enough supplies of water to offset increased requirements in the future. They are blessed with numerous rivers and regular periods of rainfall. The only potential problem is getting the water where it is needed. The island countries do not possess anywhere near the quantity of rivers and streams that are found on the mainland, but they also are blessed with bountiful rainfall. All in all, water availability probably will not pose a serious problem for the Caribbean basin countries over the forecast period.

POLLUTION CONTROL AND LAND RESTORATION

The economic and population growth experienced by the Caribbean basin countries will have several negative effects on the environment unless steps are taken to minimize them. As noted earlier, one of the most obvious negative environmental effects of increased population in that setting is deforestation. Regardless of whether the forest is destroyed so that the land can be used for agriculture or for housing construction or for fuel, the results are the same: a deteriorating ecosystem and increased risks of landslides, erosion, and siltation where it is not needed. If fuelwood is in short supply in rural areas, there is a tendency to utilize animal dung in its place. This diminishes the amount of nutrients returned to the soil and reduces its fertility.

The rapid shift in population from rural to urban areas is likely to outdistance the emplacement of facilities to dispose of waste, with potentially serious health consequences. The composition of an area's waste changes as the population becomes more affluent, and the disposal systems in place in many of the Caribbean basin countries could prove inadequate. Not only will the inhabitants be eating differently, they will be demanding more and different consumer goods, the production of which will yield wastes that cannot be disposed of in the traditional manner. In many of the Caribbean countries, sewage treatment plants perform a minimum of treatment before the waste matter is dumped into a nearby river. Industries are allowed to dump matter into the waterways indiscriminately. Improper treatment of sewage and other material increases the prospect of these substances getting into the food chain or the drinking water system.

An almost certain result of increasing affluence in parts of the region will be larger numbers of cars on city streets. Since manufacturers are not constrained to provide air pollution controls on cars sent to that market, the cities will experience increased levels of carbon monoxide, unburnt hydrocarbons, nitric oxides, and lead. The problem will be compounded in that the inadequacy of the streets will yield large traffic jams (as is common in Port-of-Spain), further exposing the environment and the inhabitants to the noxious fumes. Chronic traffic jams also could serve as a disincentive to potential investors or could force companies already doing business in a country to seek out another, less-congested country from which to conduct their business.

High levels of economic growth experienced by some of the countries will result from new oil finds due to the heightened oil exploration now evident in the region. Increased exploitation of the region's oil reserves also serves to increase the risk of a major oil spill. Oil production in Trinidad and Tobago and Barbados is concentrated offshore, as is a majority of the exploration ventures. A pipeline has been constructed across Panama to transport Alaskan oil from the Pacific to the Atlantic; even without new finds, increasing economic activity will require greater oil utilization in the region and, consequently, more oil tanker traffic. A serious oil spill in the Caribbean will not only cause grievous harm to the environment, it would also have serious economic consequences in that two of the region's mainstays--fishing and tourism--would be dealt severe blows.

When the mining companies operating in the Caribbean were all foreign-owned, a mine was exploited to the fullest extent possible, following which operations moved to another location. No steps were taken to restore the depleted mine to some semblance of its previous appearance. As more and more of the regional mining operations become state-owned--or the state takes a majority interest--there may be some limited change in this pattern, but depleted mines will scar the region in greater numbers as we move closer to the end of the forecast period. The foreign currency earned from the operation of the mines is needed in much more readily "beneficial" areas than land restoration.

Economic growth in the Caribbean basin is most likely to be derived from the sectors that contribute the most pollution and environmental damage--the extractive and manufacturing sectors. The only real answer is to tighten emission control standards and restore land stripped by mining. But this obviously will be expensive, and prospects for increased "luxury" expenditures on pollution control in most of the economically pressed countries of the region appear dim.

Population trends in the Caribbean basin also are potentially quite relevant to this dilemma. The cost for pollution control, as a percentage of future income, will vary with the size of the population. The higher the

GNP per capita, the lower the relative cost of pollution control for the same effort. This, of course, does not even consider possible limitation of the growth in the total volume of pollution with slow versus rapid population growth. Clearly, trends in population growth, economic growth and resource usage are tightly interwoven in the Caribbean basin region.

POLITICAL INSTABILITY

There are several different theories or explanations on the sources of political instability in countries. Some focus on relative deprivation of sectors of the population, others emphasize group dynamics, while still others focus on "trigger events" or the rise of charismatic opposition leaders. In each of these explanations, however, there is a notion that dissatisfaction and changing levels of well-being are an important component, and rising population and demographic change can exacerbate the existing political dynamics. It is important to realize, however, that any assessment of the political effects of population change is not usually direct or straightforward. Political change is a complex phenomenon, and the effects of population change may be mediated through the social, economic, and political systems before they are manifest. Thus, the effects of population growth will vary significantly depending on the political, social, and economic conditions of particular countries. For example, the political effects of the growth of the young male population (ages 15-25) can have vastly different consequences on a country if the economy is growing and jobs are available than if it is not growing and high levels of unemployment prevail.

Although the exact nature of the relationship is not generally understood, population growth and demographic change can have an impact on political stability. The types of impact include:

- Changes in age structure; infrastructure demands on a government may result from changes in the age structure of a population. Increasing numbers of young and/or elderly may severely increase the demand for social services--housing, health care, education, welfare. Because of rapidly increasing population, the government may be unable to meet demand. The potential for political instability may also result from an increase in the number of young males (15-25) without a corresponding increase in job opportunities. This will increase the number of unemployed and underemployed and can provide the impetus for political violence.

- Changes in population size and density; an increasingly large number of people in a small geographic area places strains on the government; the problems associated with overcrowding can contribute to political tensions.

- Changes in differential population growth rates of social, tribal, and ethnic groups; the effect of the distribution of power and the relationship among social groups is affected by differential population growth rates. As one social/ethnic group gains in size, its role in society can change and its impact on political events can be severe.

- Changes in migration; this has ramifications similar to changes in age structure. Infrastructural demands are increased as population migrates from rural to urban areas. The prospect of urban violence and crime increases as rural males migrate to urban areas seeking jobs that may not exist.
- Changes in family size; with larger families, demands on housing increase and overcrowding results. The size of land holding also is affected by increases in family size. Due to lack of land, migration to urban areas increases.

These factors may lead directly to political instability because of their possible effect on the distribution of power in a particular country. Demographic changes may also lead to instability because they have an indirect effect on the economic well-being of the population. Economic growth may not be able to keep pace with the growth of the population, adversely affecting income per capita growth. Since income distribution is far from equitable in many of the Caribbean basin countries, as Chapter 3 indicates, political stability may be increasingly threatened by the resulting relative deprivation of portions of the population. Overcrowding in the major urban areas, unemployment, low and maldistributed income per capita, and arable land scarcity contribute to political instability in El Salvador, Grenada, Guatemala, Guyana, Haiti, Honduras, Jamaica and Nicaragua in particular.

In addition to affecting political stability within a country, population growth and other demographic changes can affect relations between countries. Conflicts between countries or populations over land or resources have occurred frequently in the region. Demographic pressures and domestic economic weaknesses have been ingredients in the 1963 conflict between Haiti and the Dominican Republic, between Guyana and Venezuela since 1962, and between Guatemala and Belize on the one hand and Guatemala and Mexico on the other. The clearest example of regional conflict fueled by demographic pressures, however, is the conflicts between Honduras and its neighbors, El Salvador and Nicaragua. The 1969 "soccer war" between Honduras and El Salvador, for example, essentially stemmed from the pressures on the land and employment opportunities created by rapid population growth. Some 300,000 Salvadorans migrated across to Honduras, where they thrived. Honduran resentment of the immigrants grew, however, and they were finally expelled. The border closing contributed to political tensions, which were then touched off by the soccer match.

Although rapid population growth does not lead inevitably to political instability or regional conflict, it can in many cases be a key factor in the process that produces instability. Slower rates of population growth, on the other hand, contribute to stability by easing solution of some of the potentially destabilizing problems and alleviating some of the pressures that help breed conflict.

TOURISM

Both pollution and political instability can have a substantial impact on Caribbean basin tourism, which is one of the most important industries in the region. It is a significant generator of foreign exchange income and employment, and is the one industry that most of the Caribbean basin nations share in common. Central American nations have been major tourist destinations in the past, but are now declining because of political instability and violence. Table 4.14 shows the number of tourist arrivals, gross receipts from international tourism, and the ratio of gross receipts to total current account earnings. It is clear from the table that tourism receipts in Central American countries have levelled off or declined in recent years, and that they typically account for a smaller portion of current account flows than in the island nations. The major tourist destinations are evident from Table 4.14--the Bahamas, Barbados, the Dominican Republic, Jamaica, Panama, and Trinidad and Tobago--although the contribution of tourism receipts to current account earnings ranges from over 50 percent for the Bahamas to under 5 percent for Trinidad and Tobago. This ratio is an indicator of the importance of tourism as a foreign exchange earner, and the lower percentages for major tourist destination such as the Dominican Republic, Jamaica, Panama and Trinidad and Tobago reflect the importance of other export sectors. This discussion will focus on the island nations of the Caribbean, which constitute a relatively well-defined and cohesive tourism market group. The market characteristics of tourism in the Caribbean and the local socioeconomic impact of tourism are the most important factors determining the effect of tourism on the long-term prospects for the region.

Several factors that characterize international tourism in general are relevant to tourism in the Caribbean. Key factors distinguishing the demand side of international tourism are the income and price elasticity of tourist expenditures.[7] The tourism "product" is a package of services including transportation (usually air), lodging, restaurant and ancillary recreational services. A relatively minor component of the package is merchandise purchase by tourists. Although the annual vacation is a well-established feature of affluent industrial societies, international travel is still largely a luxury good. It is income elastic, meaning that aggregate expenditures on international tourism increase greater than proportionately as income increases. It is also price elastic, or sensitive to changes in relative price, so that total expenditures decrease in response to changes in relative prices.

In the Caribbean, these factors have influenced the development of tourism in a largely positive manner, but may pose constraints in the future. The major source of demand for tourism in the Caribbean is the United States and Canada. The steady increase in disposable incomes in these countries up until the early 1970s provided the basis for the growth of travel to the Caribbean. The slowing down of growth rates in the mid-1970s, and continued economic stagnation in the early 1980s, has limited the primary impetus for growth in tourism. International travel is often the first item to be cut from household budgets, and tourism expenditures have dropped sharply in the current recession. Revenues from tourism in the 1981-1982 season were off sharply from previous levels for all countries in the region except Jamaica, which enjoyed a resurgence of tourist trade with the United States due primarily to improved political relations. The current outlook for slow economic growth in the United States and Canada suggests that the national impetus for growth in Caribbean tourism which resulted from increasing incomes in North America will not be present in the 1980s. The income elasticity of tourism, despite the cyclical nature of demand, does promise more potential for

TABLE 4.14
International tourism in the Caribbean: tourist arrivals and receipts

Country	Tourist Arrivals (Thousands)			Tourism Receipts				Tourism Receipts/ Current Account Earnings			
	1970	1975	1978	1970	1975	1978	1980	1970	1975	1978	1980
Bahamas	1,298.3	903.1	1,176.1	--	312.6	489.8	584.3	--	.44	.59	.51
Barbados[a]	--	221.6	316.3	40.3	77.2	136.7	249.1	.40	.35	.41	.44
Costa Rica	--	297.2	340.4	22.1	51.7	72.4	86.8	.08	.09	.07	.07
Dominican Republic	--	221.8	304.4	16.4	58.8	87.9	115.9b	.06	.06	.10	.10b
El Salvador	167.2d	266.0	293.1	8.5	18.5	36.7	24.9b	.03	.03	.04	.02b
Grenada	30.4	21.1	32.3	--	8.0	--	--	--	--	--	--
Guatemala[a]	35.6d	454.4	415.6	12.1	76.0	65.9	58.8	.03	.10	.05	.03
Guyana	--	--	--	3.4	2.5	3.4	3.9	.02	.01	.01	.01
Haiti	--	77.3	112.0	8.5	21.8	54.2	64.7	.15	.20	.25	.22
Honduras	--	--	--	4.1	10.7	16.8	24.5	.02	.03	.02	.03
Jamaica	309.1	395.8	381.8	95.5	128.5	146.9	241.7	.18	.11	.13	.17
Nicaragua	--	189.1	210.0e	13.2	26.3	25.3	18.3b	.06	.06	.03	.03b
Panama[c]	155.3	282.7	201.9	78.2	97.4	147.5	170.0b	.20	.08	.08	.08b
Suriname	--	40.6	--	3.4	7.6	17.8	18.7	.02	.02	.04	.03
Trinidad and Tobago	86.9	132.6	190.0	23.9	65.4	97.9	106.1b	.04	.05	.06	.05

Source: Arrivals, United Nations Statistical Yearbook; Receipts, IMF, Balance of Payments Yearbook (line entry–"travel credit").

aReceipts from tourists only.
b1979.
cReceipts exclude travel transactions with Canal Zone, except 1970.
d1971.
e1977.

greater market expansion than most primary products and agricultural exports, whose demand does not increase proportionately with income levels in the industrial countries.

The price elasticity of tourism expenditures in the aggregate disguises characteristics of market demand in particular destinations. On an aggregate level, demand for tourism in the Caribbean is relatively undifferentiated by destination--the islands are offering the same basic type of holiday package. However, the islands are differentiated as a group from competing destinations in the southern United States and Mexico, and from one another in the types of facilities they offer, local culture, and the market they aim for. This differentiation is necessary to overcome greater air travel costs, and generally higher prices prevailing in the islands, particularly when compared to Florida. While the Caribbean has been successful in positioning itself at the higher end of the winter tourism market for North America, relative price factors are still important. A major determinant of relative prices in international tourism is exchange rate movements. Most Caribbean currencies are pegged to the U.S. dollar, which has increased the cost of a Caribbean vacation over the past two years when compared to travel to Mexico or Europe because of the dollar's appreciation. The depreciation of the dollar was a factor buoying tourism to the Caribbean in the 1970s, as travel to Europe, in particular, became more expensive for Americans. The currency link with the dollar introduces a relative price effort over which Caribbean countries have little control, as in most cases their major trading partner is the United States.

The demand for tourism in the Caribbean is highly seasonal, and is concentrated in the winter months from late November through March. This is a structural characteristic of the type of holiday the region offers, although attempts have been made to sponsor festivals and other attractions in the off-season. There has been limited success in the promotion of summer tourism to the region by black Americans. The seasonality of tourism in the Caribbean causes several problems. Underutilization of capacity in the off-season reduces the overall returns from investment in tourism facilities and necessitates higher prices in the peak months than would otherwise be necessary. Seasonal unemployment among workers in tourist facilities is a severe problem, especially where complementary types of seasonal economic activity, such as agriculture, cannot absorb workers. The concentration of revenues in a few months also affords little opportunity for recovery from a poor season, as there are limited opportunities for generating additional revenues in the off-season.

An additional factor affecting demand is the sensitivity to political instability, violence and general social unrest. Tourist destinations make great efforts through their promotional materials to portray their countries as blissful, untroubled tropical paradises. This fragile image can be shattered instantly by news reports of domestic violence and political and social unrest. Even more damaging are incidents of violence directed at tourists. Thus, the murder of American tourists in St. Croix in the early 1970s, political violence and unrest in tourism in the mid-1970s, and the current political unrest in Central America have all caused severe problems for the tourist trade. A related, but less-tangible element is the perceived attitude of nationals toward affluent foreign tourists, as transmitted through returning tourists, travel agents and tour operators. Tourism can recover nearly as quickly as it can dry up, however, in response to political changes, as has been illustrated by the resurgence of tourism in Jamaica in 1982.

These factors point out the sensitivity of the demand for tourism to a wide variety of influences. While there still remains potential for growth in tourism to the Caribbean, it is not an assured market. The sensitivity of the market to the pervasive structural factors of cyclical changes in income in North America, relative price trends and exchange rate movements, seasonality, and the perceived political and social stability of the destination country are all constraints on the expansion of tourism. Thus, characteristics of the market for tourism in the Caribbean must be set alongside the local economic and social impact of tourism development.

As an export industry, tourism is unique in its impact on the host country: tourists travel to the destinations to consume the product "package." The most important factors determining the impact of tourism on host countries are the net foreign exchange earnings, employment effects, infrastructure and capital requirements, and what can broadly be defined as the social impact of tourism. The effects of these factors vary according to the level of development of the host country, the scale of the tourism industry relative to the local economy, and government policies affecting the industry.

The gross receipts from tourism shown in Table 4.14 are not an accurate measure of the actual foreign exchange earnings. The imported goods and services required to supply tourists with their accustomed standard of living must be subtracted from this figure to give the net inflow of foreign exchange resulting from tourist expenditures. These imported inputs usually include food, remittances of expatriate workers, fuel, souvenir items, imported vehicles and other machinery, and the foreign exchange cost of constructing tourism facilities. The ability of a country to supply these inputs domestically is a function of the size and level of development of its economy. Thus, for many of the smaller island nations, the net foreign exchange receipts from tourism will be substantially less than gross receipts, with the proportion as low as 50 percent[8] However, even on imported goods sold directly to tourists, tariffs and local value added through associated services or retail markups will still capture foreign exchange. The scarcity of foreign exchange in most Caribbean nations places a premium on the earnings available from tourism, yet these must be measured against a country's ability to supply locally the goods and services tourists desire.

Tourism is a service industry, yet the capital requirements of investment in facilities and infrastructure indicate that it is not necessarily labor-intensive. The bulk of employment in tourism is in relatively low-skill trades such as restaurant and hotel operations, retail trade, transportation and recreational services. The development of a skilled labor force to these sectors probably contributes little to skills that have relevance to industries outside of tourism. Hotel and restaurant management requires well-developed skills in business administration that normally do not grow naturally out of employment in skilled or semiskilled labor. For this reason, there is still a heavy reliance on expatriate management in the Caribbean. Countries such as Jamaica have developed tourism management curricula at universities, which have enabled nationals to assume managerial positions in the tourism industry. Most countries require the hiring and training of local nationals, but without suitable candidates with appropriate backgrounds these efforts have not been successful at establishing a national cadre of managerial talent in the tourism industry. Although tourism does provide jobs, there may be little developmental impact of tourism-related employment beyond the income received, in terms of the creation of a broadly based skilled labor force.

Tourism requires a substantial capital investment in facilities and infrastructure. Hotel, restaurant and recreational facilities must be of a caliber to match the type of tourism developed and are normally in excess of local standards. Where infrastructure networks in roads, airports, water, sewer and electricity are not well developed, substantial investment will be required to cultivate any volume of tourist traffic. The benefits of this infrastructural modernization also may accrue to local residents, but in reality they usually are channeled toward tourist facilities. The capital invesment required must be financed, often from abroad, which may compound debt servicing problems. Where infrastructural development is required, this poses an additional financial burden on local governments. In addition, some element of planning is required, in terms of anticipating future growth, coordination of tourist facilities with one another and with local economic activity, and in supplying necessary infrastructure. The haphazard construction of hotels can lead to a loss of the original attraction of an area for tourists and environmental problems from overutilization of water and sewage systems.

The social impact of tourism involves a number of complex results of the interaction of radically different cultures. The presence of large numbers of affluent foreign tourists in a poor country can be disruptive and exacerbate existing tensions. Disparity in income levels among people in the same area has been associated with high crime levels, including specifically the presence of foreign tourists.[9] Affluent foreigners on vacation may inspire resentment among workers who serve them, and the general population, whose expectations exceed their opportunities. Crime and resentment of tourists ultimately will result in the contraction of the industry. Increased crime and hostility have been evident to some degree in most developing countries including the Caribbean to varying degrees. Some governments have responded with education programs to emphasize the economic importance of the industry and change residents' outward attitudes to foreign tourists. The "smile" campaign in Jamaica in the mid-1970s was a good example of this type of program. In addition to crime and hostility, beggary often also becomes a problem. To some degree, these negative social impacts of tourism vary with the magnitude of local economic benefits from tourism. If the industry is largely locally owned and managed, complements other industries, and does not compound existing social conflict, the impact from tourism itself may be minimal. Due to the small size of most of the island nations, the presence of even small numbers of foreign tourists is highly visible. The development of mass tourism carries with it the potential for increased social unrest that, ironically, can negatively affect the industry without ameliorating the source of unrest and dissatisfaction.

Tourism has become a mainstay of many Caribbean economies over the past two decades. For many countries, the only resources they can exploit are the attractiveness of their natural environments and a relatively "unspoiled" way of life. Tourism can preserve these natural attributes through placing an economic value on them; or it can destroy them through poorly planned, overzealous development. Tourism can provide badly needed foreign exchange and employment opportunities, but only to the extent those countries can supply the requirements of the tourism industry indigenously. The demand for tourism, although it holds the promise of expansion because of its income elasticity, is also sensitive to a number of factors beyond a country's control. These factors suggest that in the long run tourism can be an important adjunct to economic development and modernization.

An overreliance on tourism can, however, expose a country to changing market conditions, encourage social unrest and yield little in terms of secondary effects on other sectors. Some countries, however, such as the Bahamas and the smaller former commonwealth nations, may have little choice in terms of developing export industries.

SUMMARY

This chapter demonstrates some rather clear and often disturbing interrelationships among demographic, economic and resource use trends in the Caribbean basin. The combination of strong population growth pressures, weak economic performance and in many cases a limited and diminishing natural resource base will increasingly constrain the governments in question from promoting increased economic development and relieving human misery.

Population will generally grow at a faster rate in the region than additions are made to arable land, so all of the countries will record declines in arable land per capita. The largest percentage declines will occur in El Salvador, Honduras, Nicaragua and Grenada, but others, most notably Haiti, will find difficulty in maintaining adequate agricultural production because the decline in good farmland per capita will be severe.

The contribution of agriculture to the gross national product will remain large in many Caribbean basin countries, but will decline throughout the region due to a variety of factors. The decline will have some positive aspects to it, as countries dependent on agricultural products subject to high price volatility are able to diversify their economies. But the problem of obtaining a proper balance between agricultural production and consumption in the future will not be an easy one to resolve for several of the countries. Barbados, Costa Rica, Guyana, Haiti and Jamaica will continue to experience a negative imbalance in agricultural trade, harming their overall balance-of-payments prospects. Of these, Costa Rica is the most threatened because agricultural production constitutes such a large component of the GNP.

Growth in income per capita also will be limited by the strong population growth pressures in the region. El Salvador, Guyana, Haiti, Honduras and Nicaragua will remain the poorest countries in the region, in all probability still failing to attain the $1,000 income per capita mark by the year 2000.

Increased energy imports are expected to be burdensome for much of the region, particularly in terms of their effect on the balance of payments. The total energy consumption for the region is expected to increase from the present level of about 1 million barrels per day of oil equivalent to over 2.7 million barrels per day.

If care is not taken, strong population pressures, economic growth, and energy demand will have a significant negative impact on the environment in the Caribbean basin. Several countries are already facing forestry

150

depletion, due to fuelwood usage and conversion of forest areas to agricultural use. This depletion will accelerate in part due to population pressures; the most seriously affected countries will include Cuba, the Dominican Republic, Guatemala, Haiti, Honduras and Suriname.

The increase in population and urbanization in the region will also lead to pressure on water availability, particularly in the islands. While data are scarce, it does appear that supply levels will be able to meet the increased requirements, however, assuming water pollution does not increase markedly.

Overcrowding in the major urban areas, unemployment, low and maldistributed income and arable land scarcity will contribute to political instability in the region. El Salvador, Grenada, Guatemala, Guyana, Haiti, Honduras, Jamaica and Nicaragua are the countries that appear most threatened. Increased pollution and political instability, in turn, will have a substantial impact on Caribbean basin tourism--one of the key industries in the region.

NOTES

1. FAO, FAO Production Yearbook.
2. These sources include: United Nations, Yearbook of National Account Statistics (New York, 1980); and United Nations, Yearbook of International Trade Statistics (New York, 1980).
3. This set of categories is adapted from an approach taken by P. F. Palmedo, R. Nathans, C. Beardsworth, and S. Hale, Jr., "Energy Needs, Uses and Resources in Developing Countries," a report prepared by the Policy Analysis Division of Brookhaven National Laboratories for USAID, March 1978.
4. A. Lambertini, "Energy and Petroleum in Non-OPEC Developing Countries, 1974-80," World Bank Staff Working Paper No. 229, February 1975.
5. United Nations, Yearbook of World Energy Statistics, 1979 (New York, 1981).
6. Gerald O. Barney (Study Director), The Global 2000 Report to the President of the U.S. Entering the 21st Century, Volume II: The Technical Report (New York: Pergamon Press, 1980), p. 141.
7. Jacques R. Artus, "An Econometric Analysis of International Travel," IMF Staff Paper, Vol. 19 (1972); S. Y. Kwack, "The Effects of Income and Prices on Travel Spending Abroad," International Economic Review, Vol. 13 (1972).
8. Ruth C. Young, "The Structural Context of the Caribbean Tourist Industry: A Comparative Study," Economic Development and Cultural Change, Vol. 25 (1977), pp. 657-671.
9. Isaac Ehrlich, "Participation in Illegitimate Activities: A Theoretical and Empirical Investigation," Journal of Political Economy, Vol. 81 (1973), pp. 521-565; Donald G. Jud, "Tourism and Crime in Mexico," Social Science Quarterly, Vol. 55 (1975), pp. 524-530.

5
Implications for
U.S. Interests and Policy

We are now in a position to address several key questions about the implications of demographic, economic and natural resource use trends in the Caribbean basin countries for U.S. interests and policy. Five basic questions seem especially pertinent here, particularly as U.S. policymakers consider major initiatives in the Caribbean basin region:

1. What threats to the United States or U.S. interests will stem from demographic, economic, and natural resource use and economic trends in the Caribbean basin?
2. Given the potential for political instability in certain countries, what are the implications for U.S. security, trade and investment relations and political relations?
3. In what ways can U.S. foreign assistance and expertise help to alleviate population pressures and environmental deterioration?
4. To what extent can foreign assistance requirements be met by private sector investment?
5. What is the potential for increased trade and investment in the Caribbean basin?

POTENTIAL THREATS TO U.S. INTERESTS

Some of the social, economic and environmental trends described in this study are quite alarming. The total population in the Caribbean basin is projected to increase by nearly 50 percent to more than seventy-seven million by the year 2000, and the populations of El Salvador, Guatemala, Haiti, Honduras and Nicaragua will experience an annual population growth rate of 2.5 percent or greater during this period. Unfortunately, the effects of increased demographic pressures will be accentuated by continued economic weakness in many of the countries. Even if one uses the fairly optimistic economic growth assumptions suggested by the World Bank, five countries--Nicaragua, El Salvador, Guyana, Honduras and Haiti-- will still be limited to an annual income per capita level of less than $1,000 in the year 2000, according to our projections.

Other countries, most notably Costa Rica, the Dominican Republic, Jamaica and Suriname, find themselves in a fragile economic state because of a combination of high-priced imports of oil and manufactured goods from the West and low world market prices for their own raw material and agricultural exports. Costa Rica's external debt situation has become alarming, as a consequence, and the populations of the other three face the prospect of increased economic deprivation unless the trade picture improves considerably.

The rich bauxite deposits of Guyana, Jamaica and Suriname will mean little if the world bauxite market does not improve substantially. Of the three, Jamaica's position appears the most promising because of recent U.S. policy statements, but the rising levels of external debt and unemployment are worrisome.

Belize, Panama and Grenada have also suffered troublesome balance-of-trade deficits in recent years, and the immediate prospects for improvement are not good. Sugar prices have hurt Belize, and foreign investors are wary because of the threat of incursions by Guatemala. The beneficial economic impact of British troops stationed in the country to guard against this threat, however, has helped to offset the imbalances. Similarly, Panama's trade deficits, largely stemming from expensive petroleum import requirements, have been offset somewhat by the income generated from the canal and its related support services. External debt is growing and unemployment is severe, but there is some long-term prospect for improvement, as Panama's mineral resources are exploited to a greater degree.

Grenada's economy is also fragile, and the long-term prospects are not good. But the fact that the economy is not overly dependent on export income from any one commodity has helped to keep Grenada out of economic crisis.

Cuba is well endowed in several metals, and our forecast suggests that its trade in nickel is likely to grow substantially, thanks to new production capacity and expected increases in exports of the cobalt byproduct to the Soviet Union. But, from all available indications, Cuba's recent economic performance has been stagnant at best, and recent declines in sugar income have forced officials to attempt to reschedule external debt payments to several Western nations.

The economy of Barbados has also been hurt by sugar prices, as well as from a decline in its income from tourism, but it appears rather less fragile than most of the neighboring economies. The economic strong points in the Caribbean basin, however, are Trinidad and Tobago and, to a lesser extent, the Bahamas.

Severe population pressures together with economic weakness tend to set the stage for political instability in many of the Caribbean basin countries. Many of these countries have a long tradition of political violence, and long-standing conflicts or grievances will be exacerbated by population and economic pressures. As these pressures increase, and welfare services and economic opportunities decline or fall short, the political legitimacy of regimes is increasingly challenged. As dissatisfaction deepens and spreads, violence tends to intensify. Whether this increased violence is anomic or organized political action, domestic security will become a major issue for incumbent regimes, and the question of political stability in the region will become an increasing concern to U.S. policymakers. In this sense, the countries that appear most vulnerable are El Salvador, Guatemala, Guyana, Haiti, Honduras and, perhaps to a lesser extent, Belize, Costa Rica and the Dominican Republic. Pressures in Grenada and Nicaragua are also quite severe and there is great potential for political violence.

As stressed in Chapter 4, the roots of political instability are complex and not well understood, but it is clear that demographic pressures and economic deprivation often do play an important role. Moreover, there is an abundance of potential "triggering mechanisms" at work in the region, in the form of long-standing territorial disputes and national rivalries, opposition and guerrilla movements, insurgent activities by foreign governments, and flagrant human rights violations by authoritarian regimes and political movements. Many of the regimes must also be concerned about the activities of significant exile groups and communities operating from neighboring countries. The recent militancy and successful bombing attacks by Haitian exile groups operating from the Dominican Republic and Venezuela, as well as from New York and Miami, illustrate this kind of challenge.

There are clear threats to U.S. interests in this potential increased political instability. Regime changes in themselves obviously can harm political and economic relations between the U.S. and Caribbean basin countries, as we have seen in Cuba, Nicaragua and Grenada. To the extent that certain types of new regimes are deemed undesirable by U.S. officials or potentially threatening to stability, prosperity and democracy in the region, the demographic and economic sources of discontent threatening several friendly governments must be viewed with alarm. Much of Central America is in turmoil, and present active conflicts threaten to spread. While there may be few core or primary U.S. interests directly threatened by this potential for increased conflict and instability, there are U.S. interests at stake.

First, U.S. trade and investment in the region is substantial, though it obviously does not account for a large percentage of U.S. GNP, particularly given the rather limited role played by foreign trade generally. In both 1981 and 1982, U.S. exports to the seventeen countries under study exceeded $5.4 billion. More important, however, is the amount of U.S. and world trade that passes through the region. A substantial portion of U.S. petroleum imports presently flows through the Caribbean Sea and Gulf of Mexico. If we add to this the total amount of annual commercial traffic passing through the Panama Canal--some 171 million tons of commodity cargo in 1981, projected to grow to nearly 250 million tons by 2010[1]--there is considerable incentive to promote peace and stability in the region.

Altogether, nearly two-thirds of U.S. petroleum imports and more than half of all U.S. imports of strategic minerals pass through the Panama Canal or the Caribbean Sea and Gulf of Mexico. Moreover, the ease at which the canal can be blocked, given the state of many of the locks, the length of the canal and the limited security forces available, poses in the minds of some strategists a more direct threat to U.S. security by potentially stopping transit by U.S. warships and military supplies. Some would argue that this threat is declining in importance, due to present U.S. defense technology and strategy and the probable nature and locus of future conflict involving the United States. In addition, the largest U.S. aircraft carriers cannot presently use the canal. But current U.S./NATO plans depend on these waters for resupply shipments in the event of war with the Soviet bloc in Europe. Increased turmoil and Soviet presence in the region, particularly new Soviet military bases, would thus seem a reason for disquiet among U.S. policymakers.

The threat of new Soviet military bases and other activities in the region may not be immediate, but it does seem clear that the Soviets have taken an increasingly offensive and "armed struggle support" posture toward the region since the "peaceful transition" policy to Soviet alignment in Latin America ended with the 1973 Chilean coup. Correspondingly, the close integration that occurred in the mid-1970s between Soviet policy and activities with Cuban operations has made this offensive posture rather more feasible.[2]

A final threat to U.S. interests stems directly from current and prospective demographic pressures and economic weakness in several Caribbean basin countries. This is the threat of continued, massive legal and illegal immigration into the United States from the region. The best available data lead us to estimate that the total annual immigration into the United States (legal and illegal) is 1.2 million persons. Of this total figure, approximately 45 percent or some 540,000 immigrants per year come from Latin America and the Caribbean and nearly 150,000 of these are illegal immigrants from eight Caribbean basin countries (Barbados, the Dominican Republic, El Salvador, Guatemala, Guyana, Haiti, Jamaica and Trinidad and Tobago). Absorbing large numbers of refugees and illegal immigrants is difficult at any time; in a time of high unemployment and budgetary cuts in entitlement programs, it is traumatic.

Much of the illegal immigration into the United States stems from the demographic and economic pressures present in the Caribbean basin. Our projections for growth in the labor force size and annual new job requirements in the region illustrate the extent of the pressure and the strong likelihood that it will worsen in the future. At present, the total size of the labor force in the Caribbean basin is 18.5 million; this is expected to grow to move than 30 million by the year 2000. As a consequence, annual new job requirements will grow from the present level of about 600,000 per year to more than 850,000 per year by 2000.

Growing political concern about this problem has been reflected in recent attempts to pass a major revision of immigration laws that, among other things, would impose penalties on employers hiring illegal aliens. But the threat of increased illegal immigration will be severe and long term, unless the demographic pressures in the Caribbean basin are moderated and the economies strengthened.

Illegal migration between the countries of the Caribbean basin is also an area of concern. Accurate data are scarce, but differences between neighboring states in relative opportunity and political freedom have led to significant migration in recent years from Cuba, El Salvador, Grenada, Guatemala, Haiti, and Nicaragua to other countries in the region. Large flows of refugees--political and economic--create conditions for international friction and conflict, as they begin to undermine the services and opportunities that the new host governments are already straining to provide for their own nationals. U.S. fears of further deterioration in regional stability as a consequence are not unwarranted.

TYPES OF U.S. FOREIGN ASSISTANCE NEEDED

Historically the United States has shown a serious interest in maintaining political stability and friendly regimes in the Caribbean basin-- interest that on numerous occasions has led to some form of intervention. These include numerous interventions of various types prior to World War II, as well as postwar military intervention in Guatemala, the Dominican

Republic and Cuba. More recently, security assistance to threatened regimes in the form of arms transfers, military advisors and training missions has been the preferred approach.

U.S. interventions have never been made without controversy both in the region and within the United States. As new interventions are contemplated, one can only expect regional and domestic controversy to increase and the ease of intervention to decline. In keeping with global trends, Caribbean basin countries are increasingly jealous of their independence, and new power centers are developing in Latin America (i.e., Brazil, Mexico, Venezuela and Argentina) that help to reinforce this attitude. Some erosion in the strength of U.S. influence and authority in the region is thus inevitable, and there is clear divergence in conceptions of security requirements and on what constitutes unwarranted interference. As one author recently argued:

> ...Latin American perceptions of their security needs have changed dramatically in recent years. As the countries have developed politically and economically, and as their international roles have become more complex, U.S. and Latin American national interests have begun to diverge. North American options for implementing a narrowly defined, U.S.-oriented interpretation of collective hemispheric security are increasingly limited.[3]

The task of maintaining stability and friendly governments in the region has been complicated by the emergence of increased U.S. interest in promoting human rights in recent years. As incumbent regimes are pressured more and more by domestic discontent, stemming from demographic and economic trends together with basic societal inequities, many have found it expedient to resort to coercion, repression and violence to maintain their tenure. In practice, the goals of regional stability and human rights promotion often seem to conflict, and it is difficult for U.S. policymakers to navigate between them. Disputes between Congress and successive administrations are almost inevitable, as a consequence, and a coherent U.S. policy toward near-term threats to stability in the regime is exceedingly difficult to create.

Security and economic assitance to El Salvador has, of course, been affected by this conflict; the President has been required by Congress to certify that the Salvadoran regime has made progress in reducing human rights abuses as a condition for continued assistance. But the conflict also limits the kind of response U.S. policymakers can make to new Haitian requests for security assistance. While concerned about the heightened instability that recent violent attacks against the Duvalier Government suggest, there is reluctance to press for new weaponry and support at a time when Congress has been highly critical of the lack of political freedom in Haiti. Haitian officials have thus already begun to look for alternative sources of arms supplies. U.S. security assistance to Guatemala has been similarly constrained in the past several years.

The Caribbean basin region does appear to be passing out of a long period of U.S. neglect, however. Tables 5.1 and 5.2 together present the U.S. record of security assistance to the region through 1981. Key threatened countries have been singled out for expanded security assistance recently in a near-term effort to protect perceived U.S. interests.

TABLE 5.1
U.S. military assistance deliveries to Caribbean basin countries
(thousand 1981 dollars)

Year	Barbados	Dominican Republic	El Salvador	Guatemala	Honduras	Nicaragua	Panama
1970		4,573.7	107.9	3,487.4	195.2	1,373.9	713.9
1971		4,583.9	596.1	1,545.0	934.3	1,506.1	1,248.2
1972		1,282.6	465.6	1,066.1	400.4	325.9	249.1
1973		1,037.4	196.9	3,066.3	411.5	1,645.9	1,952.3
1974		1,110.7	66.3	3,090.9	202.9	1,164.9	391.6
1975		1,237.7	92.8	482.5	144.7	347.0	365.6
1976		532.8	770.2	478.1	228.8	514.0	293.7
1977		247.2	173.6	162.7	384.8	126.7	148.6
1978		18.7	180.1	66.3	337.2	428.0	273.8
1979	7.9	13.3	67.9	1.3	69.2	118.5	85.2
1980	69.5	253.1	196.6	76.5	50.6	151.9	47.1
1981	53.7	8.6	10,495.3	7.5	0	0	11.8

Source: Department of Defense.

TABLE 5.2
Total U.S. arms sales deliveries to Caribbean basin countries*
(thousand 1981 dollars)

Year	Costa Rica	Dominican Republic	El Salvador	Guatemala	Haiti	Honduras	Jamaica	Nicaragua	Panama	Trinidad & Tobago
1970	0	141.2	333.9	713.9	0	0	20.5	210.6	12.8	0
1971	0	72.9	12.1	2,058.4	0	41.4	17.0	1,496.4	34.1	206.8
1972	2.3	37.2	0	14,499.5	0	62.9	6.9	153.6	18.6	0
1973	41.6	689.4	80.9	3,983.4	0	236.4	13.1	98.5	8.8	0
1974	0	64.3	257.1	2,980.5	498.1	1,695.1	56.2	285.2	1,769.4	0
1975	0	55.7	480.6	6,268.3	92.8	1,091.1	37.1	406.4	3,026.5	0
1976	235.7	52.9	558.4	5,192.9	34.2	8,034.5	116.1	1,050.2	2,605.9	0
1977	0	3.1	402.0	3,392.8	159.6	600.7	1.6	563.1	380.1	0
1978	30.3	102.3	856.0	3,473.1	452.5	664.4	10.1	1,128.4	237.8	0
1979	354.1	10.6	45.3	4,536.7	334.1	1,196.8	2.7	57.2	327.5	0
1980	144.8	161.3	1,444.7	2,625.7	98.0	684.1	1.2	15.3	224.9	0
1981	0	0	2,098.4	540.5	12.9	1,881.4	0	5.4	182.7	16.1

Source: Department of Defense.

*Not including commercial export deliveries.

There are clear threats to U.S. interests stemming from demographic, economic and resource use trends in the Caribbean basin. But there also are significant opportunities for a constructive U.S. role in the long-term rehabilitation and development of the region through increased U.S. economic and technical assistance, trade and investment. The initial excitement created by the announcement of a Caribbean Basin Initiative indicated that a major program of economic and technical assistance and trade reform would be warmly welcomed by hard-pressed regional leaders. The precise character of what such an initiative should entail, however, has been the subject of considerable debate, and the prospects for a major long-term program are uncertain.[4] The issues involved in the debate cannot be addressed directly point by point in this paper, but the rest of this chapter will deal with many of them as we discuss the types of U.S. foreign assistance that would seem most appropriate in light of the findings reported above.

Minimizing the Pressures of Rapid Population Growth

Clearly, the most crucial driving force behind the increased difficulty that many Caribbean basin countries will be facing in the future is the rapid rate of population growth. As noted in Chapter 4, population growth has clear effects on food requirements, resource depletion, harm to the environment, economic development and political stability. Minimizing this population pressure, then, should be a primary goal of U.S. foreign assistance to the region in the immediate future. For several of the Caribbean basin countries the effects of population pressure have already reached crisis proportions, but for all ten of the rapid population growth countries, delays in strong family planning efforts by the governments in question and delays in increased technical assistance from the United States to support these efforts will seriously affect social and economic development and stability in the near future.

But what realistically can be done? What kind of impact on this serious population pressure can be expected from these countries? Table 5.3 presents the current total fertility rates (the average number of children born live per woman) for the ten countries of the Caribbean basin that seem to have some degree of a population growth problem. The basic aim is obviously to reduce the total fertility rate to replacement level (slightly more than two children per woman) as quickly as possible. This kind of progress will take time, and there is considerable momentum behind population growth in countries that have had high fertility rates and a consequent large proportion of children in their populations for a long time. Even if the total fertility rates in these countries were to drop tomorrow to replacement levels, the populations would continue to grow substantially for some time; the number of young women entering their reproductive years will continue to exceed the number moving out of their reproductive years. As a consequence, even if each couple were to have only two children, the number born each year would continue to exceed the number who die each year for about forty years. Figure 5.1 illustrates the impact of the momentum of population growth for Honduras.

Nevertheless, the rate of population growth can be slowed in a relatively short time. Cuba's birth rate declined nearly 40 percent during the period from 1965 to 1975, and a reduction in the growth rate can have significant social and economic effects. For example, an international

159

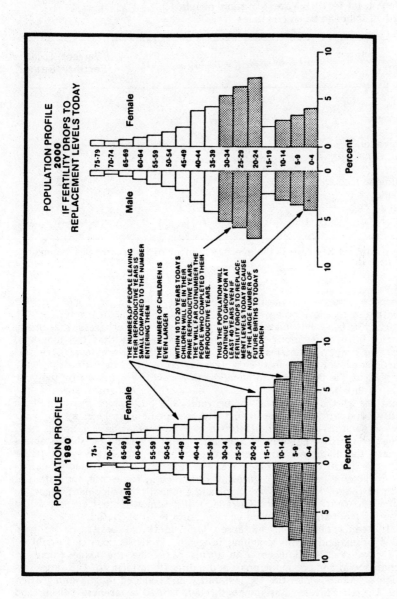

Figure 5.1 Momentum of population growth in Honduras

160

TABLE 5.3
Current total fertility rates* in rapid population
growth Caribbean basin countries

Country	Current Total Fertility Rate*
Honduras	6.4
Nicaragua	6.2
Haiti	5.7
El Salvador	5.6
Guatemala	5.1
Belize	4.8
Dominican Republic	4.2
Grenada	4.2
Guyana	3.3
Costa Rica	3.1

*The total fertility rate is the average number of live births per woman.

conference convened by the United Nations in Colombo, Sri Lanka, in 1982 set a target for developing countries to achieve replacement fertility by the year 2000, a not unreasonable goal given the progress that many countries have made along these lines. If we assume that the ten rapid population growth countries of the Caribbean basin were to achieve this replacement level target in twenty years or so, a significant impact on the total size of the population in each country would be apparent by the year 2000. Table 5.4 illustrates this by comparing the total size of the populations of these countries in the year 2000 both under continued high fertility[5] and with a decline in fertility to replacement level by the year 2000. In each instance, the difference in total population size under these alternative fertility patterns is substantial, and in the cases of Guatemala and Haiti the differences are nearly two million persons. Moreover, if the alternative fertility pattern (replacement level by 2000) is used to calculate new income per capita figures (as displayed in Table 5.5), the potential impact of reduced fertility on social and economic development begins to become apparent. Haiti and Guyana, while somewhat better off, would still be far from an average income per capita level of $1,000.

It seems clear that increased U.S. technical assistance to help develop or expand family planning programs in these countries could be amply rewarded, both directly in terms of easing the achievement of national, social and economic goals and indirectly in terms of U.S. interests through a reduced potential for instability and reduced illegal immigration to the United States. Assistance through USAID awareness raising and population and development planning programs should be intensified in the region, as should contraceptive supply, clinical assistance and education efforts.

TABLE 5.4
Total population of the rapid population growth
Caribbean basin countries under alternative sets
of fertility assumptions (1982 and 2000)

Country	Total Population in 1982	Total Population in 2000 With Continued High Fertility	Total Population in 2000 With Replacement Fertility by 2000
Guatemala	7,694,000	12,636,100	10,892,300
Dominican Republic	6,249,500	9,276,900	8,341,600
Haiti	6,110,800	9,628,200	7,665,200
El Salvador	5,094,600	8,718,100	7,215,200
Honduras	3,947,500	6,923,800	5,836,200
Nicaragua	2,922,100	5,172,500	4,287,200
Costa Rica	2,315,300	3,345,400	3,192,400
Guyana	921,800	1,236,200	1,194,900
Belize	169,200	257,600	233,800
Grenada	116,600	171,400	162,400

TABLE 5.5
Income per capita of rapid population growth
in Caribbean basin countries under alternative
sets of fertility assumptions (1982 and 2000)

Country	Total Population in 1982	Income Per Capita in 2000 With Continued High Fertility	Income Per Capita in 2000 With Replacement Fertility by 2000
Costa Rica	$1,684.40	$3,004.40	$3,148.30
Guatemala	1,056.30	1,655.10	1,920.10
Dominican Republic	1,016.10	1,774.40	2,004.10
Belize	931.90	1,446.90	1,593.90
Grenada	676.10	1,087.40	1,147.60
Nicaragua	653.40	898.90	1,093.10
Guyana	555.10	617.60	670.70
El Salvador	547.40	811.50	980.50
Honduras	531.80	754.00	894.50
Haiti	233.00	369.50	465.30

Maximizing Resource Development Without Destroying the Environment

Assistance in developing new and renewable sources of energy and alternative sources of income through new resource exploitation may be an equally viable strategy for helping to solve the long-term financial problems of several of the Caribbean basin countries. The cost of imported energy, even in the current period of glut in the world petroleum market, is a crushing burden for countries with limited alternative energy sources that are trying to develop economically. As noted in Chapter 4, all of the Caribbean basin countries can be expected to have substantially expanded commercial energy requirements in the next twenty years. Increased transfers of technology in new and renewable sources of energy, as agreed to at the 1981 United Nations conference on the subject in Nairobi, Kenya, could well go far to stabilizing troubled Caribbean economies.

Substantial research and development in alternative sources of energy has taken place in the United States and other industrialized countries since the 1973 OPEC oil embargo and subsequent price rises. Considerable progress has in fact already been made in developing geothermal energy, passive and active solar energy systems and synthetic fuels. Transferring the technology stemming from these advances and financial assistance for developing them should be a major priority for increased assistance to Caribbean basin countries, where energy research and development is practically nonexistent. As solar energy systems become more efficient and economical, for example, widespread application in the sunny Caribbean could dramatically reduce projected imported oil consumption. Oil exploration efforts, in partnership with major U.S. firms, could help to turn around several economies, and could well provide new sources for U.S. oil imports that would help further reduce U.S. dependence on the volatile Persian Gulf region.

There are clearly other important areas of resource development efforts that must be pursued in the Caribbean basin, if the effects of the region's fragile dependence on a few agricultural crops subject to devastating price fluctuations are to be counteracted. The region is certainly not blessed with an overabundance of natural resources that can be exploited economically, particularly in several of the island states. But Panama has considerable undeveloped copper reserves, as well as other metals, and the real potential of other Central American states has not been fully explored. Efficient and environmentally conscious development of the region's bauxite resources would substantially improve the economic prospects of Guyana, Suriname and especially Jamaica, as the trend impact analyses reported in Chapter 3 suggest, particularly if this effort is coupled with economic revival in the industrial West and conscious decisions to return to the Caribbean basin for future bauxite purchases.

Many of the Caribbean basin countries have been blessed with substantial forest resources. Deforestation is a growing threat, however, and there is considerable potential here for corrective U.S. technical assistance. Under various AID programs, the United States already provides extensive forestry assistance to developing countries, but there is some question as to whether these programs have been appropriately designed and effectively meshed with other development programs.[6] This area is potentially very sensitive, since it deals with problems generated by subsistence farmers and because it has not generally attracted much concern from key national leaders in the region. To be effective, increased forestry assistance will have to be carefully integrated with individual country development and environmental management plans, and considerable education and consensus-building efforts may be required. A crucial question to be raised in each case is whether host country commitment to limiting deforestation is in fact sufficient to sustain forestry projects initiated under U.S. funding.

In this, as in many other economic and technical assistance efforts, there is a need to coordinate more effectively among donor nations and international agencies. Now that there is some prospect for assistance to Caribbean basin countries from Canada, Mexico, Venezuela and Colombia, coordination is imperative. The need for foreign assistance in the Caribbean basin is massive, and the potential pool of aid available is rather limited. It is thus crucial that duplicate and conflicting projects are eliminated and that great care is taken to ensure that development projects enjoy widespread local support and are appropriate for the country concerned. There is no margin for waste.

THE POTENTIAL ROLE OF PRIVATE SECTOR INVESTMENT

A major feature of the Caribbean Basin Initiative as originally proposed was to attempt to stimulate a significant role for private sector investment in the development of the region. This emphasis has been criticized by several prominent scholars in testimony before various Congressional committees. Professor Albert Fishlow of Yale, for example, warned that excessive reliance on investment decisions by the private sector would be insufficient to the task and would be unlikely to encourage equitable or efficient development.[7] Moreover, there may be significant differences between U.S. government interests and policy regarding the region and the interests of private firms.

Nevertheless, the potential supplemental role that private sector investment might play is substantial, and there is a real need to attempt to improve the climate for business and investment in many Caribbean basin countries. The nature and extent of this role obviously must be carefully examined from the perspective of the governments concerned. There will undoubtedly be substantial opposition from certain quarters, given previous negative experience and common fears about the power of "multinationals." Attitudes are changing, however, and there is growing recognition that foreign investment will be an important tool in future economic development and employment. Even the Sandinist regime in Nicaragua has shown signs of interest in attracting foreign business investment. These signs include a new foreign investment law that permits foreign companies to own up to 100 percent of new operations in Nicaragua and an apparent good faith effort to resolve past investment disputes.

Increased foreign investment could help to provide a means for diversifying the economies in Caribbean basin countries. For example, this is the intent of recent efforts by the Bahamian Government to attract new foreign investment. Incentives for potential investors include freedom from corporate, capital gains and personal income taxes, and import duty relief for plant machinery, tools, equipment, and raw materials. The government is also considering the establishment of foreign industrial free zones in Nassau and the Family Islands to go along with the existing free zone in Grand Bahama.

Despite the apparent growing receptivity, the prospects for substantial U.S. investment in the Caribbean basin are uncertain. Some strong interest is evident for investment in Jamaica, a development that could well boost future bauxite production and exports, as the trend impact analyses reported in Chapter 3 suggest.

The original CBI proposal called for substantial tax benefits for U.S. companies investing in the region, but this aroused no serious support in Congress. The Caribbean Basin Economic Recovery Act, finally signed into law on August 5, 1983, does allow tax deductions for business convention expenses in beneficiary countries. This did at least lead Holiday Inns to plan an expansion investment in Jamaica. In addition, the 12-year, duty-free access provisions of the act have apparently stimulated some Asian interest in new investment in the region.

U.S. government assistance to potential investors in the region is already presently available. The Overseas Private Investment Corporation (OPIC) assisted thirty-two U.S. investments in the Caribbean in 1982, issuing insurance coverage and financial commitments for over $36.8 million. In early 1983, a six-day investment mission to Jamaica sponsored by OPIC and the Bureau for Private Enterprise of the Agency for International Development generated nineteen new investment projects by U.S. firms. This kind of government promotion activity and assistance should be encouraged and expanded.

THE POTENTIAL FOR INCREASED TRADE

Similarly, the potential for increased trade is questionable. As noted above, the Caribbean Basin Economic Recovery Act does allow the President to eliminate duties on all products, with certain exceptions, from countries he designates as beneficiaries. It was strongly opposed by the AFL-CIO which feared that it would result in job losses for U.S. workers. But the final version of the act contained few new benefits for the Caribbean basin nations, since most of the covered products from the region already enjoy duty-free status under the General System of Preferences (GSP). The GSP is due to expire at the end of 1984, however, and the act thus extends duty-free benefits for at least ten more years.

It is still too early to tell what the result of the trade provisions will be, but it seems unlikely that they will be enough to improve substantially the economics of the Caribbean basin. Moreover, recent passage of quotas on sugar may cause serious harm to countries already suffering from low prices. The Dominican Republic, for example, has in the past exported more than 90 percent of its sugar to the United States, an amount accounting for more than one-third of its export earnings. It has been estimated that the U.S. quota system meant a loss of more than $100 million for the Dominican Republic in 1982. The Bahamas, Barbados and Guyana also are substantially dependent on sugar trade and are thus very vulnerable to this kind of action. The growing climate of protectionism in the United States, indeed in the developed world generally, is a severe threat to economic growth and stability in the Caribbean basin.

Yet the quantities of goods flowing into the United States under a liberalized trade regime are not likely to be a substantial burden. The economies in question are miniscule in comparison to the major U.S. trading partners, and the short- and long-term effects of liberalization in trade with the region are not projected to have a significant impact on the U.S. economy.[8] As noted in Chapter 1, the United States experienced a negative balance of trade with the region in recent years, but this was essentially due to petroleum purchases from Trinidad and Tobago. Panama, the Dominican Republic, Trinidad and Tobago, Guatemala, Jamaica and the Bahamas accounted for the largest amounts of exports from the United States.

Increased regional integration in the Caribbean basin may provide a partial solution to the trade imbalances faced by many of the countries. The long previous record of attempted integration schemes met with only limited success according to any tangible measure. Regional cooperation involving Mexico, Venezuela and Trinidad and Tobago in efforts to lessen the impact of expensive petroleum imports for countries in the basin is a promising development, however, and there is prospect for increased intraregional trade.

Unfortunately, trade relations in the region are not without episodes of protectionism. An example of this problem is the recent decision by Trinidad and Tobago to restrict or deny imported goods from Jamaica. The government's argument is that Jamaica's "parallel or unofficial market" operates as a de facto devaluation and gives an unfair competitive edge to Jamaican goods. Unfortunately, in fact, too many of the countries in the region quite simply have the same products to sell.

NOTES

1. This projection was made for planning purposes in the course of preparation for the Conference on Future Transportation Alternatives Across the Panamanian Isthmus convened by The Futures Group for the Department of State, October 13-14, 1982.

2. For a detailed discussion of these changes, see Robert S. Leiken, "Soviet Strategy in Latin America," The Washington Papers, Vol. 10, No. 93 (1982); see also Chapter 3 of Bruce W. Watson's book: Red Navy at Sea: Soviet Naval Operations on the High Seas, 1956-1980 (Boulder, Colorado: Westview Press, 1982).

3. Margaret Hayes, "Security to the South: U.S. Interests in Latin America," International Security, Vol. 5, No. 1 (Summer 1980), pp. 130-150. See also: Colossus Challenged: The Struggle for Caribbean Influence, edited by H. Michael Erisman and John D. Martz (Boulder, Colorado: Westview Press, 1982).

4. See, for example, the articles in the Summer 1982 issue of Foreign Policy by Abraham Lowenthal, Peter Johnson, Rafael Hernandez-Colon, Baltasar Corrada, Sidney Weintraub, Richard E. Feinberg and Richard S. Newformer; see also: Robert Pastor, "Sinking in the Caribbean Basin," Foreign Affairs, Vol. 60, No. 5 (Summer 1982), pp. 1038-1058.

5. This continued high-fertility pattern assumes the slight decline in the total fertility rate that one would normally expect as a consequence of normal social and economic development--more women entering the labor force, etc.; but it assumes no increased family planning effort.

6. See, for example, U.S. General Accounting Office, Changes Needed in U.S. Assistance to Deter Deforestation in Developing Countries, GAO/ID-82-50 (September 16, 1981).

7. Testimony before the Foreign Relations Committee, U.S. Senate, March 31, 1982; see also: testimony by Abraham Lowenthal before the Committee on Foreign Affairs, U.S. House of Representatives, April 1, 1982.

8. See: U.S. Department of Commerce, International Trade Administration, <u>Economic Impact of the Caribbean Basin Free Trade Area</u>, March 1982.